REJECTED F.C.
Volume 2

Histories
of the ex-Football League Clubs

By Dave Twydell

Published by:
YORE PUBLICATIONS,
12 The Furrows,
Harefield
Middx. UB9 6AT

British Library Cataloguing-in-Publication Data
A catalogue record for this book is
available from the British Library.

ISBN 1 874427 21 6 (2nd Edition. Part of former 'Rejected F.C. Volume 2'
                    Re-set, additions, plus minor revisions)

(ISBN 0 9513321 2 0 'Rejected F.C. Volume 2' an extended version of this reprint)

Printed by:
Biddles Limited,
Guildford
Surrey

"There is much to be said for failure.
It is more interesting than success."

Max Beerbohm
(From 'A small boy seeing Giants')

Dave Twydell: Was born in Ealing, London during the Second World War and attended Walpole Grammar School, Northfields. During those formative days collecting train numbers was preferable to watching football! Qualifying as a Chartered Structural Engineer in 1968 he worked in both Zambia and South Africa as well as England. His first publication was a joint effort, a booklet entitled *'Brentford's Three Visits To Wembley'*. As well as a lifetime follower of Brentford, non-League football has always been supported. The first (self-published) book, *'Defunct F.C.'* was soon followed with *'Rejected F.C. Volume 1'*, a companion to this book. Three more books were written/published before redundancy in 1991 led to the setting up of 'Yorc Publications' on a full time basis. *'Yore Publications'* includes wife, Fay and married daughter Kara Matthews. Around 20 football books and several booklets have since followed, principally Club histories by other Authors.

(June 1995)

Cover Photo: Peel Park, Accrington in the mid-1960's - by then the Stand was near derelict.

ACKNOWLEDGEMENTS

My grateful thanks to many people throughout the Country, particularly those connected with, and those with an interest in, the Clubs themselves. The list below represents the help I received for the original (first edition) 'Rejected F.C. Volume 2', and the subsequent reprints (Volumes 2 and 3), without which this book would never have been possible. There are others who provided additional items to whom I collectively offer my gratitude.

The staff, and particularly the Local History sections of the following Public Libraries: Accrington, Barrow, Darwen, Durham, Gainsborough, Merthyr, Middlesbrough, Northwich, Southport, Stratford (London), Wallasey, and Wigan.

The staff and facilities provided by the British Library in respect of the Newspaper Library in Colindale and the Map Library of London.
Aerofilms Ltd.
The following individuals (Random Order):
Mark Grabowski, Alan Clegg, Tony McWilliams, Tom Sault, Sidney Booth, David Watkins, David Howgate, Harry Glasper, Brian Mackin, Arthur Appleton, John Rowlands, (the late) Ken Edwards, Michael Braham, Bryan Horsnell, Louis Burgess, Chris Ambler, Ray Spiller, and last, but far from least; my checker, principal critic, consultant, etc. i.e..... my Wife Fay.

References have been principally obtained from countless local Newspapers - both past and present.
Other publications to which reference was made:
Reports of the Association of Football Statisticians.
Non-League Directory (various years) by Tony Williams
Non-League by Bob Barton
Encyclopedia of British Football by Phil Soar and Martin Tyler.
Great Soccer Clubs of the North East by Anton Rippon
The Book of Football (Published 1905)
The Story of the Football League published by the Football League (1938)
The Official History of the F.A. Cup by Geoffrey Green
Association Football and English Society 1863-1915 by Tony Mason
Hot Bed of Soccer by Arthur Appleton
The Early Days of the Vics. by G.A. Hughes
Daily Express A-Z of Mersey Soccer by Keith & Thomas
The History of Middlesbrough by William Lillie
Merthyr Tydfil: Drawn from life. Various Authors
Magic Moments of Merthyr Tydfil A.F.C. by David Watkins.
The Giant Killers by Bryon Butler
A Century of Soccer (Blackburn Rovers) by Harry Berry
History of the Lancashire Football Association
Barrow-in-Furness Football Club. The Rise and Fall of a Civic Symbol by Tony McWilliams
A Team For All Seasons (Northwich Victoria) by K.R.Edwards
Leeds United - A Complete Record by Malcolm MacDonald & Martin Jarred

All of the above can be recommended for future reading, several of which are still available either new or second-hand.

Every effort has been made to acknowledge - where applicable - the sources of specific items and to ensure that copyright has not been infringed.

CONTENTS:

INTRODUCTION

As with Volume 1, *'Rejected F.C. Volumes 2 and 3'* contain reasonably detailed histories of all the ex-Football League clubs. However, many readers will feel that there are a few omissions. A few words regarding my interpretation of 'Rejected F.C.'.

Wigan Borough and Leeds City: Neither of these clubs appeared in the original Volume 2, for at the time I felt that although both are completely separate Clubs from their successors (both of whom are still in the Football League), any histories of the two current clubs would, or have, included the details of their forerunners - particularly since the two pairs had common Grounds. However, this omission has now been rectified in the reprints. Rotherham Town fall into a similar category, but their inclusion a soon to be published Rotherham United F.C. history is assured.

Conversely Middlesbrough Ironopolis existed separately and at the same time as the current Middlesbrough F.C. (and had a completely different home Ground), and they are therefore worthy of inclusion. Other names, e.g. Small Heath, Ardwick, etc., are of course simply the forerunners of current, renamed, Football League Clubs, and certainly do not therefore warrant coverage here.

Despite the automatic promotion and relegation of Clubs between the Football League and the GM Vauxhall Conference that was instigated in 1987, a continuous stream of ex-League clubs has not materialised as such (only Aldershot - resigned - and Newport County to date). A detailed history of Aldershot F.C. - the nucleus of which formed Aldershot Town F.C. - is I understand very likely, and Newport County F.C. (from whom was created Newport A.F.C.) has been covered in depth in *'Amber In The Blood'* (Published by Yore Publications). In any event my interpretation is that these have not been 'rejected' (i.e. the normal interpretation of being voted out), and therefore would not be included. This scenario of not including relegated clubs has been vindicated, with Lincoln City who immediately bounced back into the Football League, followed by Colchester United and Darlington.

'Rejected F.C. Volume 2' (first edition) has been extended - as stated above - with the inclusion of Leeds City and Wigan Borough, and the whole work divided into these two new volumes (2 and 3). In addition a very few minor errors (noted by myself or advised) have been corrected, additional illustrations have been included, and in general the histories have been updated. Since the original Volume 2 ran to 480 pages, splitting this into two new, and equal volumes, was I believe the sensible course to follow.

Most readers will have a general interest in the ex-League clubs, and therefore will be familiar with the same notes contained in Volume 1. However, I believe the following words of explanation are worthy of repeating:

A book of this nature requires a few words of explanation, or in this case more than just a few!

I have adopted a certain approach and highlighted certain aspects which may - I hope to only a small minority - be considered shortcomings. Having no prior knowledge or specific interest in any of these Ex-League Clubs, it may seem an impertinence for an 'outsider' to chronicle their histories. But a 'one club' devotee is liable to become dogmatic and wish to include every fact and figure - an objective that this book does not set out to do, nor has the space to include; I would stress that this comment is not made in a derogatory manner, since I owe much of my material to several such experts. There is without doubt a place for such historians to fully record the facts and figures, and I fully applaud their efforts. I do not consider that 'my' histories that follow, in any way compete with the full Club details that were, are, or will be available, but rather complement same; if one or more particular Clubs are of sufficient interest, then where available buy a copy, and read on. But significantly in the majority of cases no such fully detailed books exist at the time of writing, and in some cases are unlikely to in the future. Whilst not complete, I hope a significant part of the gaps are filled.

My aim was simple; a passion to dig out the main facts and relate them as I would wish to read them - in a simple style. Written as it is, with enthusiasm and from the heart, then I hope I have achieved my goal, and hopefully fulfilled the expectations of you the reader.

The following paragraphs are not meant as excuses for any shortcomings but short explanations on how I approached the subject, and the factual interpretation:
This not a Football Book!
It is a history book about Football Clubs.

1. The Beginning
An area often glossed over, from which errors are stated and easily become established fact. I have delved as far as is reasonable, and come up with what I consider are the true facts, as well as being interesting and necessary points that help to establish each Club within the framework of the game at that time.

2. Football League Days.
The essence of this book, and the area where basic information is fairly easy - in a statistical form - to obtain elsewhere. A long list giving details of week to week matches, goalscorers, attendances etc., I believe, makes boring reading! This is a 'reading' book, therefore such events have in general been glossed over ... except ... those clubs whose Football League careers were limited in time. In such cases I have deliberately elaborated on their brief existence. In these instances, one Club's History, may on the face of it, be out of proportion in detail compared to others; this was deliberate for in these cases, little, can be read elsewhere - therefore it's here!

3. After the League.
This has generally been tackled in a somewhat cursory manner. In most cases the Clubs still exist and/or the historical period is relatively recent. And so once again the information is more readily available elsewhere.

4. The Ground(s).

In one respect perhaps the most important item. Very little information on the majority of these Clubs' Grounds is generally available elsewhere, and yet as the decades roll by, and the supporter watches his team, what remains unchanged ? the Ground! The Players, the Managers, the Directors and even the Supporters are replaced and often forgotten - but the two prominent and constant factors are the name (admittedly sometimes with changes) and the Ground - again with some exceptions.

'The Ground' however, must be taken in it's right context. In the late 19th Century, the home venues throughout were generally little more than a fenced field with perhaps some banked earth terraces and a small wooden seated covered area; dressing rooms were nothing more - no running water - or non-existent; the local Publican often offering his facilities with the expectation of increased custom. With a large number of Clubs emanating from Cricket Clubs, the latter's terminology remained; a 'Pavilion' was, at the football ground, the covered seated area; what we would now call the 'Stand'. To add to the confusion, what was frequently and originally entitled a 'Stand', was very often an uncovered - terraced in timber - seated or standing area!

As the start of the 20th Century loomed, then passed, the slopes, became concreted, the Pavilions became Grandstands, and the standing areas often became covered.

With imagination (and this book), the inquisitive can find the exact locations of these Grounds, and where little or nothing remains, conjure up in their own minds, perhaps, a picture of those former days.

5. The People.

With a number of exceptions these have been ignored! Who should be referred to, and who cannot - due to space - be included? This is a job for the expert of each Club, where there is one, and for the statistical publications.

6. Attendances.

A great fascination for many, particularly when comparisons can be considered within the long time span encompassed here. Whilst it is interesting to make these comparisons, the figures given must be taken in their right context. Crowd figures given before the Second World War were more often estimated. A 'round' thousand stated, usually relates to the estimate given at the time by a Newspaper Reporter or Club Official, and therefore can only be approximate. 'Gates' invariably related to the cash receipts taken, and therefore with the knowledge of the entrance charges, a reasonably true attendance can be calculated. Conversely, precise attendances can be considered as accurate and official.

7. The Leagues.

For simplicity and clarity, in all cases the original, and early revised, titles of the various Leagues prior to any prefixed or new titles due to Sponsorship have been referred to.

Geographical Locations of the ex-League Clubs

"REJECTED F.C."
Book Location Key

+   Volume 1
O   Volume 2
●   Volume 3

+ Ashington
+ Gateshead
● Durham
Workington
● Midds. Ironopolis
Barrow
O
Accrington + Nelson
O
Darwen O + O Leeds
Southport Bradford
Bootle Wigan + Stalybridge
New Brighton Glossop Gainsborough
Northwich

Burton
+ +
Loughborough

+ O Merthyr
Aberdare
Thames
O

¤ THE LIFETIMES OF THE EX-LEAGUE CLUBS ¤

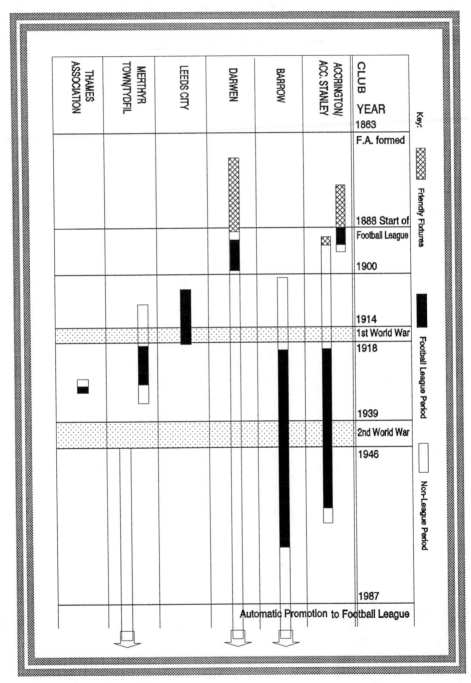

THE LEAGUE—Third...ent v. Merthyr Town

KICK-OFF 2.30 p.m.

SATURDAY, OCTOBER 30th, 1926.

NEW BRIGHTON v. DURHAM CITY

Paddock, 1/6; Stands, 2/- and 2/4; Boys and ...c, 5d.

...same should be made to Mr. B.

Re-election plea again

The end of the Stanley era.

EXETER 7, BARROW 1

BY A SPECIAL CORRESPONDENT

The Burnley-road stand on Peel Park Ground, which formerly belonged to Accrington Stanley Football Club, is being demolished and sold for scrap.

Football League . . Division III.—Southern Section

Merthyr

2nd Division

1 M'chester City
2 New Brighton
3 Leicester Fosse
4 Burslem
5 Small Heath
6 Glossop
7 Newton Heath
8 Walsall
9 Woolwich Arsenal
10 Barnsley
11 Lincoln City
12 Burton Swifts
13 Grimsby Town
14 Luton
15 Gainsborough Tr
16 Blackpool
17 Loughboro'
18 Darwen

LEAVING DARWEN.

ENTHUSIASTIC STATION SCENES YESTERDAY.

...re were scenes of great enthusiasm at ...Railway Station yesterday, when the ...ven team and officials left in the morning. Many ...usands of people assembled, and the send-...was most hearty. Hopes of victory were ...spressed on every hand, and mascots and ...ere much in evidence. The official ...morning is as follows:

...of Commons, ...Sir Her-
...Palace

HOLKER STREET GROUND

T. AVISON LTD

GROCERY AND PROVISIONS

Wednesday, 7th Sept.,
NEW BRIGHTON v STO...

Official Programme

ACCRINGTON 1961:

(back) Smith, Tighe, Forrester, McInnes, Swindells, Sneddon.
(front) Hudson, Logue, Harrower, Bennett, Devine

ACCRINGTON

Accrington:	*1878 - 1896*
Stanley Villa:	*1891 - 1893*
Accrington Stanley:	*1893 - 1916*
Accrington Stanley (1921):	*1921 - 1962*
Accrington Stanley:	*1962 - 1966*
Accrington Stanley (1968):	*1968 to date*

Football League Periods

Accrington:	*1888 - 1893*
Accrington Stanley:	*1921 - 1962*

ACCRINGTON

1878 - 1888	*Friendly Matches*
1888/89 - 1891/92	*Football League**
1892/93	*Football League Division 1*
1893/94 - 1894/95	*Lancashire League ***
1895/96	*Lancashire Combination ****

* Founder Members
** Also competed in Lancashire Palatine League (South Div.) - Latter part of season
*** Did not complete fixtures

ACCRINGTON STANLEY (STANLEY VILLA)

1891 - 1894	*Friendly Matches*
1894/95	*Accrington & District League*
1895/96	*North-East Lancashire League*
1896/97 - 1899/00	*North-East Lancashire Combination*
1900/01 - 1902/03	*Lancashire Combination*
1903/01 - 1914/15	*Lancashire Combination Division 1*
1915/16	*Lancashire Combination (North Section)*
1916/17 - 1918/19	*Ceased Activities*
1919/20 - 1920/21	*Lancashire Combination*
1921/22 - 1938/39	*Football League Division 3 North*
1939/40	*Football League North-West*
1940/41	*Blackburn & District Combination +*
1941/42 - 1943/44	*Ceased Activities*
1944/45	*Football League (North)*
1945/46	*Football League Division 3 North (West Region)*
1946/47 - 1957/58	*Football League Division 3 North*
1958/59 - 1959/60	*Football League Division 3*
1960/61 - 1961/62	*Football League Division 4 ++*
1962/63 - 1963/64	*Lancashire Combination Division 2*
1964/65 - 1965/66	*Lancashire Combination Division 1*

+ Designated the 'A' Team - principally local Amateurs
++ Last season, fixtures not completed

ACCRINGTON STANLEY (1968)

1968/69 - 1969/70	No activity (see text)
1970/71 - 1977/78	Lancashire Combination
1978/79 - 1980/81	Cheshire County League Division 2
1981/82	Cheshire County League Division 1
1982/83 - 1987/88	North-West Counties League Division 1
1987/88 - 1990/91	Northern Premier League Division 1
1991/92 - to date	Northern Premier League Premier Division

Football League Records:-

Accrington

	Pl.	W	D	L	F	A	Pts	Position	Av.Att.
1888/89	22	6	8	8	48	48	20	7th	3610
1889/90	22	9	6	7	53	56	24	6th	3055
1890/91	22	6	4	12	28	50	16	10th	2980
1891/92	26	8	4	14	40	78	20	11th	3770
1892/93	30	6	11	13	57	81	23	15th	4000

Lost play-off match to Sheffield Utd.
Relegated to Second Division, but resigned from League.

Accrington Stanley

	Pl.	W	D	L	F	A	Pts	Position	Av.Att.
1921/22	38	19	3	16	73	57	41	5th	8000
1922/23	38	17	7	14	59	65	41	8th	7440
1923/24	42	16	8	18	48	61	40	13th	5660
1924/25	42	15	8	19	60	72	38	17th	5110
1925/26	42	17	3	22	81	105	37	18th	4248
1926/27	42	10	7	25	62	98	27	21st	4100
Successfully re-elected									
1927/28	42	18	8	16	76	67	44	9th	4741
1928/29	42	13	8	21	68	82	34	18th	4398
1929/30	42	14	9	19	84	81	37	16th	4236
1930/31	42	15	9	18	84	108	39	13th	3191
1931/32	40	15	6	19	75	80	36	14th	3521
1932/33	42	15	10	17	78	76	40	13th	2933
1933/34	42	13	7	22	65	101	33	20th	2989
1934/35	42	12	10	20	63	89	34	18th	2785
1935/36	42	17	8	17	63	72	42	9th	3351
1936/37	42	16	9	17	76	69	41	13th	3733
1937/38	42	11	7	24	46	75	29	22nd	4344
Successfully re-elected									
1938/39	42	7	6	29	49	103	20	22nd	3419 *
Successfully re-elected									
1946/47	42	14	4	24	56	92	32	20th	3976 *
1947/48	42	20	6	16	62	59	46	6th	6230
1948/49	42	12	10	20	55	64	34	20th	6001 *
1949/50	42	16	7	19	57	62	39	13th	5891
1950/51	46	11	10	25	42	101	32	23rd	4562
Successfully re-elected									
1951/52	46	10	12	24	61	92	32	22nd	6378

1952/53	46	8	11	27	39	89	27	24th	5549

Successfully re-elected

1953/54	46	16	10	20	66	74	42	15th	7321
1954/55	46	25	11	10	96	67	61	2nd	9766
1955/56	46	25	9	12	92	57	59	3rd	8946
1956/57	46	25	8	13	95	64	58	3rd	8736
1957/58	46	25	9	12	83	61	59	2nd	7187

Founder members of Third Division

1958/59	46	15	12	19	71	87	42	19th	6267
1959/60	46	11	5	30	57	123	27	24th	4083

Relegated to Fourth Division

1960/61	46	16	8	22	74	88	40	18th	3530

1961/62 - Failed to complete fixtures - resigned. Ave. Att. of fixtures played = 2688 *)

(* indicates lowest average in Football League)

Number of Football League matches played:-
Accrington: 122 (plus 1 Test Match)
Accrington Stanley: 1456 (including 1939/40 season, and non-completed 1961/62 season)

SUMMARY OF FACTS

Grounds:
Accrington

1878 - 1894	Accrington Cricket Ground
	Thorneyholme Road, Accrington, Lancs
1894 - 1895	Moorhead Park (only 1 away game played in 1896)

Stanley Villa

1891 - 1893	Probably no regular ground

Accrington Stanley

1893 - 1895	Probably no regular ground
1895 - 1897	Moorhead Park
1897 - 1901	Bell's Ground, Woodnook
1901 - 1916	Moorhead Park
1919 - 1965	Peel Park

Accrington Stanley (1968)

1970 to date	Crown Ground, Livingstone Road

Colours (Football League):
1888/89 - 1892/93 Red Shirts, White Shorts
1921/22 - 1933/34 Red Shirts, White Shorts
1934/35 - 1951/52 Red Shirts, White Sleeves, White Shorts
1952/53 - 1956/57 Red Shirts, White Shorts
1957/58 - 1961/62 Red Shirts, White 'V', White Shorts, Red Stripe
Nickname:
The Reds (Accrington and Accrington Stanley)

Significant matches:
Accrington
First League Game: 8th September 1888 versus Everton (away) - lost 1-2. Attendance 12,000
Last League Game: 15th April 1893 versus Aston Villa (home) - lost 0-1
(play-off match, April 22nd versus Sheffield United at Nott'm Forest - lost 0-1)

Accrington Stanley
First League Game: 27th August 1921 versus Rochdale (away) - lost 3-6. Attendance c. 8,000
Last League Game: 3rd March 1962 versus Crewe Alexandra (away) - lost 0-4. Att. 4,272
(Season not completed)
Record Attendances
Accrington (Probable):-
2nd January 1893 v. Blackburn Rovers (League) approx. 10,000 (£294.80 receipts)
Accrington Stanley:-
15th November 1954 v. Blackburn Rovers (friendly - 1st modern floodlit game) 17,634.
11th April 1955 v. York City (League) - 15,598.
(A unique trio was completed with the record attendance of Accrington Stanley (1968) - since
exceeded in 1990 - in 1987, 1,200, in friendly v. Blackburn Rovers!)

MAIN ACHIEVEMENTS

Accrington
International Players (England):   G. Howarth (1887-1890 - 5 Caps)
                                      J. Whitehead (1893-1894)
Founder members Football League

F.A. Cup: 2nd Round (last 16) 1889/90, 1890/91, 1891/1892, 1892/93
                  1st Round (last 32) 1888/89, (as non-League Club) 1893/94
Lancashire Cup Winners: 1880/81, 1887/88, 1888/89

First Club to resign from Football League

Best League Win: 1889/90 versus Derby County (home) 6-1
Worst League Defeat: 1891/92 versus Aston Villa (away) 2-12

Accrington Stanley
Founder members Football League Division 3 North
F.A. Cup: 4th Round 1926/27, 1936/37, 1958/59 (as non-League Club)
                  2nd Round (Modern equivalent - 4th Round) 1906/07
                  1st Round (Modern equivalent - 3rd Round) 1909/10, 1910/11
Football League 3rd Division Runnersup 1954/55, 1957/58
(Wartime) Football League 3rd Division (West Region) Champions 1945/46
Lancashire Combination Champions: 1902/03, 1905/06
                                    Runners-up: 1903/04, 1912/13
                  Division 2: Champions: 1963/64, (Wartime)
                  North Section: Champions: 1915/16 (1st comp)
Lancashire Junior Cup Winners: 1920/21
1933/34 season: beat New Brighton 8-0, and lost 0-9 to Barnsley - both at Home.

Accrington Stanley (1968)
Lancashire Combination Division 1 Champions: 1973/74, 1977/78
Cup winners: 1971/72, 1972/73, 1973/74, 1976/77
Cheshire County League Division 2 Champions: 1980/81
Challenge Shield Winners: 1979/80, 1980/81
Founder-members Northern Premier League Division 1 (Second Division)
F.A.Cup: 2nd round 1991/92 (1-6 to Crewe A. at 'home' - played at Ewood Park)

ACCRINGTON F.C. - Winners of Lancashire Cup 1880-81

(Back): S.Ormerod, D.Talbot (captain), J.Lonsdale, W.Latham, J.P.Hartley, J.Yates, J.Riley.
(Middle): R.Howarth, J.Hindle. (Front): R.Horne, W.J.Whittaker, T.French, W/Eastham.
(Talbot, Yates, Whittaker, Horne & Hartley were all members of the original committee in 1878,
and all (plus Lonsdale) played in the Club's early matches).

A modern view of the Accrington Cricket Ground from the cemetry road entrance.
The white pavilion on the right. (Taken from a video shot - 'Rejected F.C. The Video')

Of all the Clubs that once graced the Football League, the most charismatic must surely be, Accrington Stanley. Perhaps it is the evocative title, or the fact that the town's connection goes back to the very first year of the Football League in 1888. Although there was a long time span of nearly eighty years in which Accrington were associated with the Football League, the original founder-members (Accrington) and the later Third Division North team (Accrington Stanley), were two completely separate Clubs.

The formation of a Football Club in the town came as no real surprise, since the surrounding area was already well endowed with Clubs, at a time when the new sport was thriving. At a senior level, Darwen started the ball rolling with their formation in 1870 (although their prowess as an Association Club did not manifest itself until six years later), while at nearby Blackburn, the Rovers were founded around 1875, and the now defunct Olympic two years later. Right on Accrington's doorstep was Church F.C. (1874), and Enfield (at Clayton-le-Moors), while in that now distant past other, lesser, teams existed in Accrington, Blackburn and Darwen.

In common with so many other clubs, the Accrington football team was formed from a local Cricket eleven, who decided to provide their players with a winter sport. The Football team was first created in 1876, when the Cricketers were playing - coincidentally - at Peel Park (the home many years later of Stanley). It is most likely that the football was of an uncompetitive nature and probably a mixture of both Association and Rugby forms. It was not until 1878, that the definite choice of Association rules was accepted, following a meeting at the Black Horse Public House in Abbey Street.

The Club's first President, Colonel Hargreaves, was chosen, and the Club's colours of Scarlet and Black were adopted. From the outset they were known colloquially as "Th' Owd Reds", or simply "The Reds". The home venue was to be the Accrington Cricket Ground, and the footballers first games coincided with the cricketers move to their new headquarters at Thorneyholme Road. The football venue was located in Cemetery Road, which was used as the ground address; the resting place was adjacent, but on the other side of the railway. Other, less ambitious, football clubs soon sprang up in the large town, including Accrington Wanderers who played near Peel Park and Accrington Borough whose Ground was at Moorhead Park - where Accrington F.C. were to see their final days.

Attendances of up to 3,000 were not uncommon at the Accrington Cricket Club matches, and within a short space of time these numbers were to be equalled by the Football team. The first game, on the 28th September 1878, was suitably a local derby contest with Church Rovers (probably not the more senior Church team), and such was the low key nature of the encounter that a match report was not even published in the local newspaper alongside other games. But the records show that the Reds claimed a win by two goals (one disputed) to one!

The official (hand written) completed fixture list from the Club's first season.

One week later the press were aware of the next Accrington match, and reported that the game was 'end to end' football, in which good play by The Reds in the second half lead to a two-nil victory after a scoreless first half. The opponents were Clitheroe (formed one year earlier), and the game was played at their local Cricket Field. The match had started at 3.30pm, with the homesters Captain - A.H. Aitken - kicking off. Accrington were represented by:- Heaton, Whittaker, Horn, Higham, Talbot (Captain), Lonsdale, J.S. Clayton, Hartley, Lightfoot, J.Clayton and Yates. After a 1-2 away defeat to Witton St.Marks, the Reds second home game was played on October the 19th. By this time there was an awareness of the new Football team, for, *"a large number of spectators"*, were present for the visit of Harwood. By half-time there were no goals, but with more determination in the second period, Lonsdale scored, for Accrington to record another victory. Haslingden Rangers were the next team to experience a defeat to the newcomers, by three goals at the Accrington Cricket Field, and this match was followed by the Reds two goal home victory over Cob Wall.

On November 1st, just a few weeks after their first ever game, Accrington were to play in one of the earliest Floodlit matches; surely an experience in such a short time from formation, that has never been equalled! The match was played at Alexandra Meadows, the home of Blackburn Rovers.

The 'Exhibition of Electric Light', as it was advertised, was provided by two Grammes Machines which were supplied by Parker & Bury of Manchester, with each producing 8 hp. Two Serrin lamps (one near the refreshment tent, and the other by the scoring tent) were used, with each giving 6,000 candlelight power - although it was reflected on afterwards that four lights would have been better. The choice of Accrington as opponents was an honour for the fledgling Club, but it mattered little who was playing or the eventual result to the enormous crowd that had gathered for this novelty encounter. It was estimated that between seven and eight thousand packed into the Ground, with a further 20,000 fascinated witnesses gathered in Corporation Park, which lay to the East of the enclosure. A white ball was used and the scene was described as being, *"charming and fairylike"*. Although the result was of little consequence, the Reds were easily overcome by the stronger and far more experienced Rovers, by four unopposed goals (one disputed), after a two goal half-time lead.

Not to be outdone, this wonderfully successful adventure was repeated in Accrington two weeks later, while betwixt times, matches with another Haslingden team and a return with Church Rovers were both won. On Wednesday the 20th of November, a more moderate gathering of some 3,000 - that viewed the proceedings from every vantage point - assembled to see the Electric Light exhibited in Accrington for the first time, although most of whom were just happy to witness the night-time glare! However, the experiment was not without its problems. An engine providing the power was damaged at the Railway Station, and Bury & Parker had to rapidly substitute a portable steam engine, which had been loaned by the local Gas Company. The first and only gas powered electric floodlights?

With a full moon aiding the artificial luminescence, the two lamps - at opposite corners of the pitch - provided a good light. However, the pitch was not conducive to good football as early snow two days previously had thawed by the kick-off time of 7.50pm. The visitors, Church, scored immediately, but Accrington equalised after ten minutes, whereupon the light near the dressing tent went out! The subsequent repairs caused a delay of 30 minutes, during which time the players amused themselves by kicking the ball around and playing leapfrog! The Accrington Brass Band also played a selection of tunes.

No more goals were scored before the break, but three quick goals in the second half gave Church a 3-2 lead before the homesters equalised 2 minutes from time. Hot coffee (no alcohol) was served during the proceedings, and the spectators went home well satisfied with this novel break in their hardworking lives. 76 years later the successors of Accrington F.C. became one of the first Clubs to install a more permanent floodlighting system. The lighting novelty was not repeated in Accrington, and the fad soon died out elsewhere, although further experiments were tried some forty years later, at which time they were frowned upon by the Football Association.

Just five more defeats were experienced during the rest of the season, which ran on until mid-April. But these set-backs were hardly disgraces; twice they lost to Blackburn Rovers, twice to the equally powerful Darwen side, and by 0-2 to Enfield. The third meeting with the Rovers, on March the 29th (a 1-4 defeat), was a 'Complimentary Benefit' match, a suggestion of payments being made to Blackburn's clandestine professionals. A total of 25 games were played by the Reds (including the two floodlit experiments), of which 17 were won, 1 drawn and only 7 lost, a good record for a Club's inaugural season in which several quality sides were encountered. The strangest contest of all was the last game, which was billed as a 'Scratch Match'.

The title was a very apt description, since the opposition consisted of players from Edinburgh (the Reds probably already having thoughts of emulating Darwen with their Scottish professional players), Blackburn, Church and other Accrington Clubs. With the fast approaching Cricket season, it was necessary to play the game in an adjacent field to the Thorneyholme Ground. An attendance of 600 spectators was present, and after Accrington had gone into a commanding 5-2 lead, the match came to an abrupt end, since all the players were tired out as they had been playing for some two hours!

The 1879/80 season saw the Club with three teams - a Reserve eleven was run in the first season - and with plenty of supporting players available, the Club hoped to be able to raise their standards to that of the major Clubs in Lancashire. The first match was played at home to Padiham, before an encouraging attendance of 400, but the Reds actions for the second game were to displease the local fans. The game in question was the first round in the Lancashire Cup, not only Accrington's first truly competitive game, but also the inaugural season of the Competition. Hallewell - from the Bolton area - were the visitors, but for this attractive match, the admission charges were raised, and the locals responded by boycotting the encounter! But this didn't stop the homesters in recording a 4-1 victory.

October, saw the first encounter with Astley Bridge - another team from Bolton, who were founded in 1875 - was played at Thorneyholme Road. Early in the match, a goal was claimed by Accrington which was disputed by the visitors. A final decision was asked of the Referee, a Mr M. Smith who had been agreed upon as the official by both teams. But when he allowed the goal to stand, the Astley team responded by refusing to continue with the game unless Mr Smith was replaced. After much discussion a replacement was eventually approved, but it was not long before Astley again raised objections to some of the substitute official's decisions - the visitors eventually lost the game 1-5! It is little wonder that the game became a rough contest, with the spectators adding their vocal comments, and becoming, *"noisy and using coarse language"*.

Despite the many players at the Club's disposal, the match at Bolton was lost by a single goal - due to only eight Accrington men turning up! But two weeks later the full team made amends by beating Witton St. Marks, 3-0, in the next round of the Lancashire Cup before a home crowd of over 500. The Reds went on to win in the final, when Blackburn Park Road were overcome in an exciting game at Darwen - by 6-4 - with receipts of nearly £52 being taken at the gate.

Accrington were making steady progress, and in the 1880/81 season, among the total of 28 games played, 21 were won, 1 drawn and only 6 lost; the goal difference showed a high scoring record of 112-47. One year later, the final record showed:- 37 played, of which only 20 were victories (plus 12 defeats and 5 draws), but the Club had 'upgraded' their fixtures, and by this time were matched with higher rated teams. During the 1881/82 season, 34 different players had been used in the first team, with J. Yates as an ever-present (and scoring 23 goals), J. Hargreaves missing only two games, and J. Hindle missing three.

At this time doubts were expressed by the Lancashire Football Association, regarding the use of 'foreign' (i.e. non-local) players, with the suspicion that professionalism was being practised - this argument was to have serious repercussions some two years later.

A run through to the final of the County Cup was again made, with victories including a four goal victory against Witton in the semi-final, at Darwen. This had been the second attempt to resolve the tie, as the Reds had already won by 2-1 - aided by a special trainload of supporters in the 3,000 crowd - but a successful protest by Witton regarding the use of an unregistered player, had required the match to be replayed. The final was lost to Blackburn by 1-3, before a 5,000 attendance at the Cricket Field, Turf Moor (Burnley F.C.). The biggest advance of the season was the Club's first entry into the F.A. Cup, and although the second round was reached, they were easily beaten at that stage by the all conquering Darwen team, with a 3-1 scoreline.

The owners of the Ground, the Cricket Club, allowed the Reds in 1882 to build a seated stand to one side of the football pitch location. Although this amenity was welcomed, there were repercussions when, one year later, the Football Club was instructed that they must dismantle it after each home match! But there were bigger problems on the horizon. By now, the Club found that in order to compete successfully with their near neighbours - notably Blackburn Rovers and Darwen - they would need to improve the quality of the players. There was only one way that this could be achieved, and that was by 'importing' and paying footballers (usually from Scotland); the team became a professional outfit. This trend had already been started by Darwen some four years earlier, and was rapidly copied by others, but Clubs involved in such actions were pursuing a dangerous course, for professionalism as such, was yet to be recognised by either the Local or the National Football Associations. The Club maintained, not very convincingly, that the Scotsmen were playing for the Club for the love of the game, and were in fact refusing payments! But it soon transpired that they were paid the not inconsiderable sum of up to £5 per match. Despite such payments being undoubtedly made by other Clubs, particularly in Lancashire, it was Accrington who became the scapegoats. In November 1884, they were expelled from both the Football and the Lancashire Associations, banned from playing in all Cup games, and even prevented from playing friendlies against other affiliated Clubs - although the latter was soon relaxed.

Most of the other 'professional' Clubs sympathised with the Reds, and many refused to declare that they were not paying their players. The F.A. was still very much dominated by the 'pure' amateur South, and in a show of solidarity the rebels declared their intention of forming a British Football Association. With such actions in mind, Accrington, along with no less than 35 other Clubs, met late in 1884. With the risk of the disintegration of the F.A. - the overall ruling body - the Association met in early 1885, to discuss the legalising of professionalism in the sport, and amid much confusion, discussion and debate, the matter was finally resolved in July 1885. Subject to certain restrictions (which appear to have never been rigorously administered) regarding players birthplaces and/or residence, the F.A. finally capitulated to the North's demands, when it was announced that, *"Professionals shall be allowed to compete in all Cup-ties"*.

With this concession sanctioned, a veritable flood of Scots descended on England, all keen to earn a good and pleasurable living playing football. In December 1884 alone, Bonnar and Conway (both from Thornliebank), McBeth from St. Bernards and the Arthurlie Player, Stevenson all joined Accrington F.C.

The 1882/83 season, had been a busy and generally successful one, both on and off the field, but the Club were not without competition in and around Accrington. Other local teams included Stanley Rovers, but they had no connection with the later Stanley Villa. Peel Bank Rovers, and the Accrington Remnants and Ramblers were others that vied for spectators. But with the Reds overall advantage, with their paid players, they were rapidly becoming the undisputed 'top dogs' in the town. Early games included a 2-3 defeat at Northwich Victoria, a six goal win at home to Padiham, and six goals shared with Bolton Wanderers in Accrington before a 4,000 crowd. There was a shock in the F.A. Cup however, when the up and coming Blackburn Olympic triumphed by 6-3 in the F.A. Cup, a game played at their 'Hole-'i-th-wall' Ground.

The next season saw an increasing interest in matches versus Scottish teams - and the subsequent poaching of their players. St. Bernards were beaten 4-2, despite the Reds being two goals in arrears after only seven minutes, and other home games included, Dumbarton (the Scottish Cup holders) which finished as a 0-4 defeat, and a 2-1 loss to Pollock Shields Athletic of Glasgow. There was little progress in the Lancashire Cup, when, before a 5,000 attendance at the Accrington Cricket Field, the nearby Church team ran out 3-2 victors, after the Reds had beaten South Shore (from Blackpool) in the previous 3rd round by 3-0.

The somewhat disharmonious relationship continued with their Cricket Club landlords, when it was suggested in April, by the latter, that the two should combine to form 'Accrington Cricket and Football Club' - an opposite proposal to that down the road, where Darwen were about to become independent. At a meeting on the 1st of May 1883, which was attended by 300 members, it transpired that the Football Club was generally against the proposal, as they felt that they would have no say in any decisions from an all Cricket Club Committee. The Cricketers reminded their tenants that they held the lease on the Ground, and pointed out that £350 had been spent on levelling the field and drainage, that would not have been necessary for solely their own sport; however, they did propose two separate Committees, but with just one Treasurer. This was countered with the statement that the Football team had contributed over £300 (including £159 in the current season) over the past five years. One faction considered that it could work but only with one combined Committee which could include a good Football Club representation. Those against were all for breaking the ties completely and finding another Ground.

A deputation was sent to the next Cricket Club meeting, and after much debate the amalgamation proposal was thrown out with a vote of 21 to 13. So the two Clubs were back to square one. The Cricketers couldn't afford to throw out their paying tenants, and the Football Club knew that there was not another economical and suitable home venue elsewhere. The next season saw the Cricketers demanding payments for the Football Club's use of the 'footstands' (probably raised timber terracing, or duckboards as they were also known). But additional expenditure could be ill-afforded, especially with £80 still owing, from the original £170, for the purchase of the covered stand. The economic realities of running a professional outfit were already being felt, although in 1886 raffles which attracted a large number of entries were started, with the first prize of a house! Meanwhile on the pitch, interest was ever increasing.

A 5,000 attendance was attracted to the Cricket Field for the visit of Preston, a game in with an exciting comeback for the homesters when they won 3-2, after being two goals in arrears. Run of the mill Friendlies were not so well supported however, with 2,000 being typical for the match versus Padiham.

By the 1887/88 season the club could boast of having one of the best teams in the North, for they could now hold their own with their contemporaries. At Thorneyholme Road, Glasgow Northern were beaten 4-1, Thornliebank were thrashed by ten unopposed goals on the 2nd of January, Wolverhampton Wanderers by the same score (although it later transpired - much to Accrington's indignation - that the opposition was their Reserve team), and Bolton Wanderers by 3-1. Football was also proving to be an attraction for spectators; over 6,000 at Newton Heath (a one goal win), and no fewer than 12,000 at Preston where the Reds lost by two goals. The return game with the North End was greeted with much excitement and a new record attendance of around 8,000 was present to see the locals lose by 1-2 in a game noted for the good passing moves from the visitors (a new innovation), but with erratic shooting from both teams.

The Lancashire Cup run was terminated in bizarre fashion. At the end of January 1888, Darwen were surprisingly overcome by 4-0 on their own Ground in the 3rd round, which took the Reds through to the semi-finals. The opposition, Witton, held Accrington to a 1-1 draw at Fleetwood before a 2,000 attendance, in freezing conditions, but in the replay at Blackburn - in front of 5,000 spectators - they were beaten 2-1. Witton protested, claiming that the winning goal by Conway was offside. An enquiry was held, at which the complainants claimed that both the Umpires and the Referee had misinterpreted the rules. Amazingly all the Officials were present at the hearing, and with the aid of diagrams, they were proved correct in their decision. The appeal was thrown out! This took Accrington through to the final, when an even more ludicrous situation arose. Preston North End were to be the Reds opponents, at the Leamington Ground Blackburn, but the North End complained at the choice of venue, it being so close to Accrington. The Lancashire F.A. would not back down, and Preston scratched from the Competition.

On the 25th of April, Accrington met Witton at Blackburn, supposedly to contest the newly arranged final, and the Reds lost 0-4. Since Accrington had already beaten Witton (in the semi-final), the Lancashire F.A. decided to award the winners medals to Accrington, and to 'use-up' the runners-up medals decreed that Witton should play Darwen Old Wanderers (the other losing semi-finalists), at which the former were the victors. Hence the Cup winners were Accrington - despite losing in the final to the team they beat at the semi-final stage - and Witton were the runners-up although losing in the semi-finals but winning the 'final'! It is little wonder that the time was ripe for the formation of the Football League, when very stringent rules were applied, including the requirement to play arranged fixtures on pre-set dates.

By 1888, it was recognised amongst the professionals in the North of England, that something was necessary to maintain spectator interest in the Sport. Whilst Cup matches were very attractive, they were too few in number, particularly for Clubs that were eliminated at the early stages, and frequent date changes and replays resulted in chaos as regards to keeping to pre-arranged friendly fixtures.

The formation of the Football League was the brainchild of William McGregor, who was on the Committee at Aston Villa. He wrote to five Clubs in March 1888 with his proposal that each should play each other, home and away, on set dates. Bolton Wanderers reply included the suggestion that the number of teams should be extended to eight more, including Accrington, but the Reds were not a popular Club with some - and notably Preston! In the final event, due to only 22 available dates for matches, just twelve were chosen.

On the 8th September 1888, Accrington travelled to Everton to play the joint first ever (there were five) League matches. Despite such an auspicious occasion, although probably not recognised at the time, the day was far from successful for the Reds. They delayed the kick-off by 20 minutes due to their late arrival, and lost the game 1-2. The Reds won the toss, and played into the sun, and Lewis of Everton kicked off.

An even first half produced no goals, and despite Accrington being the stronger team in the second period, they conceded a goal. Then disaster struck when Horne had to go off injured with a fractured rib. His replacement, McLellan, immediately conceded a second goal, and Everton with superior numbers took control of the match. The scoring was completed when Holden obtained a consolation for Accrington. The team consisted of:- Horne, Stevenson, McLellan, Haworth, Wilkinson, Pemberton, Lofthouse, Bonar, E. Kirkham, Holden and Chippendale.

A poor distribution of fixtures resulted in the Reds playing three more away fixtures before their debut at home. Blackburn Rovers were met at Alexandra Meadows on the 15th of September, when a large crowd witnessed a highly entertaining 5-5 draw. Seven days later a trip was made to Derby for the first ever meeting of the two Clubs, and a 2,000 crowd saw two goals shared. On the penultimate day of the month, the first win was recorded - 4-2 - after a two goal lead at half-time, at Stoke, before around 3,000 spectators.

October the 6th came, and the first home League match for the Reds. The occasion was marked with a crowd of 4,000, including Mr Hermon-Hodge MP, all keenly anticipating the competitive match with Wolverhampton Wanderers. The crowd were not disappointed with the thriller that followed. Barbour first scored for the Reds, but the Wolves fought back strongly to make the score 2-1 in their favour. By half-time each team had scored again, but after five minutes into the second period Accrington equalised, then went into the lead following a fine shot from Brand. Just before the end, the visitors scored again to tie the match 4-4. Thorneyholme Road Cricket Field had witnessed its first, and highly entertaining, Football League game.

On week later, Derby County were the visitors, and their late arrival appeared to unbalance them for by half-time they were four goals in arrears. The second half proved more even, when both teams scored two goals each, to complete another high-scoring match. On October 27th, the Reds lost by the narrow margin of 3-4 at Aston Villa (despite being ahead just before the end), and then recorded a draw with another visit to the Midlands, at the Stony Lane Ground of West Bromwich Albion; the Referee at the latter game, made a number of decisions which displeased the small crowd of 1,000 or so.

Two more away visits followed, firstly to Notts County, where before an 8,000 attendance six goals were shared - after Accrington had missed their train, causing the game to start 38 minutes behind schedule - and on November the 17th, the match was lost by 0-2 at Preston, where yet again the Reds arrived late! There were only 2,000 spectators present for the return visit at home to West Bromwich, at which Accrington recorded a 2-1 victory.

After twelve matches had been played - eight of them on foreign soil - a reasonable record of three victories, six draws and three defeats had resulted, with a goal difference of 31-28. On December 1st, after taking a two goal interval lead, the Reds ran out easy winners by 5-1 over Burnley, before a 3,000 home crowd. But the tables were turned next week at Pike's Lane, Bolton, when a 1-4 reverse was suffered. By Christmas on encouraging sixth place in the League table was achieved, and confidence was at a high following a home friendly demolition of Partick Thistle to the tune of 10-0.

The Club's attention was then drawn towards the F.A. Cup, and the visit of neighbours Blackburn Rovers. A year earlier in the same competition, one of the best games ever seen at Accrington had resulted in a victory for the visitors, and this latest visit was awaited with keen anticipation. But bad weather put paid to a bumper crowd, and before only 3,000 spectators a dour 1-1 draw was played. In the replay, Accrington were outplayed, losing by five unopposed goals, but before a gate of around 8,000 which produced receipts of £110. The second match was the 39th meeting of the two - the first in 1878 - a fixture which usually favoured the Rovers.

By the season's end, the Club could look back with reasonable satisfaction. The Football League placing was fair, 7th of 12 Clubs, and the Lancashire Cup was won for the third time. In all games, 18 victories, 9 draws and 12 defeats were recorded. But the strength of the opposition had been emphasised with the corresponding record of a year earlier when 25 wins, 8 draws and only 8 defeats had resulted.

The 1889/90 campaign got off to a good start with two Friendly victories over Irwell Springs (7-1) and Southport Central by five goals. After three League games, the Reds were undefeated, but the fourth - away to the Wolves on October the 5th - ended in a 1-2 defeat. Seven days later disaster struck with the visit of Notts County to Accrington. A crowd of only 2,000 (financially things were already far from healthy), saw the homesters take an early lead, but this was soon cancelled out. By half-time the Reds were 1-4 in arrears, and at the end of the game a humiliating 1-8 defeat had been experienced. Several forward changes were made for the next match, although defensive alterations would have seemed more appropriate! By the end of October the Club were languishing fourth from bottom in the League, and confidence sagged even further when they, as holders, lost 2-4 to Bolton in the County Cup competition. But an encouraging 6-1 defeat of Derby on the 16th of November - the best result of the season - saw the start of a moderate recovery which finished with Accrington lying sixth in the table.

The 1890/91 season gave cause for concern for a drop down to 10th was the final outcome. Although the home record was reasonable - five wins, one draw and five defeats - on their travels the Reds only recorded one victory (2-1 at struggling Derby County), and were thrashed 5-1 at West Bromwich, 5-0 at Notts County and by one more goal at Bolton.

One year later the situation was no better, and the lack of success was giving grave cause for concern. Once again the home record was reasonable - only three defeats in thirteen matches (the League had been extended by two) - but on their travels, there were some very emphatic defeats; 0-5 to Wolves, by nine unopposed goals at Notts County, and a complete disaster at Aston Villa with a Football League record 2-12 reverse. It was recognised that the hardworking Committee had kept the Club's head above water - although the season had seen a financial loss - and the other Clubs had faith in the team, for the Reds were comfortably re-elected for the second successive season.

In the F.A. Cup, the only shock saw Accrington beat Bolton Wanderers by 5-1 after a 2-2 draw, in the 1889/90 campaign. But they then proceeded to lose to Wolverhampton in the second round. The same stage was reached one year later, after a 1st round 4-1 victory over the Crusaders Club, followed by a 1-3 defeat to Sunderland in the next sortie.

The 1892/93 season was to be the last in the Football League for Accrington F.C., a period which saw an incredible turnaround in the Club's fortunes. The campaign started in terrible fashion with a first game home defeat by six goals to the all powerful Sunderland team, followed by a 2-5 reverse at the Wednesday (Sheffield) one week later. But with only four more defeats by the end of the year, the Reds gradually climbed the table. December had been highly successful, with four home victories, one away draw, and no defeats, which led to the Club's highest ever placing of 5th in the League. On January the 2nd, the visit of neighbours Blackburn Rovers, attracted the (probable) record attendance at the Cricket Ground when approximately 10,000 packed into the enclosure, and paid £295 to witness a 1-1 draw, which raised the team one place in the League. By now the Club were rejoicing at their recovery, and at the A.G.M. in January it was reported that the increase in home gates had allowed some of the Club's mounting debts to be paid off. The joy was to be shortlived, for there was to be a terrible change in the Club's fortunes on the horizon.

The F.A. Cup had its financial rewards, for after beating Stoke - who were accompanied by 500 rattle waving supporters - at Accrington by 2-1 (which saw the Reds endure a desperate defensive battle towards the end), the Club was drawn to play Preston North End at Accrington in the second round. The prospect of meeting 'Proud Preston' captured the local's imagination as no other game had. A special foot-stand was erected opposite the seated stand which could accommodate 3,000, and a record attendance was confidently expected. The team even went into training for the week before the big game - on

'Favours' were popular from the early 1890's, they were similarly used as the later rosette

February the 4th - with cigarettes and beer banned to the players after the Wednesday of that week! The gate receipts produced at the final tally only amounted to £284 - less than for the earlier Blackburn visit for the League match - and despite an enthusiastic reception and continued support during the game, the homesters lost 1-4.

This match was to herald the disaster that was to follow. From the fourth place on January 2nd, five straight defeats to March the 5th sent the team tumbling down the League to 13th (second from bottom). No more victories were achieved by the season's end. Ironically during this period of disaster, the Club's inside right - Whitehead - was capped for England in the match against Wales.

Of all the defeats, the worst was at Aston Villa. The Club had shot into a remarkable four goal lead, and even with 25 minutes left on the clock were leading by 4-1, yet they finished up on the wrong end of a 4-6 defeat! The last game was played at home in the return with the Villa team on the 15th April. With the necessity of competing in the play-offs by now a certainty, the fans had all but deserted the Club. Despite having the best of the game, the forwards were woeful, and although leading by one goal, an error by the 'keeper near the end produced a final 1-1 draw. The team for this last Football League match consisted of:- Mason, Hodge, Ditchfield, Bowie, Matthews, Shuttleworth, T. Lea, Whitehead, Cookson, H. Lea, Kirkham.

In a desperate attempt to raise the Players morale, gold medals were offered as inducements to win the play-off game against Sheffield United at Nottingham one week later. Despite the earlier poor finishing of the forwards, there was just one change in the line-up from that of the Villa match, with Stevenson replacing Matthews. But it was all to no avail, and with the forwards again well off form - notably many missed chances by Cookson - the Club bowed out to a one goal defeat. The Accrington support at the game consisted of just two Committee men!

This was the first season of the Second Division and the play-off system, a method whereby the promoted and relegated teams between the Divisions was to be determined. Accrington expressed the hope that the First Division would be extended and that they would get good support for them to remain in the top tier. But extra Clubs were not to be and therefore their defeat to Sheffield United had automatically meant their relegation.

Rather than just accepting this lowering in status, doubts were raised as to the League to enter for 1893/94 - would it be the Second Division or the highly rated, but undoubtably lower standard Lancashire League? This was the main topic in a 'Future of Accrington F.C.' meeting that was held in June. Such indecision, in modern times, would be unthinkable - the choice of League or non-League status - but the Club considered the financial implications of their future. The previous few years had not been financially secure, and large debts had mounted. Ironically, the 1892/93 season had produced greatly increased gate receipts (£1,892) than on year earlier, and an overall loss of only £42 was shown. The Club had to consider that a reduced status would almost certainly produce less gates, whereas the more localised Lancashire League would decrease expenditure substantially.

At the meeting a collection for the Club was made, and at a further meeting at the end of July it was revealed that not only had an appeal for additional funds produced little money, but also the Committee were unwilling to act as guarantors against further losses; it was estimated that even with cost-cutting, around £1,000 would be required for the next twelve months.

The Club considered that they had little option but to resign from the Football League and submitted their reasons to the governing Committee. Although their resignation came at the eve of the new season (Middlesbrough Ironopolis who had been unsuccessful in the Second Division election was offered, and accepted, the now vacant place), their leaving was based on sound and sensible reasons, but the Football League thought otherwise, and adopted a severe and somewhat high-handed attitude.

They ruled that the Reds must pay the additional expenses of £7-7-0d, that they had caused in relation to re-arranging fixtures, and further, that no Football League team could be played in any friendly matches until such time that the money was paid! The Club refused to pay up. Additionally their late resignation gave the Reds possible bigger worries in their gaining acceptance into the Lancashire League. But no doubt the Club's previous status influenced the County League into welcoming the club with open arms.

The Club's continual refusal to pay the - perhaps albeit unfair - but none the less moderate fine to the Football League, led to the Club having a dearth of fixtures - the Lancashire competition only had twelve teams. This in turn resulted in the players leaving for other Clubs, one of the first being Whitehead to Blackburn Rovers for an enormous, but much needed, fee of £100. Eventually they capitulated and paid up their fine to the F.A. in late November, but by this time the team had lost all their capable and experienced men. During this period of despondency, the Club had contributed to one innovation in the Football World, that was soon to be repeated throughout, when they were credited with being the first English team to incorporate three half-backs - an idea probably copied from Scotland.

The August trial games had attracted healthy crowds of up to 1,000, and when the season commenced, there was optimism in the air and the confidence that they would carry away the Championship of their new competition and be elected back into the First Division of the Football League. Southport Central were met in a friendly game on September the 2nd - a 1-5 defeat - followed by the first Lancashire League match two days later at home to Blackpool, which resulted in a 1-3 scoreline. A poor start led to the crowds quickly deserting the sinking ship. The first game had attracted an excellent following of around 3,000, and this figure was maintained when Bury were the visitors in the fourth League match - but half of the crowd were the visitor's supporters!

The Committee announced that they would spend money and acquire players, but by December the attendances had dropped to barely 300 - with many changing their allegiance to Blackburn Rovers - and it became increasingly questionable as to how the Club were still managing to survive, let alone spend money. Despite the financial problems, there evolved a great improvement on the playing front.

But when Burton Swifts were the visitors to the Cricket Field before the turn of the year (admittedly the weather was very poor), less than 100 spectators paid just £1 in total to watch the game.

Early in the new year, the club had risen to 3rd in the League and had recaptured some of their lost support with attendances having risen to over 1,000. But the earlier problems had taken effect and with so few League matches, the club were by now, well in debt. But then the troubles multiplied. Unruly crowds had by now became a feature of Reds' matches; the players and linesmen were attacked at West Manchester, and at Bury the visitors in the crowd threw stones and kicked the team at the end of the match - with the Police having to escort the players off the pitch! The club were obviously not blameless for they were quickly earning the reputation of having a rough and undisciplined tem, governed by a weak committee. No doubt the men had cause for grievance, since by the end of March, they were owed money and a Godsend contribution came by way of the club's £80 share of an excellent £170 gate following a match with Everton. A topsy-turvy season resulted in a high placing in the League, but finished with empty coffers!

Some additional income came by way of a late season competition, The County Palantine League (South Division) in which five teams competed. Despite their problems, the Reds reached the semi-finals of the Lancashire Cup and played well in the match against the F.A. Cup finalists Bolton Wanderers, at Everton, before an incredible 10,000 attendance (receipts £236) and only lost by a single goal. The game was not without incident since bad sportsmanship came once again to the fore and Bolton limped off at the end with no less than six injured players! The F.A. Cup run ended in the first round proper with a three goal defeat to Sunderland. Somewhat ambitiously, the club re-applied for election to the Football League, but it was no surprise when they received only seven votes. The bad reputation of the club was noted by their landlords, the Cricket Club, and with unpaid debts and a reminder of the money spent at the ground on the football team's behalf, they were forced to leave at the season's end.

A move was made to Moorhead Park, where the ground had been enclosed and a Grandstand built. Expenses were halved as the club were to share the venue with an up and coming Junior side, by the name of Accrington Stanley!

Any hopes of the Reds return to their former standing in Lancashire football were severely shaken when the opening League game was lost by 1-4 at Fairfield, which was followed by a poor scoreless draw in a Friendly at home to Nelson on September 5th. Even so, the home debut at the Reds new home was greeted with much enthusiasm, and councillor J.S.Higham did the honours by ceremoniously kicking-off.

Apart from these two poor to indifferent results on the field, there was plenty of justified criticism aimed at the committee who appeared to be running the club in a very casual fashion. There was little done to advertise the inaugural match, despite the auspicious occasion at this new venue - just two flags were flying over the ground announcing the match. But worse was to come in the club's first home League game.

There was a grand cycle parade on the day and as a good publicity move, the players joined in. However, the parade started late and instead of moving onto Moorhead as soon as possible, they dallied (in the pub?) for so long that the football game kick-off was delayed for 45 minutes! Prior to this, the spectators who had arrived at the ground found that there were no tickets for sale and no explanations. Clitheroe were beaten 2-1, and they took a dim view of the proceedings and reported Accrington to the League.

A generally poor start was made to the season, although attendances - at least initially - were encouraging; nearly 2,000 for Bacup's visit and 3,000 (£43 receipts) for table-topping Blackpool's appearance - the latter resulting in a single goal win for the Reds. Nearly 4,000 were present for the F.A. Cup qualifying round game for Bacup's second visit - the first time that Accrington had had to play at such an early stage - but a four goal defeat put paid to any run in that competition.

As the team's performances got worse, so did the attendances, with only an £8 gate for a friendly with Rotherham and barely 700 present for Chorley's visit on December the 8th. Only 600 turned up to see an incredibly one sided game with Heywood Central, who were beaten 13-0. By Christmas, finances were so bad that it was thought likely that the club would have to field an all amateur team by the season's end.

The New Year led to a moderate recovery on the field however, to give the team a mid-table placing, but the latter half of the season saw another poor run. It was something of a surprise to see the team reach the semi-finals of the Lancashire Cup again, but they lost at this stage to Preston by 1-6, at Blackburn in front of a 6,000 crowd. With little money to pay for the professional players, ever increasing numbers of inexperienced amateurs were tried, which led to worse results and inevitably, ever decreasing support.

"The Reds with this weakened team, are struggling on the best they can till the close of the season. Although interest in their doings is fast reaching vanishing point, and the players themselves can hardly have much relish for their work." These sentiments were expressed by the local press on April the 15th. At the same time, the club management were talking about putting the club in the front rank again by next season, a desire that was no more than a pipe dream.

Following a 3-1 defeat by Fleetwood, there were just three more League games left and the first two were lost heavily by seven unopposed goals at South Shore and 0-6 versus Chorley. The last game on April the 17th, resulted in a surprise home win over Southport Central, especially as the scratch team consisted of only ten players and was played before no more than 50 spectators.

Incredibly, the impoverished club managed to make a start in the 1895-86 season and even managed to undertake some ground improvements, including the re-erection of the grandstand which had been blown down by storms during the previous December. The local press stated that: *"The wonder is that it* (Accrington) *exists at all"*, and considered that the club should be, *"put on ice"*, for one or two years.

Local amateur players were used for the first match - now in the Lancashire Combination - but were not disgraced in their 1-2 reverse to Burnley's second eleven. The first home match was a poor 2-2 draw with Oswaldtwistle Rovers before barely 100 spectators - which consisted mostly of visiting fans - and on October 5th, the preliminary round of the F.A. Cup was played against West Manchester at Old Trafford, despite a home draw, and the Reds lost by 0-4. The club managed to put together the elements of an experienced team, and the next game ended in a victory over Rawtenstall to lift the team to a mid-table position, but the attendance was only a pathetic 150.

On October 12th, the last ever League game was played in the return with the Oswald-twistle team. Due to a dispute over wages to the paid players, the Accrington secretary Mr J. Heys, sent a telegram to the host club informing them that the game could not be played as the Reds were unable to raise a full team. The match was immediately postponed, but five minutes later, another telegram announced that they could play after all! A scratch Accrington team was hopelessly outplayed and lost by 2-7, after a 1-3 half-time score, with Smith providing the Red's last goal. At this point, the League record showed a 13th placing - with one victory, one draw and three defeats - and a goal difference of 12-18.

From this point on, no matches were played and it was reasonably assumed that the club had folded. Then to everybody's surprise a team was got together for the first round Lancashire Cup-tie at Darwen on January the 18th. The prospect of the match raised little interest and was watched by only 800 spectators. The Reds actually managed to include an ex-England International (Forrest), but the team was hopelessly overwhelmed. The first half produced six goals to the homesters and was doubled after 90 minutes, a game in which Accrington rarely crossed the halfway line. This, to all intents and purposes, heralded the end of Accrington F.C. since no more matches were ever played.

Meanwhile, for the other club playing at Moorhead Park, things were beginning to look much brighter.

Accrington Stanley F.C. are said to have been created from the Stanley Villa club - supposedly a team formed in the early 1890's and named so due to the fact that several of the members lived in Stanley Street. Documentary evidence cannot confirm these facts, since the club did not first play in a League - at least worthy of report in the local press - until 1894. It is very likely that at a time of growth in the sport, notably in Lancashire, Stanley Villa - as a junior status team - were just one of a myriad of clubs playing friendly games only in the locality.

It is a fact, that as the Accrington F.C. club were in the process of a rapid decline, the Stanley team - renamed as Accrington Stanley (at least from 1894) - were enjoying a great deal of additional support, and they first entered a league of any standing in the 1894-95 season. Although the competition was only the Accrington and District League, it was a large step up the ladder to recognition and a local journalist stated that: *"The club may be justly regarded as the premier junior team in the District".* At least the ground-sharing of Moorhead Park would have suggested that the club were financially viable, probably more so than their joint tenants at the ground!

The "Stanleyites" - as they were known in these early days - started the season well with three League match victories, and by Christmas were proudly heading the table with seven wins and only one defeat. As the Reds sunk even further into oblivion, the Stanleyites were blossoming and by the season's end, were runners-up in the Accrington and District League - albeit, a competition composed of only seven teams. The new Accrington club continued their rise in status with entry into the North-East Lancashire League for the 1895-96 season.

Even higher grade teams that were now met did not prove too much for the team, and by the turn of the year they were in third position in the League table. Support was also increasing and a season's best crowd of 600 was present for the visit of Peel Bank Rovers from Oswaldtwistle, and a 500 attended when Darwen Olympic came to Moorhead on the 8th of February. This Darwen team was also encountered and beaten in the semi-final of the North East Lancashire Cup, which was played at Blackburn in front of 1,500 spectators. Although there was to be no victory in the final, the club could look back with satisfaction following an eventual runners-up place in the League table.

For the 1896-97 season, the Stanleyites joined the newly created North-east Lancashire Combination, and for this new challenge most of the previous campaign's players were retained. Their gradual rise in status was well summed up in the local press: *"By the decline of the Reds, Accrington Stanley have become what may be termed the premier team of the town, although they do not represent the same class of football we were once privileged to witness in the day of the Reds".* It was to be some years before this distinction was reached.

The first match in September 1896 was played at Burnley Wood Top, followed by a home game when Clayton Rovers were beaten 3-1. For the first time the club entered the F.A. Cup, but any hopes of a lucrative run were cut short in the 2nd qualifying round at Chorley, when the much superior side run out five goal winners. Support at early season home games was depleted due to several games being played on very wet or cold days, with receipts of only £3 for the first match and barely 200 spectators when Nelson were the visitors. But the team managed to hold their own in the competition without winning any honours, finishing in the top four in the final table. A run through to the semi-finals of the North-east Lancashire Cup was made, but lost at this stage to Wood Top Rovers. One unfortunate trait of the Club was their apparent unpunctual behaviour. Games were rarely started on time - shades of their predecessors - resulting in matches of less than 90 minutes duration during the winter months.

The 1897-98 season saw a change in home venue when the club moved to Bell's Ground at Woodnook, in the South part of the town, a venue previously occupied by the Bell's Temperance Club. The facilities were very spartan compared to the well enclosed Moorhead venue, but the Stanleyites were unable to afford the rental and their move to a cheaper ground, coupled with their sharing the same with an amateur team - Accrington Villa - was more in line with their pocket.

An interesting match was played at the new Bradford Association Club - neither of the later Football League clubs of that town since they were formed some years later - and this was followed by another friendly, at home, when a very poor Burnley Athletic were beaten 12-1. The team's general winning ways continued and on October 16th, Trawdon Forest (another unbeaten team), were the visitors. Trawdon were soundly beaten 6-3 after a commanding five goal half time lead, before an excellent attendance of 1,500, probably a record to this time. The first defeat was experienced a week later in the Lancashire Junior Cup. The importance afforded to the Press was shown when it was suggested that a small stand be built, for spectators - but primarily for the journalists. Once again, the F.A. Cup produced little, for the first match was won 4-0 at Carlisle City, this was followed by a 1-4 defeat at Horwich. Although no major honours were won, the club continued to make steady progress, with the only real blemish being the occasional crowd trouble at their matches!

By the 1900-01 season, the club had become an established semi-professional outfit, and by now were known as the Reds, in recognition of their predecessors who had held the title as Accrington's top football team. This period also saw a rise in status, with an acceptance into the strong Lancashire Combination, and the club's president - Captain Harwood - instigated the annual presentation of medals to the most successful non-reserve team in the competition. The Reds only just missed out on winning these medals in their first season when they finished a respectable 9th place in the table.

ACCRINGTON SANLEY F.C. 1902/03
(Back): Chadwick (committee), Finney, Coupe, Boulton, Emmett (Trainer).
(Middle): Morgan, Golding, J.Bradshaw, W.Bradshaw, Gardner. (Front): Watkins, Brunton, Hargreaves.

The campaign had seen the club attract bigger crowds and with the team in their best ever financial position, they were ready to put the question of a suitable ground on a better footing. The Woodnook Ground was hardly worthy of the club's high status, and for the 1901-02 season a move was made back to Moorhead Park.

The first real black spot for the Reds occurred in 1901, when they were temporarily suspended from the Lancashire F.A., following the improper retention of £6 that related to receipts at a Junior Cup-tie. The penalty was severe, as four named officials were suspended from football for five years. This inevitable upheaval in the running of the club, rather than inhibit it appeared to promote it, for at the end of the 1902-03 season, the first major honour was won, with the Championship of the Lancashire Combination, the first ever by a non-League (first team) side.

One year earlier their debut match back at Moorhead produced a record gate of around 2,000 (receipts of £44), the best ever attendance for an Accrington team since the days of the earlier Reds. The opponents were Blackburn Rovers in a friendly fixture (a scoreless draw resulted) a club who uniquely managed to attract record attendances for all three Accrington teams over the years. With a successful team - the Reds reached top spot at Christmas - support continued to rise and the record crowd was nearly doubled in numbers with Bury Reserves' visit, when four goals were shared. With their banishment from the Lancashire F.A. at this time, only the F.A. Cup was entered, although a local Charity Cup match was played at home to Burnley, and lost by three unopposed goals, but before a surprisingly poor crowd of less than 1,000.

" PLAY UP, STANLEY!"

September 1901.... the end of the Victorian era, and its craze for strange inventions. The newspaper paid for the first (and probably last) aerial night advertising. A hot air ballon was used and illuminated by electric lighting. This promoted the newspaper on one side and the Club on the other!

(Accrington Observer and Times)

As the early years of the 20th century passed, the Club achieved further honours with the runners-up position in the Lancashire Combination at the end of the 1903/04 season, and another Championship win two years later. The Club had by now become very ambitious and had the idea of raising £2,000 with the formation of a Limited Company, and with a subsequent application for election to the Football League mooted in November 1906, but the scheme never transpired. During this season, the second round of the F.A. Cup was reached, but lost by a single goal at Bradford City. This contest brought the Reds up against the legendary goalkeeper Willie Foulke, who was previously with Chelsea. This veritable giant of a man had to change his Jersey as it clashed with the red of Accrington, but a suitable light coloured replacement could not be found, and the problem was eventually overcome by the use of a sheet - borrowed from a nearby house - which was wrapped around his giant frame!

The Cover and line-ups from a programme in the 1905/06 Lancashire Combination Championship winning season.

With the League runners-up position in 1913, the Club were arguably the best non-League Club in the Combination, the only other non-reserve teams to emulate their performances being Rochdale - Champions in 1911 and 1912 - and the single table topping successes of Oldham Athletic and Stockport County. Although the Reds made no bids to join the Football League, the three other Clubs did, and in 1907 Oldham were successful and joined the Second Division, despite only their single Combination Division 1 title success.

The 1914/15 season became the last peacetime campaign for several years, and following their last match on April the 24th, when they shared two goals at Chorley, the Reds finished in 6th place, with a League record of 15 victories, 7 draws and 10 defeats. A dim view was taken by the Country, as a whole, of football continuing, and a halt to all former competitions was made for the 1915/16 season. However, a wartime Lancashire Combination was created, and Accrington Stanley played in the Northern section.

Performing now as a purely amateur outfit, there was an encouraging number of hopefuls who turned up for the trial games, and a good crowd was present for the first match on the 4th September 1915, when Adlington were beaten 6-1; admission for matches was now reduced to 3d, (just over 1p) with an extra 1d for the Stand.

Other Clubs in the ten team competition included Blackburn Trinity, Leyland and Nelson, but the Reds proved themselves the best of the bunch by reaching the top of the League after eleven games and finishing in that position at the end of the 'first competition' - the campaign being split into two separate 'seasons'. But the wartime difficulties in respect of movements (to away games) and eventual lack of players and crowds due to many fighting in the war, were to prove too difficult for many Clubs to continue. Additionally players had to work longer hours which resulted in late kick-offs (which both 'Reds' Clubs had become adept at coping with!). Further declining crowds and fielding depleted teams resulted, and at the season's end Accrington had to admit defeat and were one of those that chose to cease their activities.

The formation, in 1911, of the Central League for the reserve teams of the Football League clubs, was to result in a lowering of the standards of the Lancashire Combination, and the loss of lucrative home games against the top clubs' second strings. This in turn reduced the gate receipts of most clubs, of which Accrington were one, and the 1915/16 season was to prove a financial disaster. By 1919, the Club were deep in debt and could not even hold claim to their own home Ground. It was only thanks to a few, who showing zeal and enthusiasm, pulled the Club round when they were on the point of becoming defuers (Accrington) Stanley were efhird Division Noed during the early part of 1916, and immediately started plans to resuscitate the Club and find a suitable venue for home matches.

By the start of the 1919/20 season, the secretary - Mr S. Pilkinton - and his small band had secured a new ground. Peel Park was chosen, an ideal location due to its convenient position to the town. Although the purchase price was £2,500 and only £300 had been raised in the short time since the Club's reformation, it was considered a better investment than the increased rental required at Moorhead Park. Although money was at a premium, the new Committee managed to provide boarding to surround the enclosure - except for the School side where the wall was considered a suitable barrier - but anything further had to wait. The sparseness of Peel Park resembled the Bell's Ground at Woodnook, but with the difference that this enclosure was owned by the Club.

Initially the club were to play as an Amateur team, and for the trial matches the Club stepped back in time some thirty years by making use of the Accrington Cricket Field as the venue, where they were able to take a collection. On August the 30th the first competitive match was played, with a team that consisted almost entirely of fairly inexperienced local players with one notable exception - George Chapman, the ex-Blackburn Rovers man. The initial League match at Tranmere was very onesided for the raw Reds could not compete with the experienced Rovers and Accrington ran out as 0-7 losers. True to form, the visitors turned up for the match late! They arrived at Preston 18 minutes after the scheduled kick-off time, and had to finish the journey in a fleet of taxis.

The first post-war F.A. Cup match, at Nelson, produced nothing other than the Reds share of a healthy £169 gate. Meanwhile in the League the bad start to the season was not continued, as the team won by three goals at Rochdale and 3-2 at Prescot - where the latter had a notoriously narrow pitch.

On September 20th, the Official opening of Peel Park was made with the visit of Stalybridge Celtic. Whereas the occasion may have been an auspicious one, the venue was far from it! The facilities were non-existent, just a railing around the pitch and the boarding around the Ground. There was no dressing-rooms or tent, and the players had to make use of the School for this purpose; the surface was rough and the playing area sloping. But this did not prevent a large crowd of around 3,000 (receipts £107), each paying 8d (3½p), for the privilege to be present. Even so it was generally regarded that the Committee had performed miracles in such a short time and with such limited resources.

After 30 minutes, a gem of a goal shot from an acute angle by Woods, opened the account for Accrington, and after 90 minutes they finished as 4-2 winners. The next match was also at home, to Horwich, and this produced another victory and increased gate takings of £122. Barrow was the next port of call, a happy Ground for the Reds for they had only been beaten at Holker Street on one occasion. This record remained for the visitors triumphed by 4-1, and with only ten men after Helmsley was sent off for a retaliatory foul. After 11 games the Club was holding the top spot, encouraging a crowd of 4,000 to Peel Park for a Combination cup-tie versus Rossendale, which was duly won. A slight falter followed, and by Christmas the Reds had dropped to 4th place. This position was not improved upon and no Lancashire Combination honours were won by the season's end. The next campaign was to be the last for Accrington Stanley - and others - as a non-League Club. But the farewell of the first team from the Lancashire Combination was something of a disappointment, for a mid-table position at the turn of the year was not improved upon, as a late run of injuries produced some poor results. The final place in the table was only 6th, with 16 victories, 9 draws and 9 defeats; Nelis was the leading goalscorer with 15. The last game of the season had been played on the 7th of May, a friendly match versus Dick Kerr's - an organisation that later became renowned for its Ladies Eleven.

ACCRINGTON

STANLEY F.C.

WINNERS LANCASHIRE JUNIOR CUP, 1920-1921.
Winners Rossendale & District Cup, 1913-14, 1914-15.   Winners Lancashire Combination, 1902-3, 1905-6.   Winners Best Non-Reserve Medals, 1901-2, 1903-4.

1d. OFFICIAL PROGRAMME. 1d.

Smoke "Old Bob's" Mixture
—— 11½d. per Oz. ——

WOOD & Co. Opposite TOWN HALL Accrington

BAZAAR JOTTINGS.

Our Bazaar will definitely take place in the Town Hall, last week in April which is now about three months off.

So far we have done splendidly, we hope to raise at least £2,000 towards the ground extensions.

The Bazaar Club has now reached the handsome total of £700, and through the efforts of our committee we have raised over £300 in concerts, whist drives, etc.

It is only eight months since we decided on this method of swelling the Club's Funds, and up to now it has been very successful

If you have not already got a ticket for the Gent.'s Suit or Lady's Costume do so.

We have a workroom in Woodnook P.S.A.

Institute. We want many workers (not forgetting the donors) so come along and put your shoulder to the wheel. If you can't come let us know, we shall only be too pleased if you will take some home.

Persons being members of our Club are asked to let their collector know if any special article is required so that we may obtain what they want.

Make a note of March 9th—we are having another Whist Drive and Dance in the Conservative Club   The last one being a great success

We hope to give you all the items of interest about the Bazaar which is sure to be a big success. Keep your eye on this page, and order your copy of the Programme so that you will be sure of having one next week.

FOR FULL REPORTS
—of—
STANLEY'S MATCHES
READ
Tuesday's "Observer."

An early Stanley programme
(12th February 1921 versus Morecambe)

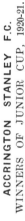

ACCRINGTON STANLEY F.C.
WINNERS OF JUNIOR CUP, 1920-21.

J. Jacques, E. Chadwick, F. Heyes, G. E. Holman, R. Cragg, C. Smithies, G. Chapman, G. Wilson, J. Yates, J. Tattersall, H. Smethurst, A. Colwell, T. Heslop, J. Richardson, T. Pendergast, J. Sutcliffe, A. Studdard, E. Hargreaves.
Seated: J. Brown, J. Hollard, J. Miller, C. Pearson, P. Nelis, P. Quigley, A. Stevenson, S. T. Pilkington (Secretary), F. Brennand, J. Parramore, W. H. Pilkington (Mascot).

There was one particular highlight however, with the Club's appearance and first capture of the Lancashire Junior Cup. Chorley were beaten in the final, and before the biggest attendance ever to attend an Accrington match. The match receipts were an easy record for the competition - £1,072 - which represented a crowd of around 20,000 at Ewood Park, Blackburn; the Reds previous appearance at this stage - in the 1905/06 season and at the same venue - had only produced gate takings of £146.

Such support was indicative of the Club's following, for throughout the season attendances at Combination matches - despite the indifferent performances - had been higher than ever before, with an average gate of over 3,000. With an income of £4,030, and expenses of £3,713, a profit of £317 over the year had been made. An incredible sum of approximately £2,000 for Ground improvements was raised from the running of a bazaar, and the town were obviously behind the team in numbers. By now the Reds had their sights set on bigger things, their hopeful election to an extended Football League.

Stanley were one of the main movers in the campaign to form a Third Division North, and at the end of season meeting of the Football League had representations to put forward the case for the aspirants. In fact a Third Division had been formed for the season just ended, but purely for Southern based clubs. Although this appears to have been a 'North and South divide' issue, it was reasoned one year earlier that the Southern League could boast of a competition worthy of Football League status, both in ability and finance, whereas there were few northern clubs that could match both ideals. But on this occasion the quest of the North was successful, and along with several Combination clubs, plus those from other leagues, the Reds were elected to form the twenty strong new Northern section of the Third Division. After a wait of nearly thirty years, Accrington could once again look forward to a team with Football League status.

The Reds had done their sums, and reckoned that with minimum gates as for the season just past, they could get by, albeit with the ground entrance money raised by 50% (to one shilling) - match receipts per game of £350 were budgeted for. But not everybody was in favour of immediate Membership of the Football League! An crowd of 300 was present at the Club's A.G.M. on the 8th of June, and many considered that Football League status for the Club would be better in two or three years time, by which time a better team could be assembled and a more healthy Bank balance could be accumulated. But conversely there were those who considered that this golden opportunity should not be lost, and suggested either the formation of a Limited Company - the popular choice of many Professional Clubs - or a subscription list with a view to raising £3,000. The meeting was generally in favour of the Limited Company suggestion, as they felt that over £4,000 could realistically be raised in £1 shares. The money would principally be used to wipe out the Club's £2,000 overdraft, improving the Ground by providing more covered accommodation, and removing the notorious 'lump' in the middle of the pitch, plus the acquisition of new players to suit the Club's elevated status; £5,700 had already been spent of Peel Park during the past two years.

The main objectors to the Limited Company option were those on the Management Committee, who considered that the great strides made in such a short time - mostly by their own efforts - should be allowed to continue in this slow but steady way. No decision was made, but another meeting was scheduled for eight days later, which to be held at the Ground.

The degree of interest in the Club can be judged by the turnout of around 1,000 at Peel Park, but it turned out to be a far from peaceful meeting. In opposition to the Limited Company method, the idea was for all those who were interested to become Members of the Club, and listed as would proper Shareholders. But Mr Harry Meynell virtually took over the meeting when he explained the businesslike way that a Limited Company Club would function, rather than the amateur and insecure 'subscriber' system. In an impassioned speech he won around the majority of those present. The Chairman of the meeting interjected, only to be overpowered by Mr Meynell, which led to uproar from both factions. With the body of opinion in support of Mr Meynell, there was no alternative but to put forward a motion for forming a Limited Company, or to abandon the Meeting - which would no doubt had led to some ugly scenes. The former option was adopted, a vote taken and an overwhelming majority voted for the proposal.

On June the 21st, at a meeting in the Town Hall, the Committee formally announced the intention of the change of name of the Club to Accrington Stanley (1921) Limited.

Just ten players were retained for the 1921/22 season, the rest of the playing staff being given free transfers. Peel Park at this juncture was barely acceptable for Football League status. Spectator comfort - just a small seated stand by now - was virtually non-existent, although additional banking was build during the close season, which increased the Ground capacity by over 2,000. Stand extensions and covered standing were, it was promised, to follow shortly, hopefully from capital raised from the sale of shares. By the season's start, 21 players had been signed, and the eleven that represented the Club in the first Football League game consisted of: Tattersall, Newton, Baines, Crawshaw, Popplewell, Burkenshaw (Captain), Oxley, Makin, Green, Hosker and Harties. The match on the 27th of August was played at Rochdale, and in a crowd of between eight and nine thousand, the Reds were well represented with over 2,000 making the journey by charabanc.

To the delight of the home fans, and the distress of the visitors, Crawshaw had the dubious distinction of being the first Accrington Stanley goalscorer in the Third Division North - but for the opposition! However, the game then swung very much in Accrington's favour and after 23 minutes Hosker equalised for the Reds. Nine minutes before half-time they took the lead, and almost from the resultant kick-off had the ball in the net again, only for it to be ruled offside. A debut win seemed on the cards, but Rochdale fought in the second half like a new team, and, including three goals in only eight minutes, accomplished a complete turn around with a 6-2 lead. Accrington pulled one goal back, but finally ended up as 3-6 losers. A very entertaining match, but not reflective of the Reds equal share of the play.

On August the 31st, just three days before the team's home debut in the Football League. the Club formerly became a Limited Company.

The first match at Peel Park produced unprecedented interest, when a record attendance at a Stanley home encounter (11,500) was present for a thrilling match for the return game with Rochdale. Makin commenced the scoring for the Reds after 15 minutes and that scoreline remained until half-time. Three more goals in the second period settled a comfortable win for the homesters.

The team made an early exit from the Lancashire Senior Cup at Barrow, but the League was the most important Competition, and around 10,000 came to the next home game versus Crewe. By now work to form a covered enclosure and extensions to the seated stand were underway - the latter was a priority since season tickets (priced at just over £2 - with nearly £1 for ordinary ground admission) had already been sold for seats that were not present!

After four games the Club lay fourth in the table, but despite this very reasonable start, the next home attendance for the 3-1 win over Chesterfield was inexplicably very much down on the previous two home games. However, after completing the double over the Derbyshire side, on October the 8th the Ground attendance record was again broken with a table topping clash with local rivals Nelson. The estimated crowd of 12,000 (receipts of £477), was in fact lower than th number expected, due no doubt to the inclement weather coupled with the lack of spectator facilities! The Reds won easily by 4-1, and one week later before a new Nelson record attendance that produced £550, a single goal win completed the double.

The first home Football League match
(3rd September 1921)

While the gate money was encouraging, a different picture was painted for the selling of shares, for by now only £1,400 had been raised. Nelson were in opposition yet again for the Reds F.A. Cup sortie, and another 10,000 plus assembled at Peel Park, and paid £538 for the privilege, but a third victory was not to be, and the Reds bowed out to the only goal of the game.

The Club carried on their winning ways in League encounters and by Christmas lay in fourth place in the table. Following the team's first drawn game, at Lincoln, five out of six points were captured over the festive season to carry the Club to the top.

But the terrible disappointment was the attendances, which had dropped, and with only an average of £225 gate money for each of the two home games. Promotion prospects gradually faded, with a number of late season defeats, including the only two at home, and a final 1-6 hiding at Walsall in the last League game. The final place in the first ever Northern section League was a relatively poor 5th, 15 points behind Champions Stockport.

The grim forbodings of those a year earlier, on whether the Club was ready for the Football League were borne out, at least in part. The season had not been a financial success, and on the playing front, after a good initial campaign, things were to get steadily worse.

The next six years produced a gradual and consistent decline in the Club's playing fortunes, with final placings of 8th, 13th, 17th, 18th and finally 21st respectively. The last of these seasons, 1926/27, surprisingly produced the Club's best run in the F.A. Cup. Accrington Stanley had rarely progressed far in the Competition, and had caused few shocks. The second round was reached in the 1906/07 season, after beating Crewe Alexandra in a replay, but ended at this stage with a single goal defeat at Bradford City. Three years later, after beating Brentford at the last qualifying round stage at the old Moorhead Park Ground, they were drawn at home in a money spinning local derby match with Blackburn in the first round proper. But with finance the main consideration, and an offer of £135 plus a half share of the gate, the game was played at Ewood Park, and lost 1-7.

The new Club did not reach the first round again until the 1923/24 season when record receipts (£580) were recorded for the visit of Charlton Athletic, after the Reds had previously overcome Rochdale and Wrexham in the qualifying rounds. The homesters held the Londoners to a scoreless draw at Peel Park but lost the replay by a single goal. One year later after disposing of New Brighton (in a replay) then Chesterfield, another large crowd of over 10,000 saw the Reds easily overcome by high-flying Second Division opponents Portsmouth, to the tune of 2-3. Despite their flagging fortunes in the Football League, the 3rd round was reached for the first time in the 1925/26 campaign. After two home ties, when first Wrexham and then Blyth Spartans were beaten, the third round produced another godsend for the treasurer, with a match at nearby Bolton Wanderers. Before an attendance of 32,875 and match receipts of £2,135, the Club were far from humiliated when they went down by a single goal, to one of the top Clubs in the Country. The 1926/27 season, the worst to date in the Football League, produced - conversely - the joint best run in the Club's history. At the third round stage a long journey was made to fellow Third Division (South) opponents Exeter City. Although lying second from bottom in the League, the team excelled themselves and truly played as a team, to record a two goal win. The attendance at St. James' Park was 13,647 (receipts of £888), and at Accrington a crowd of over 2,000 assembled for the Reserve game, in order to hear updates on the scoreline from Devon!

For the first time ever, the Reds had made it to the last 32 teams stage, and as a reward were required to make another long trip, this time to West London, for a game with a top Second Division Club, Chelsea. Amongst the official attendance of 30,142 (receipts totalled £1,785) between two and three hundred hard-core Reds' fans had made the overnight train journey. After just ten minutes the visitors were three goals down - two they claimed were offside - when an amazing comeback ensued to produce a half-time score of 2-3. The second half produced no more drama, for the Reds were completely outplayed and finally lost 2-7.

During the early 1920's, the Football League scorelines in a number of matches were often poor. The 1922-23 season had produced several bad results, including a 1-7 reverse at Grimsby on Christmas Day and a four goal home defeat to Chesterfield in November. One year later, the team produced moderately good form on their travels, recording four victories and only one bad defeat at Champions-elect Wolverhampton (1-5). The 1924-25 season, despite their lowly position, saw three away wins and no defeats by more than three goals - they even managed a 6-0 home victory over Durham City - but results took a turn for the worse during the following campaign. Although there were only four teams to score more goals than the Red's total of 81, the "goals against" column produced a dismal 105, only Walsall conceding more. The away matches caused this high number with five goals being let in on five occasions (one game of which was actually a victory over Wrexham with a 6-5 scoreline!), a 2-6 defeat at Doncaster and 2-7 at Chesterfield.

The boost to morale and the club's finances due to the Cup run in the 1926-27 season was countered by another significant and depressing season. By the New Year, the club were languishing very near the bottom of the table, a position that had by now become all to familiar.

On New Year's Day, traditionally a popular date for good crowds, an attendance of only 5,000 was present to see the team beat Chesterfield, the first win since November 20th. Just one match was lost in January, followed by a morale boosting 7-2 victory over Hartlepools on the February 5th. But this run of good form was shattered with a single goal home defeat to bottom club Barrow two weeks later, when an easy win was hoped for. There then followed a bad string of results, which included an embarrassing defeat by seven unopposed goals at Nelson.

The next victory did not come until March the 19th, and this lifted the team three points above tailenders Barrow. The only away win of the season was recorded the following week at New Brighton, and raised the club one place higher in the League. The end of the season run-in consisted of three undefeated home games, but several defeats on the team's travels, the most damning being a 1-6 scoreline at Bradford City when the Reds were totally outplayed. Although the last game was won, 3-1 over Rotherham, it was too late to prevent the club having to apply for re-election, although finishing five points higher than wooden-spoonists Barrow. This was the club's first application to remain in the League, and it came as no surprise when they were given 36 votes of confidence, the highest number for any club that season.

The 1927-28 season got off to an excellent start, when Nelson were beaten at Seedhill by 4-1, and the crowd included approximately 2,000 Reds fans. On the same day, there were an estimated 3,500 for the Reserves home match with Clitheroe. The Accrington supporters could not be faulted at this stage for their support, but this was to change! The new found hope was repeated in the first League game at Peel Park when a crowd of 8,000 was present, but they were not happy with their favourites when they lost 2-4. Although a fairly good start was made to the season, with a mid-table placing after 12 games - a big improvement over recent years - the support dropped and for Durham's visit on November the 12th, there was a crowd of only 3,500. If the Accrington support was flagging, pity their opponents in this match, who were so badly in debt they had to ask the Reds for a £25 advance of their share of the gate money in order they could travel!

Two weeks later, an exit was made from the F.A. Cup, when dogged by bad luck and the missing of two penalties, the first match was lost at home to Lincoln City by 5-2. Middle of the table form continued to Christmas, but the fans were not happy and matches over the festivities - which included home wins over Barrow (5-1), a 7-1 thrashing of neighbours Nelson and a 2-1 victory over New Brighton - were poorly supported with barely 4,000 for the latter game on Boxing Day. This changeable form and poor support continued to the season's end, but at least the final outcome of 9th in the table was a vast improvement on 12 months earlier.

The next few seasons saw the club struggling on the field yet again, as they once again occupied a near continuous placing in the lower half of the League. The 1929-30 end of the season record showed a strange twist however, for despite finishing in 16th place in the table with 14 victories and 19 defeats, their goal tally was a plus, with 84 for and 81 against. These figures were achieved from some good home victories, including a 7-1 win over Halifax and 7-2 when Carlisle were the visitors on New Year's day.

The next campaign produced an improved position in the League, a rise of three places, but a poor defensive record with 108 goals conceded. On this occasion, it was principally the away record which produced some embarrassing defeats; 1-6 to Wrexham and Doncaster, 3-7 on the team's visits to Carlisle and Chesterfield, and no fewer than eight goals conceded at Both Tranmere and Rotherham.

While the results on the pitch were variable, the financial position was consistent - bad! The club in fact, were only saved from extinction in 1932 with another very profitable bazaar at the ground. The decade of the 1930's was to prove to be one long struggle to achieve success on the pitch and to remain solvent off it. The most infamous game occurred on the 3rd of February 1934, when the team were humiliated by Barnsley with a score of 0-9, and on their own ground at Peel Park! Barnsley were the eventual Division Three North Champions and this at least alleviated the embarrassment, but to prove an even bigger surprise, was the home victory the next month over New Brighton, with a score of 8-0!

The club's best season of this dismal decade, was the 1935-36 campaign, when a 9th final placing was accomplished, but it was still a miracle that the club struggled on, with low gates caused partly by the club's virtually continuous poor play, coupled with the attractions of a higher grade football to be found in nearby towns.

During all this time, there was only one season of note as far as the F.A. Cup was concerned, when the fourth round was reached for the second, and only other time, in the club's career, in 1937. Although the run ended at Manchester City with a narrow two goal defeat, the third round saw the club achieve a surprising 3-1 victory (after extra time) at nearby Second Division Blackburn after four goals were first shared at Peel Park. Although the club's F.A. Cup exploits were rarely successful, at least when a good run was unusually made, they at least prospered from the high gate receipts.

As the Second World War approached, the team's playing record slumped again, and at the end of the 1937-38 season, re-election had to be sought once again when they finished in rock bottom position. Despite their unenviable placing in the League, bad defeats were rare, the poorest being an unopposed five goal defeat at Champions Tranmere Rovers in January. And on home territory, there were several defeats, but all by a close margin, the opening game of the season against Carlisle being the most dismal, when the Reds were overcome 1-4. However, once again their fellow Leaguers showed faith in the club by casting 41 votes in their favour, again the highest number polled that season.

The approach of the War and the cessation of normal Football League activities in the next year, may well have saved the club from being cast out from the elite, since the bottom position was realised once again one year later. On this occasion, it was a close thing, for the Reds finished all of 11 points below their nearest rivals and this time, the vote was not so confident. Whereas they retained their status, the voting showed only 29 this time in their favour.

A rare success occurred, in the Third Division Cup competition (which had been started in 1933), when the club fought through to the Northern final before losing to Bradford City. But overall, the season had been one long period of distress both on the field and at the gate. By the new year, the club was firmly anchored at the bottom with just one win and four draws from the 23 games played, and it was only a second half of marginal recovery that prevented an even more damning final record. On January 9th, the second victory was claimed - 3-1 over Wrexham before a pathetic attendance of 2,000 - and five successive defeats followed. The third victory, won on February 25th (2-1 over Crewe), provided a glimmer of hope, but it was back to normal one week later! In this latter game, the Reds were losing 1-5 at Carlisle at one stage, but eventually pulled back the score to 4-6. By April the 22nd, the team's fate was sealed, although the game that day was won by 2-1 over Rotherham, before another sub-3,000 crowd at Peel Park. With repeated poor seasons and crowds down as low as 2,000, it appeared only a matter of time before the end of Accrington Stanley (1921).

But would it have been another disastrous campaign? For when the hostilities finally called a halt to normal football, the team had won all three games and actually headed the table!

For the first time in several years, a full time trainer was appointed and perhaps it was his ability that aided the team's excellent start. After a 6-1 pre-season home friendly victory over Southport, the ever optimistic Accrington faithfull filled two trains for the first League match visit to Bradford City. A two goal win was achieved and it should have been more. The luck was with the Reds when a trip was made to Barrow for the next game, as two penalties against them were missed and they went home with a narrow 2-1 win. On September the 2nd, the last Football League game for several years was played. The best home attendance for some time, 6,000, cheered the team on to a two goal victory over Oldham.

Hastily arranged friendlies were played over the next few weeks before a formula for the continuance of competitive football was devised. During this interim period, the variable results were of little consequence and this was born out by the attendances - 3,000 at Peel Park when Rochdale were beaten 6-4 in the first game and barely 1,000 when Bradford City were entertained in the last. Accrington's wartime activities were shortlived. Although they played in the North-West League during the 1939-40 season, their earlier competitive successes did not continue, neither did the crowd numbers rise. After a scoreless draw at Carlisle, the team lost by 1-2 at home to Oldham, watched by only 1,500 spectators. Oldham were later met at home again, and this time were beaten 7-1 in the (Wartime) Lancashire Cup, but the crowd only numbered 780.

By Christmas ten games had been played, and none won! The two matches over the festive period showed a surprising increase in attendances (3,000 and 4,000), but little in the way of football. The abbreviated season finished wih only 2 victories, 6 draws and 14 defeats, plus a familiar bottom place in the table. Over this first period of the War, average gates were down to an uneconomic £30. Many Clubs were boosted by itinerant 'Guest' Players during the War who were allowed to play for nearby Clubs. But there were no 'stars' in the area who attached themselves to the Reds, and coupled with the reduced attendances, they sensibly called it a day, until Peace in Europe was once again apparent. During this short season of 1939-40, no fewer than 36 players were used, and 16 different goalscorers in League matches contributed to the total tally of 37.

A team of sorts entered the Blackburn and District Combination, and were labelled as 'Accrington 'A''. The A.G.M. in August 1940 did not even attract a quorum, and therefore the meeting had to be deferred until the next night, when again insufficient numbers were present. The rules of the Company required that the Directors should carry on as they saw fit. Feeling let down by the interim controlling body, the Club decided to continue to develop the young local players. With only six teams willing to continue in the (Wartime) Lancashire Combination, it was left to Chairman Captain S.T. Pilkington and his Board, to act in the best interests of the Company.

Afraid that non-activity would result in the dying of the Club when hostilities were over, the local League was entered with, in effect, a Reserve Team. The entrance charge was fixed at 3d, and it was hoped that this would produce at least sufficient to pay the Mortgage and Rates on the Ground. Early attendances approached 500 at home matches, and although a reasonably successful season was undertaken, the declining numbers of fans and players - due to the War demands - eventually forced the Club to go into 'hibernation' for a few years.

The approaching end of the War brought the Reds back into football action once again, when at a special meeting in mid-June, it was decided to re-enter into football compatition for the 1944/45 season, with their entry in the massive 54 strong 'North' League. After frantic preparations, not least the forming of a playing squad, the first match was played, and won 5-1, at home before a 3,600 attendance. The players available consisted of a mixture of Accrington men, locals, and a few 'guests', including Male (Arsenal), Mandsley (Blackburn) and Walmsley from Preston. The Ground had been maintained during the 'hibernation', as the local firm's team - Bullough's - had played their local league matches there.

Since only eighteen matches were played by each team in the North League, the final 'table' was somewhat academic, but significantly the Reds won only five games, and drew two and lost eleven. In the second part of the season they scraped through the qualifying competition in the League North Cup, but were soon dispensed with when Bolton beat them over the two first round legs. None the less, the home tie had produced a new record attendance of 11,791. But things took on a far healthier look in the near normal 1945/46 season. With the Third Division split into two regions, they became a Football League Championship winning team for the first time ever in their history, finishing two points ahead of Rochdale in the West section.

The F.A. Cup competition was revived, but all rounds were played over two legs. The first and second rounds produced close overall wins over Chorley and Oldham, before a dream third round tie with Manchester United. But further progress was halted when after holding their illustrious neighbours to a two all draw, they collapsed by 1-5 in the second leg.

The 1946/47 season heralded the start of a true return to the pre-war competitions, but by the season's end the club's recent successes deserted them as they sunk to a familiar low final position in the Third Division North. But at last the following campaign gave hope for the success that the Reds had never truly attained.

By the dawn of 1948, the team lay in an unaccustomed high playing in the League of 5th. But the first game of the New Year produced a disappointing 2-4 home defeat to Hull City. The attendance of 7,337, although a vat improvement over the dark pre-war days, was still somewhat low for a Championship challenging team at a time when crowds were at a peak throughout the Football League. But rather than maintaining a promotion bid, the results continued to go against the team; a three goal defeat at Barrow - the second half played with only ten men and before a crowd numbering 4,700 - 2-4 at Gateshead (attendance 7,000) and then a single goal reverse to a poor Tranmere side virtually put paid to any hopes of honours. Back in January the home match versus Oldham was to have been a 'first' for the Reds, for a live radio commentary had been planned, but the match was postponed!

The defeat by the odd goal in five, in the rescheduled home game with Oldham on March the 20th was watched by only 5,200 faithfuls and produced a drop to eighth in the League, and when Mansfield were beaten 1-0 in the next ome game the attendance fell even more to 4,596. The last game of the season ended as a victory to the visitors Rotherham, but the high-flying Millers were still denied promotion, by one point less than Lincoln City, and the Peel Park attendance of 7,000 had been substantially boosted by visiting fans. The final position of 6th for the Reds may have been something of a disappointment, but was a vast improvement from 12 months earlier. Dare the Reds hope that the turning point had at last come? They probably did... but it hadn't!

The 1948/49 season started with high hopes, and this was evidenced with an attendance of 5,500 for the practice match. Six new players had been signed, giving a total professional squad of 21 of which only 6 were full time players - a sign of the austerity that the Club was undergoing. One of the newcomers was centre-forward Sam Parker, who in this trial game literally broke the net with a thunderbolt of a shot from a penalty.

The first League match brought fellow Lancastrians Oldham to Accrington, and a 1-1 draw was played out with an excellent attendance of 8,650 present. But after no victories in the first five games - and a resultant second from bottom place in the table - the home crowd for Mansfield's visit - another two goals shared draw - had dropped to 6,233. Wrexham's visit produced another defeat although the crowd increased to 6,774, but following further reverses at well supported Halifax (attendance 11,000) and Rochdale, the Reds could drop no further in the table, with a dismal record of only four points from four draws, and eight defeats.

At last, and not before time, the long awaited win came when New Brighton came to Peel Park and were walloped 5-1, and in all the circumstances, a reasonable crowd of 6,000 was present. A 3-1 victory over Southport two weeks later lifted the team one place in the table, and a slight improvement in form continued. But support slipped away again, and the two pre-Christmas home games attracted only 3,400 and 3,700 spectators. By Christmas Day the Reds were fourth from bottom, but by the season's end they finished one place lower. Despite the poor season, back in September, the Champions-elect, Hull City, attracted a new record attendance of 13,162!

The 1949/50 season provided hope yet again, for a rise at the finish to 13th was obtained, but optimism was dashed when the team plunged to the depths once again one year later, and re-election had to be sought following a 23rd (of 24) placing. At the Football Leauge meeting, New Brighton were not re-elected - a rare occurrence to see new blood accepted into the fold - but Accrington easily maintained their League membership with 46 votes.

One year later, things were little better, for the 22nd position in the League table was the final outcome, but at least the Reds did not have to go through the indignity - and possible threat to their future - of another re-election bid. Yet again, despite a poor season, a new record crowd assembled at Peel Park - 13,268 - for the Lancashire derby match with Oldham in October. There was no solace gained the next season, 1952/53, when the Reds fortunes sunk to the lowest possible depths. The first game of the 1953 New Year required a visit to Workington, a bottom of the table clash, as the homsters were lying in 23rd place, with the Reds three points below them. A surprisingly good attendance of 7,223 was present, and the result, 0-3 against Stanley summed up their form. The next two home games produced a point from each, with a 5,000 crowd at the first clash, with Chesterfield, but which slumped to 3,000 for Mansfield's visit. When York were beaten by the only goal of the game on February the 7th, it looked as if better things were perhaps in store for the Club. By now, Accrington had joined Rochdale at the bottom, with goal average only separating the two, but a three goal defeat at second placed Grimsby (attendance 10,078), put the situation into its true perspective.

With a vital continuous run of several seasons in the doldrums, it was no surprise that the club were in serious financial difficulties, and following the 1-0 defeat of Barrow, in front of 4,300 loyal fans, Walter Crook - the manager for the past two years - resigned. With nine games left, the team were two points adrift at the foot of the table and although the 2-0 win over Scunthorpe on March 28th, relieved the points problem, an attendance of only 3,000 did nothing to alleviate the cash situation. However, the games over Easter virtually sealed the club's fate. High flying Oldham were first visited and before a crowd of 21,738, the highest that the Reds had played before for many years, a three goal defeat ensued, followed by the return at Peel Park, which resulted in another loss, by 2-0. The high attendance was deceptive, but very welcome, for amongst the 10,300 present, nearly half were visiting fans.

The last match of the season was won by a single goal over Darlington, but the wooden spoon position had already been allocated to the Reds, and the attendance of 2,250 illustrated the degree of support now behind the club. Nonetheless, an impassioned letter was written by the Town Council to the Football League, urging them to re-elect the local club, although nine years later, they were unable to depend on such support from this source!

Accrington Stanley were duly re-elected, once again by a comfortable number of votes (45), compared to fellow distressed team Workington (in only their second League season) with 36 and Wigan, the nearest of several aspirants gaining 17 voices of support. Eleven players were retained for the 1953-54 season, with ten more added before the season commenced. With another new surge of optimism, which included a hoped for brighter future on the financial front, and several ground improvements, the start of the season was looked upon with keen anticipation.

Better days were in fact ahead, and the one of the means provided came from the team's new manager Walter Galbraith. The fan's hopes were illustrated by the attendance of 5,400 for the pre-season trial game, a crowd in excess of most Football League matches of the previous season.

The club's treasurer was overjoyed with the first game which produced a 9,200 attendance, and the manager was happy too, with a 2-1 victory over Stockport County. The following Wednesday, there were 100 more fans in the crowd and the second victory of 4-2 over Workington resulted. The support of 2,000 Reds fans in the 8,375 crowd at Rochdale, were insufficient to lift the team, as they lost by the only goal of the game, and this match was followed by a 1-3 home defeat to Wrexham in front of 8,200.

In October, it was announced of the club's intention to raise £30,000 by way of £5 shares, in order to purchase a new two-tier, 4,000 seated stand, which would embrace within it, a training area and offices. Whilst the club could be commended for their forward thinking, with the large debts already hanging over the company, it was hardly the correct time to contemplate such an adventurous move, and it is little wonder that the project died a death. But for the present, the most important thing was the encouragement of support to the ground, which could only be achieved through good results, and in this respect, the situation was already turning sour, for only a mid-table placing was the position after 19 games. By now, the gates had inevitably dropped, but not so alarmingly to cause further financial losses, although the attendance of 7,850 was poor for the attractive visit of League leaders Port Vale.

The attraction of the F.A. Cup drew a new attendance record when Tranmere Rovers were the visitors, after the first round Reds victory by a single goal at Blyth Spartans and before a (probable) record crowd of 8,011. 14,390 fans packed into the Peel Park ground, when they also paid record gate receipts of £1,300. The Reds had a depleted team due to injuries, but held on for a 2-2 draw, only to be easily beaten 5-1 in the replay.

By the season's end, a vast improvement over 12 months earlier was shown, but even so, only 15th place in the League was attained. However, financially, things were looking up, with a much higher aggregate of attendances and, under Galbraith's good management, the next campaign was to prove the best in the club's history.

With only a limited budget, but with the need to strenghen the team, £6,000 was somehow found and spent on new players for the 1954-55 season. Even this modest sum taxed the club's resources, but can be compared with Workington's expenditure of £17,000, for their attempt at a revitalisation. Reminiscent of the early days of of Professional football in Accrington, the club now had a strong bias towards Scottish players, so much so that they unofficially became known as "McStanley".

The intention to erect floodlighting was fullfilled - eight forty foot high pylons at a cost of £4,000 - making the club one of the pioneers in this new phenomina, just as their predecessors had been nearly eighty years earlier. The inaugral match, a friendly with near neighbours Blackburn Rovers, on the 15th of November, attracted the all time record attendance of 17,634 (receipts £1,700).

The season had started without any indication of the success in the League that was to follow, with a disappointing 1-1 home drawn match with Southport. This was followed by a single goal win at Carlisle, and already the team had equalled the number of away wins obtained two seasons earlier! There was a setback the next Saturday, when defeat came at the hands of Barrow, but the double over Carlisle was completed four days later at Peel Park. As the season progressed, the Reds made their way up the table, aided by attendances undreamed of just two seasons earlier, being 2,000 up on average over the games during the previous campaign. The first game of 1955 was won at Peel Park over Barrow before an attendance of 9,575, in which both Stewart and Cocker scored hat-tricks in the exciting 6-3 victory. When Workington were defeated on their own ground on January the 5th, the Reds were heading the table, one point clear of second placed Barnsley; that same day the reserves defeated the Oldham second eleven, before 2,500 fans, to put them eight points clear at the top of the Lancashire combination. The second string became eventual champions for only the second time, and 14 points clear of their nearest rivals.

After defeating Bradford City at home, before another near 10,000 attendance, the team had gone a record nine games without defeat, and their losing at Wrexham on February 12th, was the first since November the 13th. The odd goal in three home victory over Scunthorpe (attendance 10,750) put the Reds three points ahead in the table, and after defeating Chester by 3-0, their 46 points had equalled their best ever in the Football League. Even defeat at Grimsby in early March, still left them five points above their nearest rivals, but this was the start of a poor run, which was to cost them promotion.

However, all was not lost when the games over Easter were played, but two draws with fellow promotion aspirants York City, did not help their cause. At Bootham Crescent, there was a massive attendance of 19,500 and in the return at Peel Park - when the Reds shared four goals after a 0-2 half time scoreline - a new record (League) crowd of 15,598 was present.

By now, promotion was gradually slipping out of their grasp, and after a shock 2-5 thrashing at home to Hartlepool, the club had the same number of points as the leaders Barnsley, but having played two more games. Worse was in store, for on April the 30th, they crashed 1-6 at Chesterfield followed by their last game, and a 3-0 defeat at Bradford City. After promising so much, the runners-up position had to be accepted, four points behind the Oakwell team.

While the final outcome may have been a dissapointment on the field, at least financially the picture was looking better with a record average home attendance of 9,965 which together producing record gate receipts; the worst attendance was 5,300 for Tranmere's visit, which could have been one of the largest crowds only two seasons earlier! The season produced many new records for the club; the most points won, plus, the most - games won, home wins, home points, away points and goals scored. A spell at the top of the table from January 5th until April the 12th, included a record seven successive victories and eleven straight home wins. Stewart and Crocker both scored over 20 League goals - the former going on to record 136 up to 1959. Without doubt, this was the *"Best Season Ever"* - the title of a book written at that time by G.A.Pratt, the club chairman.

Just three new players were signed for the 1955-56 season and with record season ticket sales of £4,400, there was a keen anticipation for the months ahead. By Christmas, there was good cause for optimism, with the team lying second in the League and crowds even higher than a year earlier, the best being 12,016 for nearby Rochdale's visit. Yet, again the campaign ended in dismay, with the club only managing a final third place, nine points behind the Champions. However, the club and the ground were honoured with their staging of the (Third Division) North versus South match, in which Reds player Ryden appeared. The frustrations continued, with the third final placing being repeated in 1957. In those brief halcyon days, the club were able to rely on good crowds, an average during this campaign of 8,689.

In the 1957-58 season, the club rose one place higher, but at least the latter produced a promotion of some sorts, as the club - along with the top 12 teams of both Third Divisions, were to form the new Third Division for the next campaign. New Year's Day had seen the club lying in 6th place, when they played at leaders Bury's ground, where before a massive 18,067 crowd, they shared two goals. With only two defeats in the previous 19 games, they were thrashed 1-6 at Carlisle. Variable results ensued during February and although the attendances were reasonable - an average to this date of 7,138 compared to 8,373 one year earlier - the run-in to the season's end saw the numbers rise. The highest, 14,436, a near record for Rochdale's visit was exceptional, but even so the crowds often rose above 8,000.

Considering there had been three straight wins over Easter, the attendance of 8,341 on April the 24th was poor - as was the match when the Reds lost a three goal lead against only ten men to draw 3-3. The Club's continued promotion challenge was then quashed with two defeats, 1-3 and 1-5, at Mansfield and Chester. With the signing of junior player, Harvey McCreadie, the Club had a total of 16 Scottish players on the Books; McCreadie signed for Luton in January 1960 for £5,500, the second highest ever fee received by the Club. The end of the season produced a rift between the Supporters and the Football Clubs, when the Chairman of the latter, in a highly Dictatorial way, insisted that any money raised by the former (no less than £40,000 to this date) should be given to the Football Club for them to spend it as they saw fit!

In all the post-war years, the Club's dismal record in the F.A. Cup had continued, with a single appearance in the third round, in 1958, when after holding Bristol City at home to a 2-2 draw before 11,976 fans, they lost in the replay 1-3. The last time this stage had been reached, and a subsequent progression into the fourth round, was 20 years earlier!

It would have been reasonable to assume that the Reds could perhaps finally clinch an upward move to the Second Division, with two places now available to them. In the early days of the formation of the two Third Divisions, the Northern group was considered to be by far the weaker. However, this was shown to be untrue in 1959, as five 'old Notherners' finished in the top 12 twelve of the first single Third Division; significantly Accrington Stanley were not one of those five. This failure, after a brief period of hope, was to prove to be the start of the end.

All the players were retained, although no fewer than 31 players were used in the 1958/59 season as the Club tried to form a consistant winning combination. No player had been an ever-present, although J.Anders only missed two League matches. Only a moderate home record ensued, and coupled with generally poor results on their travels, the final position saw the team in a disappointing 19th place, just 6 points clear of relegated Stockport County. Most results were fairly close affairs. but with two notable exceptions - an unopposed five goal defeat at Reading, and a massive 9-0 beating at Tranmere Rovers.

The two encounters with Champions Plymouth conversely produced three out of the four points at stake. Initially the attendances were very high, approaching 10,000, but inevitably this figure dwindled as the season wore on. By the New Year, after six successive victories, there followed a bad run which ended in a final fight against relegation. A rare good Cup run was enjoyed though, and the 4th round was reached, at which stage the Reds lost to Portsmouth after a home scoreless draw.

If the 1958/59 season was considered bad, this was nothing compared to the next campaign! After the previous season result at Tranmere, the next encounter there - the first of the season - was approached with trepidation, and the Reds lost 5-1. This was followed with a home match when Shrewsbury were the visitors, and four goals were shared. The same scoreline was the result the following Saturady when Wrexham came to Peel Park. The return match at Shrewsbury resulted in a 5-0 thrashing, followed by a 4-0 defeat at Grimsby. Four games, two points, and 14 goals conceded in the the first three away matches - already the writing was on the wall.

By the New Year of 1960, the Club languished at the bottom of the Division, and with gates now down to between four and five thousand, the warning bells also started ringing on the financial front once more. In October 1958, the Mayor had launched a 'Stanley' Appeal Fund', for £10,000, but over one year later this had raised only a paltry £533. The weekly wage bill had been severely pruned to £400 - from £600 - and with travel to mostly Northern clubs in prospect, relegation was viewed as not necessarily a disaster - at least on the financial front.

But the gates fell even more as the inevitable drew nearer - 3,109 for Port Vale's February visit, 2,018 when Southend came and scored four goals (it could have been ten), to an ultimate low of 925 the following week, the lowest Peel Park crowd since the 1930's. It was something of a surprise to see 2,597 turn up on April the 9th, but a five goal defeat doomed the team to bottom place in the League. The average attendance in the latter half of the season had plummetted to around 2,000, and as a show of 'no confidence', the manager was sacked, and replaced with Jimmy Harrower in a combined player/manager position. With other nearby football attractions, a fixture clash was avoided when special dispensation was given to the Reds for the playing of their home match with Brentford on the 11th of March, a Friday night. The attendance was a slight improvement, 3,500, but the increase could probably be attributed to to the novelty factor of the fixture.

By the season's end, the final goal tally read 57 for and (a Club worst record) 123 against, and with an accumulation of only 27 points, the team finished nine ponts clear at the bottom. The short early period of relative prosperity was now well behind the Club, and their debts continued to rise. An income of £300, plus an average donation from the Supporters Club (who by now had made their peace with the Club) of £150 per week, was offset with a wage bill only, of £400 per week. An earlier boon to the Club of introducing a weekly fund-raising Pools enterprise had produced a massive £27,921 in one year, but the scheme was adjudged to be illegal, and this lucrative and life-saving windfall had to be terminated.

In some respect the next season, the last complete one as things transpired, was not so bad as may have been anticipated at the time. But the first game of the season, on the 20th August, could hardly have produced a worse result, when the Reds were hammered 9-2 at Crystal Palace. Still in London, three days later, the team's confidence was partially restored when four goals were shared at Millwall. A two goal victory in the next match, at home to York City, perhaps gave some hope for optimism. However, as the season progressed, generally poor results led to a lowly position in the table, and a final 18th placing, three places above the re-election zone, but only two points clear.

The situation was becoming desperate, with poor attendances and ever increasing debts. Although not made public at the time, the 1961/62 season was to be a make or break period, and the latter won. The season started in reasonable fashion, for although the first game was lost at Tranmere (again), Darlington were then beaten 3-1 followed by a single goal defeat at Peel Park, and finally a point picked up in the Darlington return match.

Three points out of eight, not promotion form, but hardly a foretaste of the disasters to come. From that drawn match on August the 28th, only three encounters produced two points - each being by the only goal of the game - before the Red's season was curtailed on March the 3rd. Few results were really bad, although five goals were conceded at Oldham, and the Reds contributed only one to the six scored at Gillingham, but by the New Year, they were propping up all but one in the League.

By now even more fans were signalling their lack of appreciation, by staying away, and the two pre-Christmas matches each attracted sub-2,000 attendances. 1962 started with the resignation of Manager Jimmy Harrower, and undenied rumours said that the Club were around £40,000 in debt. Bad weather caused the cancellation of the potentially better supported games over the Festivities, and the cash flow was not helped by the gap of four weeks between home fixtures; but that was hardly worth the wait, as Colchester's visit attracted a paltry 1,411 to Peel Park, and resulted in a four goal defeat (what a contrast to a game two years earlier at League leaders Southampton, where the attendance was 20,356 - and the Reds received a 5-1 thrashing). Earlier, arguments between the Supporters and Parent Clubs once again had resulted in a banning of the former, an incredible slur on the fans who had contributed so much to the Club, but this rift was healed when they agreed to forget the past and strive for a better future. The involvement of Supporters Clubs have often been criticised by the Clubs themselves, but Accrington's faithful band had given and raised much in the past, and their return was to be too late to save the team.

The Chesterfield scoreless draw saw only 1,820 paying spectators at Peel Park, and 400 less one week later when Bradford City appeared, and walked off with the two points. On February the 17th, it was stated that:
"Stanley are on the brink of a precipice, only a miracle can save the Peel Park Club"
...... *"It's gone beyond anything the Directors can do, only the Public can save this old and famous Club."* Mr Pilkington the former Club Chairman added.

Both comments were true, the Directors had been paying the way of the Club from their own pockets, and the public had all but deserted them, but the miracle was not forthcoming - 3,000 to 4,000 gates were needed as a minimum - the average for the shortened season was recorded as 2,688. A Managerless two months was followed by the resignation of Chairman Edwin Slinger, and with normally well-founded rumours rift, the Football League were prompted into formally asking the Club to clarify the financial situation. It transpired that with a £5,500 loss incurred to May 1961, plus a further £5,000 since, the total owing to unsecured creditors was a massive £43,566. In addition over £400 was owed on the Players National Insurance contributions, £3,000 on unpaid transfer fees, (further acquisitions had been banned from the previous December onwards). All this with assets worth only £35,600. Another 'Save Stanley' campaign launched in December had raised only £450 in three months. It is little wonder that the 'Butcher King', Burnley Chairman Bob Lord, quickly pulled out from his promised help in putting the Club back on its feet when these figures were finally admitted. Six Stanley Directors had already resigned, one of the terms for this eventual unsuccessful rescue mission.

The plight of the Club reached far and wide, and with both Television channels publicising the Club's plight, the attendance for the Rochdale game on the 24th of February rose, but only to 2,690, this number indicating the true feeling of the town as a whole - and not the 2,000 or so true supporters - felt about the Club. The previous home game (attendance 1,775) had seen Pickup score the last ever goal for the Club in the Football League.

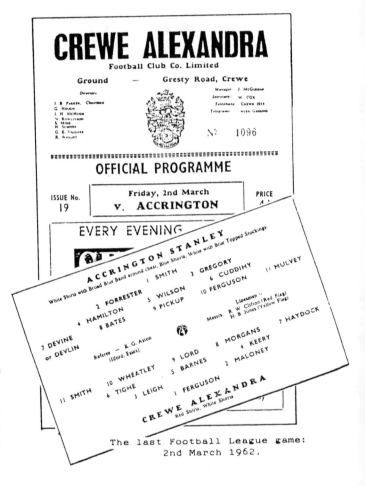

The last Football League game: 2nd March 1962.

The last game came at Crewe on the 3rd of March, before 4,272 fans, at which - in a snowstorm - the Reds lost by four unopposed goals. The Reds represented in that game were:- Smith, Forrester, Cregory, Hamilton, Wilson, Bennett, Devine, W.Smith, Pickup, Ferguson and Mulvey.

Three days later, the Players as usual reported for training, unaware that a letter had been sent to the Football League the day before tendering the Club's immediate resignation from the Fourth Division. However, following a meeting on the Thursday of that week, the resignation was withdrawn. A hastily called meeting between the Clubs Directors and legal advisors, revealed that all creditors, that had been approached, had refused to take steps that would in effect kill the Club. In a new wave of hope, aided by eleventh hour cash donations from the Public and the promise of financial help from several Businessmen plus the Club's President, the meeting agreed to fulfil the rest of the Club's fixtures. Attempts to strengthen the Board would also be made, and most importantly it was agreed to write to the League immediately withdrawing their resignation.

Bob Gordon, Alex Hamilton. Garry Richardson and skipper Bob Wilson keep in trim though the future for them is uncertain. Sadly the poster behind them announces a match that could have drawn the biggest crowd of the season today but will not be played.

The players train in vain outside the Ground, for the Exeter match which was never played.

(Accrington Observer)

A special meeting of the Football League on the 11th of March, debated the issue at length, but finally decided, and aided by their interpretation regarding the legality of the situation, that the first letter from Accrington Stanley F.C. should be accepted - seventy-two hours had meant the difference between survival and the end of the Club. One interesting issue was raised by the Club after the event, to the effect that as they were willing to play their next fixture, as were their opponents Exeter City - on March the 10th - and since the League at this time had not accepted the Club's resignation, then surely Alan Hardaker (the Football League Secretary) had no power to instruct the Club not to play; the Reds threatened to sue, but the argument was never resolved in a Court of Law.

Inevitably the letters of protest from the local public were written - and from wider afield - denouncing the Club, the Directors, the (lack of) supporters, and the Football League, but if those same people and many others who did not voice their opinions publicly, had acted earlier, then the Club may have been saved. By early April, twelve of the Club's players had left for nominal fees - Mike Furgusson later moved again for £50,000 - and although a new (legal) weekly pool was started for 'The redevelopment of Football in Accrington', it was too late. The Inland Revenue proposed the winding up of the Club which was carried through one year later - they wanted their £3,567 'pound of flesh'.

A new Accrington arose, under the Chrimanship of George Clarkson and three other Directors. Stanley's comeback was enthusiastically endorsed with seventy players asking for trials, and in the practise match - attended by a crowd of 650 - one aspirant broke his leg; the new Club were apparently to be dogged by bad luck from the outset.

Entry had been accepted into the Lancashire Combination Division 2, and on the 18th of August 1962 - while the Reds replacement in the Football League - Oxford United - were playing at Barrow - 995 spectators turned up at Peel Park to see the team play Rolls Royce. Two goals were shared, followed by a 1-4 defeat at Padiham. Despite a shaky start, crowds of around 700 were faithful to the Reds, and the next season they became the somewhat unlikely Champions.

By the next season's end they were only saved from relegation by New Brighton's resignation and a ballot which favoured them over bottom Club Prescot Town. But the earlier, and quite reasonable, support had decreased by now, so that only 300 were present for the first game of the 1965/66 season at Peel Park. This figure quickly dropped to barely three figures as the team's fortunes sunk, and by October, Peter Dewhurst the Player Manager left, at which point the Club became purely Amateur. In November the new owner of Peel Park, Mr Littler - a scrap metal merchant from Wigan - announced his intentions of selling the Ground to the Lancashire County Council. By now with virtually no support, no money, and the prospect of no Ground, the Club stated that they would finish their fixtures, and then probably fold at the end of the season.

By the dawn of 1966, the Reds were in a familiar bottom slot in the table, with just one point from fifteen games. Following a six goal home defeat to Padiham and then another crushing defeat, they had completed nine months of Football, and achieved just two victories. On the 8th of January, Glossop were entertained, and in by far the best game of the season, the Reds unexpectedly triumphed 3-2, Cockburn was the scorer of the last two Accrington goals, and appropriately enough a bottle of Port was provided for the team in celebration of the victory. Just fifty spectators witnessed the game, and this Accrington Stanley were never to play another match, for the second time in four years a Club carrying the same name failed to complete their fixtures for the season.

A new Accrington arrives at the Crown Ground.
(Video still taken from 'Football Phoenix')

In 1968, and with stubborn determination, Accrington Stanley (1968) was formed. After a number of approches from ex-Stanley supporters, Councillor Bill Parkinson held a public meeting at Bond Street Working Men's Club, and around fifty enthusiasts formed the new Accrington F.C. on the 15th of July 1968. Sensibly it was decided that the new Club should be started on a firm footing, and with a desire to get back into the Lancashire Combination, it was reckoned that £500 starting capital would be required plus running expenses of £50 per week. Mr Parkinson announced that help should be forthcoming from a number of businessmen, and the site for a new Ground, behind the Crown Inn, should be possible to establish.

A small in number, but strong in dedication, Supporters Club was formed, and the Club played its first match on the 9th of August. The team - no more than a 'scratch' one but with a strong feeling of nostalgia - was composed of most of the previous Stanley players from the 1963/64 season. The occasion was a pre-season friendly at nearby Great Harwood. Under the temporary Managership of Tom Lee, the team were not lacking enthusiasm, but the far more experienced Lancashire Combination team crushed the new 'Reds' by 9-0. The gate produced a mere £21, and it was a big disappoint-ment that only fifty or so Accrington supporters made the journey.

With great resolve three new enthusiasts set about putting the Club on a firm footing, and despite the difficulties experienced in fund raising, the small Committee together with the Supporters Club were, by June 1970, at last ready to take the plunge. At this time trialists for the team were invited to Bullough Park, and work was put in hand to develop the Crown Ground with the erection of enclosure fencing, etc. Jimmy Hinksman was appointed as Manager, and all that was left was to the newcomers acceptance into the Lancashire Combination Division 2. It was a worrying few weeks, for the Club were all geared up for a start at a Senior level, but with Kirkby Town reserves also applying for membership, it was no foregone conclusion that the Reds would be voted in. In the event, Accrington Stanley (1968) with 11 votes as opposed to the Kirkby team with only two, were given the chance for a brand new start.

Having fought their way up through several Leagues, they are now in the Northern Premier (Premier Division) League, with the avowed intention of regaining Football League membership for the team and with promotion now possible, it is conceivable that of the twenty or so ex-Football League clubs, the latest Reds are a possible candidate. With the team playing in a League just one step below the top in non-

League circles - The Conference - the name of 'Accrington Stanley' is once again ocassionally heard when the football results are given out on a Saturday evening. A run through to the second round of the F.A.Cup in the 1990/91 season, produced a familiar fixture from the past, a match against Crewe Alexandra. The national publicity gained did the club no harm, nor did their share of the takings from a 10,081 crowd for the match which was played at Blackburn's Ewood Park. Earlier, in the 4th qualifying round, the Crown Ground saw its record crowd, which numbered 2,096, pack in for the visit of Fleetwood Town. Home attendances for matches averaged around the 500 mark (1993/94 season), one of the best in the League, but still a long way short of the break even figure that would be required at the next step up.

On paper the Club may have nearly reached the ultimate goal - the Football League - and whilst their efforts and achievements over the past 25 years or so may be highly commendable - the realists acknowledge that those last two steps will be the highest and most difficult to achieve.

THE GROUNDS

1. CRICKET FIELD, THORNEYHOLME ROAD.

Not much changed since the 1880's.
The re-built pavilion and uncovered seating in the same location.

In common with so many clubs of the era, Accrington F.C were associated with and played their games at, the Town's Cricket Ground. Despite the passing of over 100 years since its inception, the ground has not changed dramatically. The present pavillion is sited where the original stood and there are traces of uncovered seating on both the North and South sides, which may date back to the early days. The ground is now smaller than it was before, with floodlit tennis courts occupying the original West end, where the football club's covered, seated stand once stood. The main entrance is now, as previously, located in the South-west corner.

With the overall boundaries of the ground remaining unchanged, and armed with the knowledge of the earlier layout of the venue, an interesting visit to this former Football League Ground - dating back to the very first season - can be very rewarding.

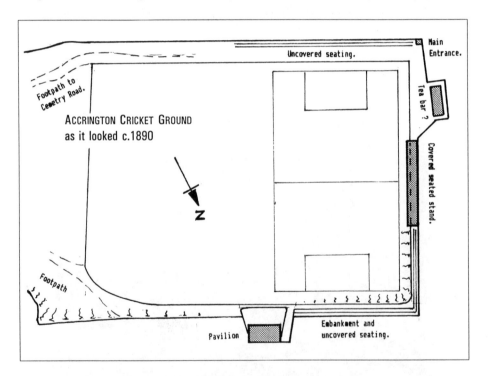

2. MOORHEAD PARK.

This ground was, for a short time, common to both Accrington and Accrington Stanley F.C. and although not used by either in the Football League, it was probably a well appointed and enclosed ground. Located at the ends of Cromwell Avenue and Orange Street, it was of an irregular shape and built in the early 1890's, but had disappeared by 1930. From the mid-1930's, a girl's high school and playing fields have stood on this site.

The main, and probably only, entrance was located at the end of Orange Street, with both open and covered seating extending about half the pitch lengh on the East side. Opposite, was a short and narrow covered (probably standing only) enclosure, with flat areas to the rest of this and the other two sides.

3. BELL'S GROUND, WOODNOOK.

This ground was used by Accrington Stanley for nearly twenty years around the turn of the century. The move from Moorhead was made to save money spent on rent, but the facilities undoubtedly could not compare with the former home venue. The Ground was located to the West end of Nuttall Street (now Bellfield Road), at the end of Hudson Street and was enclosed on the West side by the former railway line. The pitch had a pronounced slope, and although probably enclosed the venue offered little, if any, facilities for spectators. The area had ceased to exist as a Football Ground by the early 1930's.

4. PEEL PARK.

The last and most famous of this quartet of former football grounds. The stadium was within the formerly large grounds of the Peel Park Hotel. Football was played in the locality as far back as the 1870's, at which time the Accrington Cricket Club's home venue was also located in this area.

The Ground was purchased for £2,500 by the post-war resurrected Accrington Stanley in 1919, and with this debt and little capital, work was undertaken to create an enclosed ground. By the opening match on the 20th of September 1919, boarding had been erected on three sides - the adjacent school wall forming the barrier on the South West side - but spectator and players' facilities were non-existant, with the players having to change in the school. The pitch at Peel Park also had a pronounced slope and a notorious hump which was not removed until 1954. The playing surface was rough, but in a very short time, the committee had been able to provide a reasonable home venue, which also include railings around the pitch. By June 1921, a total of £5,700 had been spent on the Ground, and by this time work had started on providing a covered seated Stand on the South-east side. Although improvements to the banking on the North-east end had been undertaken (increasing the ground capacity by 2,000), it was soon recognised - at the time of the club's entry to the Football League - that extensions to the seated stand would also be required. Work commenced on this enclosure in September and the Stand was to extend some 75 yards alongside the pitch. Although a compact and well appointed stadium was taking shape, the club had a number of complaints from visiting teams regarding the small size of the playing area and the closeness of the spectators. By 1930, narrow strips of concrete terracing had been introduced on all four sides, but it was to be another twenty years or so before the upper areas were also concreted - plus the addition of extra terracing at the Huncoat End - although an additional enclosure was provided during the interim period, at the school end of the Ground, which continued around the corners. Around 1953, a major redevelopment plan for the Ground was considered, particularly the provision of a two-tiered 4,000 capacity seated Stand on the Burnley Road side, but this never materialised. In November, the Floodlight pylons were erected, making Accrington Stanley one of the earliest innovators, although the first match did not take place until one year later. By now the Ground capacity was 24,000, a figure never even nearly approached.

After a few rare years of success and relative financial stability, the Club purchased the Aldershot Military Tattoo Grandstand in April 1958, at the bargain price of £1,450. But one point the Directors had probably not bargained for was the £14,000 or so expenses required to dismantle, transport and re-erect the structure! Such a high expense just preceded yet another - the last - financially bad period, and this 'white elephant' probably contributed, to a large extent, to the Club's eventual extinction. The 60 yard long timber and galvanised steel clad building could provide seating and covered standing for 4,700 spectators. This major improvement provided an official capacity at Peel Park of 24,600, including 9,000 under cover.

After Accrington Stanley (1921) became defunct, Peel Park was sold to a scrap metal merchant from Wigan, who in turn, in November 1965, sold the by now derelict Ground to the Lancashire County Council. The planned use by the Council for a local education sports field accelerated the final demise of the shortlived successors to the '1921' Club. On the 23rd of April 1972, at 5.00am, the last act in the sad saga of Peel Park was enacted, when the original timber stand - then valued at approximately £10,000 - was destroyed by fire.

The end of the old Stand - the day after the fire in 1972.
(A video still from 'Football Phoenix')

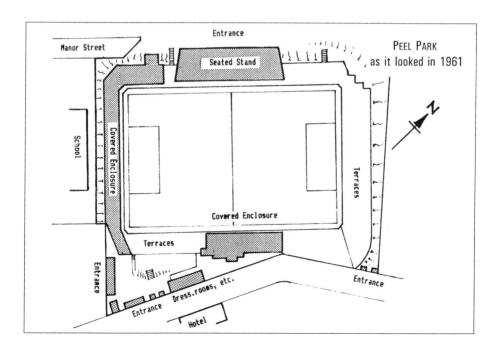

The South-east corner of Peel Park in the late 1980's.
Some walls and the dressing rooms remain, but little more.

Parts of the perimeter wall, dressing rooms and other structures on the South-east side still remain, also evidence of the terracing (now grass banked) at the North-east end, together with an old delapidated hut, once the Club's social headquarters, remains on the North-west side. Football can still be seen at Peel Park! Matches of the adjacent Primary School are played at the end of the former Football League Ground - the same pitch orientation that Accrington Stanley used in their first season in 1919/20.

PROGRAMMES:

Some Clubs in pre-1900 certainly issued programmes, but this would seem highly unlikely in Accrington's case, since - at least in 1893 - the Accrington Weekly Advertiser, produced home match, team line-ups, in the Newspaper, with the advice to: *"Cut out and take to the field for reference".*

A reference to total programme sales of Accrington Stanley for the 1919/20 season of £17, proves that they existed, but it is highly unlikely that any existing copies remain to this day. Pre-Second World War copies are very rare, and inevitably highly prized, and even post-war copies - although far more plentiful - fetch high prices. The last Football League programme issued by the Club was for the match versus Bradford City on the 3rd of February 1962.

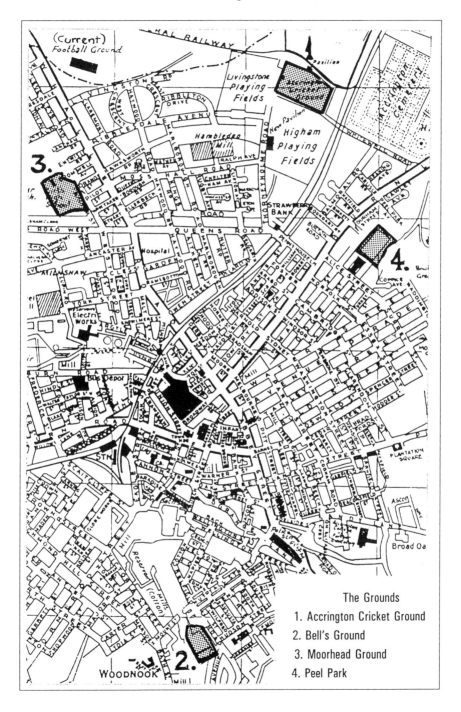

The Grounds
1. Accrington Cricket Ground
2. Bell's Ground
3. Moorhead Ground
4. Peel Park

Fixtures for the (non-completed) 1961/62 Season

August	19th	Tranmere Rovers	Away	0-2
	21st	Darlington	Home	3-1
	26th	Chester	Home	0-1
	28th	Darlington	Away	1-1
September	2nd	Colchester United	Away	2-1
	4th	Mansfield Town	Home	0-1
	9th	Carlisle United	Home	1-0
	16th	Bradford City	Away	1-0
	18th	Barrow	Away	1-3
	23rd	Aldershot	Home	0-2
	25th	Barrow	Home	2-2
	29th	Stockport County	Away	0-2
October	2nd	Oldham Athletic	Home	1-0
	7th	Rochdale	Away	0-1
	10th	Oldham Athletic	Away	0-5
	14th	Crewe Alexandra	Home	1-0
	21st	Exeter City	Away	0-3
	28th	Wrexham	Home	0-2
November	11th	Workington	Home	0-4
	18th	York City	Away	0-1
December	2nd	Gillingham	Away	1-5
	9th	Millwall	Home	1-1
	16th	Tranmere Rovers	Home	1-1
	23rd	Chester	Away	0-0
	26th	Hartlepool	Home	Postponed
	30th	Hartlepool	Away	Postponed
January	8th	Doncaster Rovers	Away	1-1
	13th	Colchester United	Home	0-4
	20th	Carlisle United	Away	0-2
	27th	Chesterfield	Home	0-0
February	3rd	Bradford City	Home	0-2
	10th	Aldershot	Away	2-2
	17th	Stockport County	Home	1-2
	24th	Rochdale	Home	0-2
March	3rd	Crewe Alexandra	Away	0-4

Unplayed Matches: March 10th Exeter City (Home), 17th Wrexham (Away), 24th Doncaster Rovers (Home), 31st Workington (Away), April 7th York City (Home), 14th Chesterfield (Away), 20th Southport (Away), 21st Gillingham (Home), 23rd Southport (Home), 28th Millwall (Away), 30th Mansfield Town (Away),

Undated (for re-arrangement) Hartlepool - home and away

F.A. Cup
1st round: November 4th	Stockport C	Away	1-0
2nd round: November 25th	Hartlepool	Away	1-2

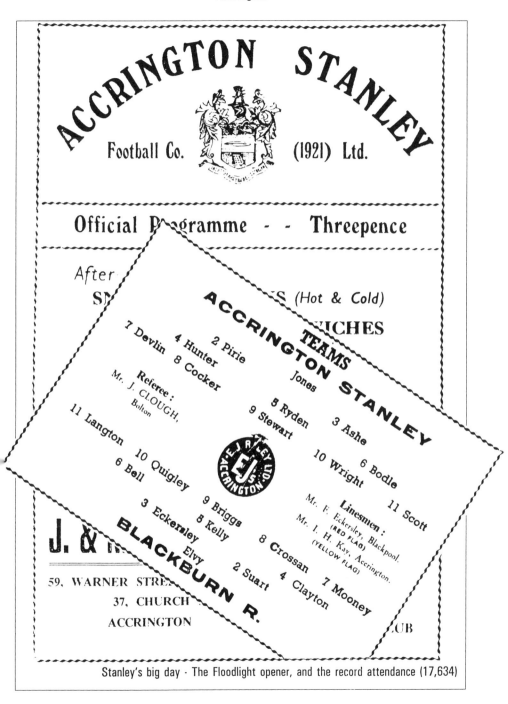

Stanley's big day - The Floodlight opener, and the record attendance (17,634)

BARROW ASSOCIATION FOOTBALL CLUB 1921-22

Back Row— J. Banks, W. McKay, J. Atkinson, H. Carter, M. Nimmo, J. Phizacklea, W. Dickinson *(Secretary).*
Middle Row— C. Matthews, R. Munro, B. Sharkey, W. Pearce, F. McPherson.
Front Row— E. Simpson, H. Pearson, W. Eaves.

Barrow F.C. - 6th May 1967 (Fourth Division promotion day)

The Barrow team in that last vital match v Brentford—Back row: Bob Knox (Substitute), George Smith, Jim Mallon, Fred Else, Malcolm Edwards, Eric Harrison, Dick Robinson (Trainer) Don McEvoy (Manager); Front row: Ron McGarry, Jim Mulholland, Brian Arrowsmith (Captain), Roy McCarthy, Tony Field, Brian Pilkington.

BARROW

Barrow 1901 - to Date

1901/02	- 1902/03	Lancashire League
1903/04	- 1904/05	Lancashire Combination Div. 2
1905/06	- 1907/08	Lancashire Combination Div. 1
1908/09	- 1910/11	Lancashire Combination Div. 2
1911/12	- 1914/15	Lancashire Combination Div. 1
1915/16	-	Ceased Activities
1916/17	-	Lancashire Combination (Wartime)
1917/18	-	Ceased Activities
1918/19	- 1920/21	Lancashire Combination Div. 1
1921/22	- 1939/40	Football League Division 3 North *
1939/40	-	(Wartime) North West League
1940/41	- 1944/45	North Western League **
1945/46	-	Football League Division 3 North (West)
1946/47	- 1957/58	Football League Division 3 North
1958/59	- 1966/67	Football League Fourth Division
1967/68	- 1969/70	Football League Third Division
1970/71	- 1971/72	Football League Fourth Division
1972/73	- 1978/79	Northern Premier League
1979/80	- 1982/83	Alliance Premier League
1983/84	-	Northern Premier League
1984/85	- 1985/86	Alliance Premier League
1986/87	- 1988/89	Northern Premier League
1989/90	- 1991/92	GM Vauxhall Conference (Alliance Prem.)
1992/93	- To date	Northern Premier League

****

* Played only 3 games in 1939/40 season, before League abandoned.
** Team composed of local players, and known as Barrow 'A' or Reserves.

Football League Record:

	Play.	W	D	L	F	A	Pts.	Posn.	Ave.Att.
1921/22	38	14	5	19	42	54	33	15th	5675
1922/23	38	13	4	21	50	60	30	18th	3745
1923/24	42	8	9	25	35	80	25	22nd	3320 #
Successfully re-elected									
1924/25	42	16	7	19	51	74	39	14th	4300
1925/26	42	7	4	31	50	98	18	22nd	2756
Successfully re-elected									
1926/27	42	7	8	27	34	117	22	22nd	4336
Successfully re-elected									
1927/28	42	10	11	21	54	102	31	19th	5386
1928/29	42	10	8	24	64	93	28	20th	6039
1929/30	42	11	5	26	41	98	27	22nd	4512
Successfully re-elected									
1930/31	42	15	7	20	68	89	37	16th	5669
1931/32	40	24	1	15	86	59	49	5th	5811

(Contd.)	Play.	W	D	L	F	A	Pts.	Posn.	Ave.Att.
1932/33	42	18	7	17	60	60	43	9th	3835
1933/34	42	19	9	14	116	94	47	8th	4561
1934/35	42	13	9	20	58	87	35	17th	3859
1935/36	42	13	12	17	58	65	38	15th	3926
1936/37	42	13	10	19	70	86	36	16th	4037
1937/38	42	11	10	21	41	71	32	21st	4532
Successfully re-elected									
1938/39	42	16	9	17	66	65	41	13th	6354
1946/47	42	17	7	18	54	62	41	9th	6542
1947/48	42	16	13	13	49	40	45	7th	7814
1948/49	41	14	12	16	41	48	40	13th	6939
1949/50	42	14	9	19	47	53	37	15th	5946
1950/51	46	16	6	24	51	76	38	19th	5778
1951/52	46	17	12	17	57	61	46	12th	6939
1952/53	46	16	12	18	66	71	44	19th	5450
1953/54	46	16	12	18	72	71	44	12th	5587
1954/55	46	17	6	23	70	89	40	17th	4774
1955/56	46	12	9	25	61	83	33	22nd	6194
1956/57	46	21	9	16	76	62	51	10th	6379
1957/58	46	13	15	18	66	74	41	18th	5733
Founder members of Fourth Division									
1958/59	46	9	10	27	51	104	28	23rd	4325
Successfully re-elected									
1959/60	46	15	11	20	77	87	41	18th	5612
1960/61	46	13	11	22	52	79	37	22nd	4299
Successfully re-elected									
1961/62	44	17	14	13	74	58	48	9th	4446
1962/63	46	19	12	15	82	80	50	9th	4083
1963/64	46	6	18	22	51	93	30	24th	3039
Successfully re-elected									
1964/65	46	12	6	28	59	105	30	21st	3204
Successfully re-elected									
1965/66	46	16	15	15	72	76	47	12th	4701
1966/67	46	24	11	11	76	54	59	3rd	5770
Promoted to Third Division									
1967/68	46	21	8	17	65	54	50	8th	6062
1968/69	46	17	8	21	56	75	42	19th	4676
1969/70	46	8	14	24	46	81	30	23rd	3649
Relegated to Fourth Division									
1970/71	46	7	8	31	51	90	22	24th	2333
Successfully re-elected									
1971/72	46	13	11	22	40	71	37	22nd	2307
Not re-elected.									

(# Indicates lowest average attendance in Football League)

****

Number of Football League matches played: 1927.
(Including 3 matches in 1939/40 season)

SUMMARY OF FACTS:

Grounds:

1901/02 - 1904/05	The Strawberry Ground, off Abbey Road
1905/06 -	Ainslie Street
1906/07 - 1908/09	Little Park, Roose
1909/10 - To Date	Holker Street

Colours (Football League):

1921/22 - 1929/30	Royal Blue Shirts, White Shorts
1930/31 - 1939/40	Royal Blue Shirts with White 'V', White Shorts
1945/46 - 1957/58	Royal Blue Shirts, White Shorts
1958/59 -	As 1930 - 1940 period
1959/60 -	Royal Blue and White Striped Shirts, White Shorts
1960/61 - 1966/67	White Shirts (Royal Blue Trim) Royal Blue Shorts
1967/68 - 1969/70	Royal Blue Shirts and Shorts
1970/71 - 1971/72	As 1960 - 1967 period.

Nickname: The Bluebirds

Significant matches:
First League Game
27th August, 1921 versus Stockport County (Home) Lost 0-2. Attend. 9,700 (record at time)
Last League Game
29th April, 1972 versus Exeter City (Away) lost 1-7. Attendance 3,050
Record Attendance:
9th January, 1954 versus Swansea Town (F.A. Cup), 16,874. (Receipts £1,680)

MAIN ACHIEVEMENTS:

F.A. Cup (Never past 3rd Round)
(As non-League Club:)
3rd Round: 1990/91.
1st Round: 1905/06, 1912/13, 1976/77, 1988/89.
F.A. Trophy: Winners 1989/90
                  Semi-finals 1987/88

Promoted to Football League Third Division - 1966/67.

Northern Premier League Champions:	1983/84	1988/89
Runners-up:	1987/88	
Northern Premier League Shield Winners:	1984/85	
Lancashire Combination Div. 1 Champions:	1920/21	
Lancashire Combination Div. 1 Runners-up:	1913/14	
Lancashire Combination Div. 2 Runners-up:	1910/11	

Lancashire Senior Cup Winners: 1955/56. Lancashire Junior Cup Winners: 1980/81
Cumbrian Cup Winners: 1982/83, 1983/84
International (Whilst playing with the Club): Miller - Ireland, (1932 and 1933)
Most Football League Goals: Billy Gordon - 145, (1949-1958)
Best Football League Win: 1933/34 versus Gateshead (Home) 12-1
Worst Football League Defeat: 1958/59 versus Hartlepool (Away) 1-10.
                  1959/60 versus Crystal Palace (Away) 0-9.

Barrow F.C. can surely have no equal for prolonged misery! The Club enjoyed (if that is the correct word) Football League membership for over 50 years, and yet in all that time achieved just one promotion, but had to seek re-election on eleven occasions; their record holds testimony to the determined enthusiasm of a series of Club stalwarts and supporters, who, over the decades kept the team in the League, only to see them lose that status soon after their brief period of rare success.

Detached in its corner of the far North-west, the town of Barrow was, relative to other areas of like population, slow to promote a Football Club of Senior status. But, in relation to the rapid increase in the town's size, particularly noticeable around the turn of the century, perhaps this delay was not so surprising. From a small village of 68 inhabitants in 1845, it grew to 12,000 within 20 years, and quadrupled that number by 1881. This phenomenal growth rate can be attributed to the industrial demands of the mid-Victorian era, and the consequent growth of the Iron industry and subsequently the Steel making trades. The coming of the railway in 1846 opened up this little community, and created work for thousands of immigrants that flocked to Furness for employment in the Iron Ore mines, the smelting trades and the final shipment of this new 'gold' from the little harbour that was to become an International Port.

By the turn of the century, this flourishing town had few indigenous folk, but was almost totally populated by 'foreigners', notably those from North of the nearby border - Scotland. It was the end of an era, a period which had seen the rapid growth of Football throughout the industrial North. It was also inevitable that the Scots brought with them their love of the game to Barrow, as they had done to so many other towns. But it was no easy passage to form a Football (Soccer) Club that would be supported sufficiently, for the 'other' code - Rugby - had already gained a secure foothold and following, the local Club having been first formed back in 1875.

A detailed list of founders of Barrow F.C. cannot be ascertained, but there was inevitably a strong Scottish influence, as these pioneers of the game had demonstrated their worth elsewhere. It was, however, a local publican - Mr. Hinds - who was the principal champion of the cause, after previous attempts to get football recognised at a Senior level, by others, had failed. Barrow Rangers who were formed in 1876 and played at the Racecourse made little impact. Another club had floundered in 1894, and some twenty years later the Furness Club had an undistinguished life that lasted only two years in the North Western League.

Mr. Hinds called a meeting at the Drill Hall for Tuesday the 16th of July, 1901, which was enthusiastically attended by many shipbuilding and engineering workers, and alongside Mr. Hinds, who took the Chair, was the ex-Preston North End player, Moses Saunders. Resolutions were rapidly passed to the effect that a Senior side, or none at all should be created, and the £280 that was considered necessary as a minimum to get the Club started and kitted out, should be raised by public subscription from membership fees of 1/6d. (12½p) per person. This figure was voiced as being a small sum, but Mr. Hinds had shrewdly taken into account that it was better to get a large following with each contributing little, rather than only a few at an amount that could only be afforded by the minority of wealthy men.

Mr. Hinds had already entered into correspondence, via the North Western Evening Mail, with the Barrow Amateur Athletic Club regarding a proposal to use the area within their running track at Cavendish Park as a Football Ground. This proposal was unanimously rejected by the Athletes as they stated that the venue was unfit for football; a strange claim since it had been used by the ill-fated Furness Club. Another objection was the fact that it was not fenced off from the adjacent Rugby Ground. The latter reason was nearer to the truth as the Athletics Club undoubtedly had a strong bias towards the handling code, for in 1895 the Rugby, Cricket and Cycling Clubs had combined, and they recognised the threat that the dribbling game could pose.

Mr. Hinds with enthusiasm and confidence in the successful formation of a Football Club had already made an application to join the Lancashire League. This was an incredibly bold step, for this organisation was not only a Professional League, but also represented one of the strongest combinations in the North outside of the Football League itself. In an attempt to sway the townspeople at large towards the Club's creation, he pointed out that a Senior team would attract many away supporters to Barrow, who in turn would spend their money locally. Mr. Dawes proposed that a Senior Association Club be formed, this motion was seconded, and the resolution was enthusiastically adopted. Seven Committee members were elected, and following advertisements for players, 30 applications flooded in from as far afield as London and Glasgow.

A suitable field had been found for home games, which was located near the junction of Strawberry Lane and Abbey Road, and became known as 'The Strawberry Ground'. In the final event, subscriptions (i.e. season tickets) were sensibly raised to five shillings (25p), and it was decided that the team would play in Black and White striped shirts and Black shorts. Arrangements were rapidly made for trams to run from the town centre to the Strawberry Hotel (which was to be used as dressing rooms) on matchdays, at a cost of 1d.

At the end of August workmen were hard at work transforming the field into a football pitch, by early September the new Club had 750 members, and large attendances were reported at the team's practise matches. In an incredibly short period of less than two months, the idea of forming a Senior football team had been transformed into a reality, and the Club's entry had been approved into the Lancashire League, the F.A. Cup, and the Lancashire Cup!

The first match of Barrow F.C. was played at the Strawberry, with Blackpool in opposition, in a friendly match on the 2nd of September, before an incredibly good attendance of approximately 4,000 spectators. These new found football fans made their way home after the match well satisfied with the home team's 3-1 victory. Five days later another good crowd, of around 3,000, came to see the first Lancashire League game against fellow newcomers Warrington, the first and last match with these opponents, for they withdrew from the League before the season's end. Once again a victory ensued, this time by a single goal.

A Lancashire Senior Cup match followed, and an attendance of 3,302 paid £57 at the gate to see the new team win by two goals. Two highly prestigious Friendly games were also played in September, when Preston North End came to Furness on the 9th, and Sheffield Wednesday on the 28th; very creditable results were recorded with a one goal win and a 5-2 defeat respectively. Between these matches another friendly contest saw a comfortable win by seven unopposed goals over Blackburn Park Road. The second League match was not played until October the 12th, at which time Barrow were brought down to earth with a 1-2 defeat to Prescot, and seven days later the first F.A. Cup match was played. Their opponents, Moss Bay from Workington, forced a 1-1 draw, and the replay - which was also played at Barrow, saw the homesters through with a 3-1 victory. Rochdale were then beaten, before the end of a very good run, with defeat at the hands of the experienced Darwen team.

By Christmas, the team lay 7th in the League after seven games, a lesser number played than other members. But this encouraging start to the Club's career, was a misleading guide to their eventual capabilities, for by the season's end it was far from a rosy picture with the team finishing tenth of thirteen teams. However, with 8 victories, 3 draws and 13 defeats, their overall record was perhaps not so bad, and with 19 points they were well clear of Haydock in bottom position who gained just 6 points. The financial situation did give cause for concern however, with a deficit being recorded over the year. The doubting Thomas's no doubt praised themselves on their foresight that a Senior Football (Soccer) Club could not exist in the town, and although the road has usually been a rough one, they have been proved wrong in the long term.

BARROW ASSOCIATION FOOTBALL CLUB 1902-1903

Probably the first (un-named) team group

Interest was maintained amongst the team's supporters with many Friendlies in the first two seasons, which included the visits to the Strawberry of such players as Herbert Chapman (Sheffield Wednesday), Jack Bell who played for Everton - in a County Cup tie - and other notable Football League players. Having successfully gained re-election to the Lancashire League, the second season was a great improvement over the first, and by the New Year the team lay in fourth place, and with the final placing of third and a record of 14 wins and only 5 defeats from their 22 games, things looked far healthier than one year earlier. Despite winning all their home games, the away form showed room for improvement, even so only 5 points separated them from Champions Southport Central. The season had started with a well attended prestigious friendly with Nottingham Forest, and only a two goal defeat, followed by a less glamorous and boring game with Nelson.

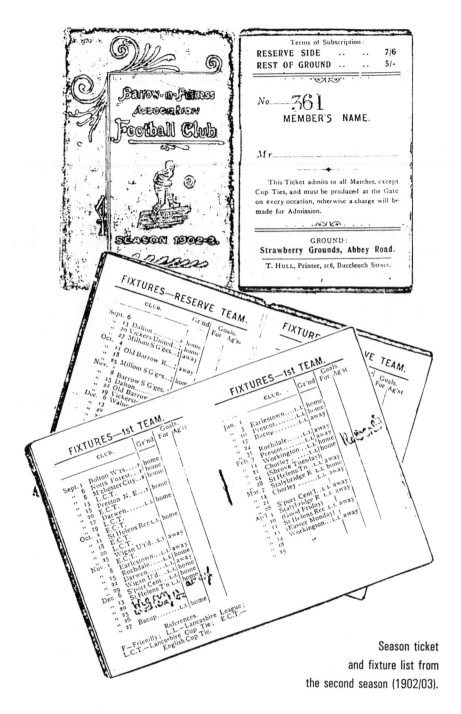

Season ticket
and fixture list from
the second season (1902/03).

With the demise of the Lancashire League in 1903, the 1904 season saw Barrow move over to the Lancashire Combination Division 2, and although the season was not a disaster on the playing front, the same could not be said of the financial situation. With the high travelling costs incurred by their isolation, and although the total gate receipts amounted to £347 plus a further £355 from season tickets and other means, a loss on the season of over £54 was realised. This loss represented over twice the gate taken for the best supported home game, with Chorley St. George. But by now the Club realised that the distant location of the Strawberry from the town centre was deterring better support. The elevation of the Ground was also a drawback as the heavily laden Trams were often unable to make the steep climb and the drivers would then need to recruit help from the passengers to help push the vehicles! A move was made to Ainslie Street, which offered two big advantages over the Strawberry. Located nearer to the town centre, it alleviated the transport problems to matches, and the £15 rent for the pitch represented around half that paid previously. Set against these factors were several bad points, principally a pronounced slope, and the poor surface of the pitch - the stay was to be only a short one.

On the 3rd of September 1904, the first match was played, and won, at Ainslie Street, with St. Helen's Recreation on League duty in opposition. The Ground was to cause problems throughout the season, and by March the last game was played at this venue. By this time the home venue had not only effected the team's playing ability, but inevitably support had started to dwindle. Logically it would have been better to have stayed out the season at Ainslie Street as it was argued by some, for with the worst of the winter rain over, the warmer weather should have help to dry out the pitch from the near quagmire that it had become. Conversely there was a body of opinion, including the local Press, that argued for a move as soon as possible.

A Ground at Little Park, Roose, was offered and this was taken up. But this was also far from ideal, since it would mean yet again a tram journey away from the town centre. While the arguments continued regarding the wisdom of a mid-season move, the team certainly reaped the benefits. An incredible run continued that started from one of the last games at Ainslie Street, when Padiham were defeated, and which was to see a gradual rise of the team up the League. In fact it is quite possible that if the Club had continued at Ainslie Street, they may well have become defunct, since financially they were at death's door, and already the Secretary had departed along with several players.

A final 16 match run saw the Club score 44 goals with only 8 against, and they ended in an eventual runners-up place to Champions St. Helens. The supporters had returned, the financial side therefore improved, and the Club were back on an even keel, with First Division football to look forward to. The Club's initial stay in this division of the Lancashire Combination was limited to just three seasons, when they were relegated back to the lower fold. At least the experience was good for these top division days brought the Reserve teams of the Lancashire Football League teams to Barrow, and on one occasion, the Liverpool second string contained no fewer than five current or past International players.

But yet again the lack of a winning team brought its money problems, and three players in particular were to offer the Club a lifeline by their transfers; Sanderson - a winger - moved on to Preston North End for £100, but he was to tragically die two years later; the move of Mawson produced even more money, and goalkeeper Mearns later starred in Barnsley's F.A.Cup Final appearance in 1910.

Once more the Directors had to dig into their pockets and it was necessary to again sell the most promising players in order to keep solvent; Dick Smith for £175, and full back Oddie both moving to Preston. The high unemployment in the area inevitably took its toll at home matches, and with crowds of only around 1,500 it was always going to be a struggle. The balance sheet at the season's end revealed gate takings of £578 and season ticket sales of half this amount. A total expenditure of £1,371 was incurred to give a profit on the season of £36, but the Club were still in the red by nearly £400.

A Baines 'play-up' lapel badge of the period

However, in January 1906, the first round of the F.A. Cup was reached for the first time, to bring some excitement to the Club. Although the result ran true to form, a 2-3 defeat at 2nd Division (Football League) Brad-ford City, the share of the gate was more than welcome. The return to the Combination Second Division in 1908 did not initially bring success, the season ending in a disappointing League placing.

The Club and its followers' dissatisfaction continued with regard to Grounds, and once again the non-central location of Roose necessitated yet another move, the fourth - but final - venue in only eight years. The Roose ground was subsequently used by the Barrow Rugby Club. The desire for a central location produced just one possibility, the Holker Street Ground that had previously been used by Hindpool Athletic. A complicated 5 year agreement was made with the money going to the Steelworks Band, who then had to pay the Furness Railway Company, the actual owners. The location may have been suitable, but the Ground itself was far from perfect. The surface had hardly a blade of grass and there were no spectator facilities. In view of the Club's overall record in these early years, the Holker Street's previous use as a rubbish tip, coupled with its location next to the Cemetery, probably summed up Barrow F.C. to that time!

The 1909/10 season started in fine style with a 5-2 defeat of Eccles Borough on the 4th of September at Holker Street. But such victories were rarely repeated through the rest of the campaign, and an appalling away record that produced just three points left the Club struggling once again for their very existence.

But this was to be the last of a poor run, at least for a few years, as the Club's fortunes took a decided turn for the better. The first game of the 1910/11 season was played at Combination newcomers Fleetwood, and the Barrow team were well represented with supporters who travelled across the bay by paddle steamer. The new season signings of Ives and McFarlane from Tottenham Hotspur, plus Atkinson from Exeter was to have a great effect, and with added new blood later, the team became a seldom beaten combination away and never at home. As the months passed, the support rose, and on some occasions up to 2,000 fans travelled to away matches, none of which could be considered very local.

The Champions were Haslingden, whom Barrow beat 5-1 in one match, and the Club took the runners-up spot to earn their second promotion. The season was not without its problems, for, following the Lancashire Junior Cup home semi-final defeat to Bacup, the disgruntled Barrow fans mobbed the Referee, which led to Holker Street being closed for 18 days during March. One potential high profit game, at home to Championship chasing Hyde, was played at Morecambe Road, Ulverston, during this period.

A somewhat poor away record prevented the Club from finishing higher than fourth in the First Division at the end of the, none the less, most encouraging 1911/12 season. One year later, the Club achieved their greatest triumph up to then, from a notable F.A. Cup run. The qualifying rounds produced a goal difference of 20 - 3, and these victories led to a first round match at Second Division Bradford.

Five hundred Barrovians travelled to Bradford on January the 11th, only to find a snow bound Park Avenue and the postponement of the match. Four days later there were only 100 visiting supporters in the 8,000 crowd at the re-arranged game, but a potential giant-killing was in the offing for two goals were shared. Much to the Barrow fans disgust, the replay was also played in Yorkshire, for a record cash inducement - stated as a staggering £650! A demonstration was organised to voice the supporters disgust in the home League game with Colne, but the Directors minds could not be changed, and one week later on January the 25th, the replay Cup game was played. Once again a shock result was on the cards, but with the last kick of the game - after five minutes injury time - Bradford earned a win with the only goal of the game.

The effort had its repercussions in the Combination, as a defeat on the following Saturday came at the hands of lowly Walkdon Central - Barrow's first home defeat since January 1909, a run which had spanned 53 games.

The receipts from the cup games aided the bank balance considerably, to the extent that a profit of £392 on the season was enough to wipe out the Club's debt, despite the Players wages topping two thousand pounds; over the period, gate money had risen to £2,725, a staggering 50% increase over the previous year. Fourteen new players were signed on for the 1913/14 season, mainly to provide manpower for the Club's first ever Reserve team, that were to play in the West Lancashire League. While the first team prospered, the second string was a financial disaster, for they showed a £252 loss on the season. But undoubtedly this reserve strength aided the Club in its best ever First Division in the Lancashire Combination. The Champions were Tranmere Rovers, over whom Barrow had achieved the 'double'!

Rather than capitalising on this, their first major success, they finished the 1914/15 season in a fifth from bottom position. The downward turn was mainly attributed to their losing most of the previous season's successful team. Together with several men who left during the summer of 1914, there was to be a total of eight who sought greener pastures during the campaign, including McKnight who was sold to Bury for £100. As World War I loomed over the horizon, many of the Club's supporters found themselves making munitions for the forthcoming struggles, this prevented them from watching football, but as the team were flagging anyway, those still able to attend became fewer in numbers. The season ended on a grim note for the Club -a lowly position and money problems again - and in the Combination, a suspension of normal matches. Many of the supporters and players, also enlisted for the coming conflict.

It was four years before Barrow were active on the field again, at which time the team rejoined the Lancashire Combination. The enforced lay-off appeared to positively help the Club, for by the season's end they had finished back up with the leaders in fifth position in the competition. The end of the season created a milestone in the Club's history, for despite the near never ending money problems, they purchased the Holker Street Ground for just £1,300; they could only hope that this big financial gamble would pay off.

Four particularly influential men signed on for the Club in the summer of 1920; Matthews, Eaves, McPherson and Nimmo, and their worth was evidenced by the Club finishing the campaign as Champions. As 1921 dawned, the Club headed the table on goal difference from Darwen, with 11 victories, 2 draws and only 1 defeat. As the season wore on, the lead increased, 3 points in early February, 5 at the end of that month, and finally 6 over runners-up Eccles United. Even with good attendances, often around 6,000, it was necessary to sell to keep afloat, and Alford left to play for Everton, for which Barrow received £450. This best ever success could not have come at a better time, for on the 7th of March, 1921, Barrow F.C. were voted into the newly formed Third Division North of the Football League. From now on it was recognised that the gate receipts would have to be at a constantly high level, £350 per home game was considered necessary for each Club in the new Division, but more for the Furness Club, in view of their geographical location which required long journeys to away matches. Things were made bleaker when it was announced that the Entertainment Tax was to be increased, by a staggering 50%, to five shillings in the pound. As an attempt to consolidate their new position, the share capital was raised from £750 to £2,000, and in July it was announced that the number of shares issued had risen from 988 to 1,949.

The last match as a non-League team, at home, was surprisingly lost by a single goal to Lancaster - another 6,000 crowd - and the final away match on April the 30th also ended in defeat by the same score, to Great Harwood. There were few disappointments that season, apart from a 1-4 F.A. Cup defeat at Durham City - the biggest reverse of the campaign - after earlier wins over Vickerstown, Cleator (12-0), Carlisle and Wath Brow. Such was the optimism at the Club that the Ground underwent substantial development - aided by a keen body of voluntary workers - and the Directors had the confidence to team-build to such an extent that over thirty players - several described as 'prominent' - were signed on for the coming 1921/22 season.

With the Club's first ever match under the Football League banner just days away, a crowd of 4,229 was present for the pre-season trial game. Unprecedented excitement greeted the team as they ran out onto the Holker Street pitch on August the 27th for the first home Football League game versus Stockport County, and a new record attendance of 9,750 was present. To set the team on its way, two bands were also there to provide entertainment, together with the Mayor of Barrow who ceremoniously hoisted the Club's new flag, accompanied by much cheering and singing.

Unfortunately the football match did not produce the desired result, a two goal defeat! It was a hard contest, but with little excitement. The visitors took a 15th minute lead, followed by a second in the same period of the second half. The team for this inaugural game consisted of: Thompson, Sharey, McPherson, Matthews, Eaves, McKay, James, Dixon, Sharkey, Taylor and Nimmo. The next game was a Lancashire Senior Cup-tie, and before 5,000 (receipts of £242) Holker Street fans this contest was also lost.

The second League game produced another poor two goal defeat, at Durham (attendance 4,000), followed by the return with the Cathedral team, and this time a single goal loss was incurred, but before another good crowd, of 9,000.

The fans could well have asked what was wrong, after the team had promised so much on paper! Three Football League matches played and each lost. But more of the same was to follow. The next game had seen Taylor score the first League goal for the team and take a half-time lead. But the final result was 1-2, as was the return with Crewe the next week. At last, on October the 8th, after six straight League reverses, Barrow achieved their first Football League victory, by 2-0 over Ashington, and repeated this result and score with the same opposition the next week. After the third win, in successive matches, the Club had moved up to fourth from bottom, but this was only a brief respite, for after 12 games, they were back on the lowest rung of the League ladder, one point behind Chesterfield. The fans inevitably became fewer in number at matches, and for Bury's visit in mid-November, there were barely 3,000 present, although the match was played on a Monday afternoon.

The F.A. Cup experiences that season were shortlived. Undefeated Lancaster held Barrow to a draw, and then went on to beat the Football League Club on their own Ground. Southport's visit to Barrow attracted a good crowd of 6,000, but this was contested over Christmas, and after the festivities, they were still at the bottom of the League, two points adrift. Constant experimenting with the team line-up resulted at last in at least moderately good form, and a final sixth from bottom placing in the table, hardly a good debut season, but at least considerably better than it looked like finishing at one time. From the large squad of players, the incoming 'names' did not fulfil expectations, and at the end, the Club tended to rely on those that has been with the Club in their previous successful campaign. Attendances however, were overall reasonable with an average for the season of around 5,500.

The second season in the Football League was little less than a disaster. A reasonable start was made after an initial defeat by the odd goal in three at Chesterfield, then two home games were won and a point obtained at Wrexham. Two defeats followed, and the record continued to deteriorate. The only really bright spot was a 6-2 win at fellow-strugglers Ashington just before Christmas. Such boosts were rare occurrences, and throughout the season only one other away win was achieved. By the end of the campaign, the Club just managed to avoid having to apply for re-election, finishing third from bottom, above Ashington on goal difference and two points above Durham City.

One year later the position was even worse, and although after 22 games - the halfway point - they were 2 points above bottom team Crewe, by the season's end this position and points separation were reversed. Both Barrow and Hartlepools, on equal points, had to seek re-election, which fortunately became no more than a formality. By the time the last home match was played - on April the 19th - attendances had dropped alarmingly and only 2,847 were present for New Brighton's visit. Results in general were fairly close affairs except for five goal defeats to New Brighton, and in the last match at Grimsby, two weeks later.

The 1924/25 season, the fourth in the Football League, started with optimism. Several new players were signed on to bring the total number of Professionals up to 21. This degree of hope was borne out with a 3,000 crowd for the practise match. The newcomers included: Robb from Cardiff, Brelsford and Laycock (ex-Sheffield Wednesday), Loughram from Hull, and the strangest - Brown - who had been playing Rugby up to this time!

The first home game was played with a near totally new eleven from that of a few months previous, and the changes seemed to work for Crewe were beaten by two unopposed goals on the first day of September before an encouraging attendance of 5,008. This followed a goalless draw at Doncaster. Five days later, Southport were beaten by a single goal, and the crowd numbered around 8,000, the best for some time. The team's undefeated start had taken them to third place. The next home game, with Durham City, was also won, but before only 3,229 fans, however, the weekday (Monday) match coupled with heavy rain, explained why the numbers were low. After the sixth League match the team had reached the top spot, but after a reverse - the first - at Halifax, their prime position was conceded and after ten matches they had dropped to fourth. With fifteen matches played, the team had plunged a further six places, and by the season's end to a final 14th position. The early season encounters had promised much, but as the results became poor, so had the attendances. Even so on the financial side things had improved compared to the gate receipts of a year earlier when only £150 average was taken, when a minimum of £350 was required.

The rest of the country came to hear of Barrow due to their drawn out F.A.Cup exploits in 1924. After disposing of non-League Darwen in an exciting, but single goal match before a 4,314 crowd, the next - and final qualifying round, required a very long trip to Kent, to play Gillingham, at this time another non-League team. Excellent defensive play before a crowd of 9,700 (receipts of £515), produced a draw, and a replay on the next Thursday, which ended with two goals shared, before only 3,670 spectators. The second replay, on neutral Wolverhampton's ground, barely paid for expenses with Barrow's share of the £135 gate (2,342 attendance), and ended in yet another draw. A third replay was necessary, when it was confidently expected that the Furness Club would remove their opponents from the competition. This required yet another long trip, but a rare experience for the match was played on the hallowed turf of Highbury. This fourth game resulted in another 1-1 draw. But at last the Kent team were overcome, even then only after a narrow 2-1 victory, after a two goal interval lead. The fifth and final match was played at New Cross, Millwall, in front of 4,242 mainly Gillingham fans. Five matches and nine and a half hours of football had created a new record marathon run in the competition, and at last the 1st round game could be played at Blackpool. 11,775 spectators paid £846 to see the underdogs earn a replay after a thrilling scoreless draw with the Second Division team. The next Wednesday, a spirited fight saw Barrow lose by 0-2, but before an attendance of 7,145 (£400 receipts), albeit it was estimated that over 4,000 were from Blackpool.

Betwixt the Cup games, several League games had been played, and had led to a three match unbeaten run after Accrington Stanley's visit, and defeat, in front of 5,400 Holker Street spectators. In the last game of the season, Barrow finished on the wrong end of a 5-1 thrashing at Rochdale, and despite the homesters final 6th place in the table, the match only attracted 3,000 to Spotland. More local players were signed for the 1925/26 season, but the team was unable to avoid a first match home defeat to New Brighton before an attendance of 5,700. The wisdom, but probable economic necessity, of using local players was tested in late September when nine of the team were all from the Barrow area - an all-time record for the Club - but a two goal defeat to Doncaster ensued. Before long it looked as if it was to be yet another season of struggles, for by the end of October the Club were languishing in second from bottom place in the League. With the Supporters Club ever active and willing, they embarked on a novel scheme to purchase for Barrow F.C. a new centre-half - Matthews from Wrexham - at a cost of £100! But such gestures were insufficient to 'lift' the team, as the F.A. Cup was left behind following a two goal defeat at New Brighton, and a familiar bottom slot in the table was the end of the year outcome.

There was hope however, for the last game of 1925 was won at home over Walsall to the tune of 5-2, but none the less left the Club with a dismal record of 3 victories, 2 drawn games and 14 defeats. The latter half of the campaign provided no respite, and once again the team finished in the bottom slot, and had to go cap in hand to the other Clubs for the second time in three years. The Clubs had faith and re-elected Barrow, although they only received 25 votes compared to Walsall's 33.

If that season was a disaster, then the next was even worse! By the end not only did the team repeat the position of a year earlier, but created some unwelcome records en-route; compared with every other team in the Football League, they obtained fewer points (22), scored less goals (34) and had more goals against them (117)!

As far as defeats were concerned, those at home were not too bad - except for a five goal thrashing by Wrexham - but away from home it was a different story; 0-8 at Wigan Borough, 1-8 at Chesterfield, 0-7 to Stockport and Doncaster, plus three matches when they conceded 5 goals.

By now it was something of a miracle that not only did the Club manage to survive, with increasingly low gates and the consequent money problems, but they also had to contend with the ever present threat of the alternative (Rugby Football) sport in the town. Even so the Club were again easily re-elected after the season's end. Never before had the Directors and Players had to endure such criticism, the latter being accused of flagrantly defying training regulations. There was one overriding factor that kept not only the team in the League, but ensured that the team did not become defunct, and that was the ever-suffering supporters, who, although by now reduced in numbers, kept faith in what could only have been seen at the time as a hopeless cause.

After the two previous seasons, that of 1927/28 was a relative success. At least at the final count the Club had moved up three places, and so just missed a third in succession re-election application - which could well have meant the end for them -but only by two points over 21st club Durham City. The season had started in an inconsistent fashion with four heavy away defeats, but with two victories, one draw and one defeat at home. By the end, several defeats on the Club's travels had ended in four, five or six goal reverses to provide another awful 'for and against' record. Perhaps the most surprising feat was the average attendance at home matches of 5,505, not marvellous, but hardly that expected of a continually struggling team.

1928/29 ended much as a year earlier, but on this occasion just one position above the dreaded re-election place. Apart from two five-nil defeats (at Lincoln and Rotherham) plus an eight goal hammering at champions Bradford City, the many defeats were at least of a moderate order, and the players even managed to record a 7-2 home win over Nelson. Unbelievably the average home gates were up on the previous campaign, to a very reasonable 6,030, but the mediocre football provided could only leave the Directors to wonder how long the true supporters would continue their allegiance. For the last game, at Stockport County on May the 4th, a special excursion train carried 250 Barrovians, but on stopping at Manchester, 243 were reputed to have alighted (presumably to go shopping, etc.), leaving seven supporters to continue on to see their team defeated 2-3!

Ever optimistic, the Barrow Director, Mr. Walker, confidently announced that there would be a big improvement in the coming months of the 1929/30 season. This proved to be 'pie in the sky' for the team yet again finished at the foot of the Third Division North table! At this end of season, the Club's continued future in the Football League was not a forgone conclusion, for at the re-election meeting they only achieved seven more votes than the highest non-League aspirant, Mansfield Town.

These continuous years of failure - nine seasons, four times bottom, four re-election applications and the highest League position a poor 14th - were difficult to explain. Attendances, and hence money, were low, but no worse than several other Third Division teams, and the players' wages were reputedly higher than most of their contemporaries. Several good players were to prove their worth after their transfers, but losing 'star' men at this level was a cross that the lower division teams had to bear. One notable missing factor, appeared to be that of a leader, a Captain that could inspire confidence. It was several months into the 1930/31 season before a saviour of sorts was recruited.

By late October the Club were in their familiar very low position in the League, and by this time four Directors had resigned. Then in a complete turnabout, those Directors rejoined the Club, applications for a Secretary/Manager was advertised (previously two separate men held these positions), and over thirty hopefuls applied. Mr. Commins - a former Clyde and Barnsley player, but latterly Southport Manager - was appointed. The new man was given more or less a free hand on the question of team selection, a task previously undertaken almost exclusively by the Directors. After a shaky start, things at last took a turn for the better and by the season's end, the team had risen to sixteenth in the League.

Even support increased - by nearly 1,000 on average - and although a loss on the season of £268 was announced, at last a scheme was devised to hold on to promising players. By now the previous fixed wages of all professionals throughout the winter months - but nothing in the summer - was switched to a rising scale for first team appearances, and the weekly wages were spread over the whole year.

The change in strategy worked, for with a good team spirit and discipline that was previously lacking, by May 1932, the team had risen to the dizzy heights of fifth in the League. Miller (the Club's only International - Irish - in their history) led the goalscorers with a record 31 League successes, and at last perhaps the Club were on the way up. But the defection of the Manager to Ireland, coupled with the irony of the best season to date, and the loss on the campaign of £389 (due to higher costs all round), a big question mark over the Club's future was still present.

Significantly further economies had to be made, and two prominent players were sold; Kelly to Grimsby for £350 and Brain for £300 to Preston. This balanced the books for a while, but resentment was felt by the faithful fans. Attendances took a downward path and a record £1,700 was lost on the 1932/33 season; yet for a while the team was in the running for promotion! The free transfer signing of Thomas Shankly from Southend United proved to be a shrewd move, for at the 1933/34 close he was not only an ever-present, but scored a new Club record 38 goals in a season. The team had managed a third season top half of the table position, although on this occasion only 8th, and due to the Club record fee received from Hartlot's £600 move to Stoke City, expenditure cuts, and a healthy increase in support, a profit on the season of £11 was realised.

The last game was one to savour. The highest Barrow win of 12-1 over Gateshead could literally be described as a 'cricket score', for down the road, the Vickerstown team managed only four runs more in their Cricket match!

The past three seasons however proved to be only a respite in the Club's sorrows. A bright start was made, and even with high unemployment in the area an initial reasonable average attendance of 5,600 was recorded for the first few home games in the new campaign. But as their successes became fewer, so did the crowd numbers drop - 4,179 for the three months to the end of the year, 2,280 to the end of March, and only a moderate rise (since the Easter games were included) to 3,729 for the last period. With a final placing in the table of a dismal 17th, such poor figures could hardly have been a surprise.

From the mid-1930's, to the break for the Second World War, lowly positions in the League once again became the norm, the best being the 1938/39 campaign when 13th was achieved, and one year earlier the worst, when a second from bottom place required yet another cap in hand re-election application. There were three managerial moves during this period. After a five year spell, Tom Lowes (the Club's former trainer) left to get more money at Walsall, and James Bissett tried his hand for a few disastrous months (during his reign the team scored just eight goals in seventeen games). The next candidate was Fred Pentland (who was previously Assistant Manager at First Division Brentford) who was recruited to try and pull the team from their miserable last place in the table, in February 1938.

As ever, each season rolled by with economy a major factor, and it was only hefty 'donations' that kept the Club going. But the last pre-War season had seen improvements all round under the skilful managing of Pentland. By the season's end, gate receipts were up by a staggering £1,300 produced from an average attendance of 6,353 (compared to around 4,900 one year earlier).

During this long period (nearly twenty years) in the Football League, little has been said of the Club's F.A. Cup record, but with no appearances past the third round, this fact is probably sufficient comment!

The 1938/39 season started with Barrow in a rare, financially stable condition, a profit having been announced of over £1 on the previous campaign! In common with most other Football League teams, just three matches were played before the long interval caused by World War Two. Football continued during the war years for most Clubs, and for Barrow the rest of the 1939/40 season was played in one of the regionalised Leagues - the North-west in their case. Barrow, at the end of this abbreviated season had the rare distinction - not only for themselves - but also compared to the vast majority of their fellow-Leaguers, of actually making a profit during this period.

The new League enabled them to play on equal terms with the likes of Preston, Blackpool and Bolton, all of whom were First Division teams. This artificial elevation not only entitled them to a 40% share of the away gates, which even during the lower attended matches - considering the status of the opposition - were occasionally in excess of the normal Third Division peacetime figures - but also the team had the rare privilege, and monetary benefits, of entertaining those same teams. In a peacetime situation, these attendances, such as the 3,753 for the Burnley home game, would have seemed poor, but in this unique situation, such crowds compared favourably as a whole. These attendances varied greatly and were dependant not only on the Club's form and opposition, but also the availability of Players and spectators; League gates varied between 6,960 (in March when Bolton were the visitors) down to just 750 on May the 25th versus Carlisle.

By the season's end a respectable mid-table placing was achieved, a high average attendance of 4,190 was produced, and a profit - albeit minor - of nearly £10 was shown. One notable crowd of 11,785 (2,000 above the previous record attendance) watched the team against Stoke City - complete with Stanley Matthews - in the second round of the Wartime League Cup; the homesters lost on aggregate 3-8, but in the earlier round they had defeated Liverpool 4-1 (2-0 at home before 5,963 fans and by 2-1 away).

Geographically outcast, the Club's poorly attended A.G.M. was told that it was not possible for the team to continue in the regional League, as other Clubs could not guarantee travelling the long distances to the Furness area in the difficult war-time conditions. It was most ironic that the Club were able to show a profit, yet be forced to retire. Even the fans has rallied around the Club, and most had not asked for the return of their season ticket money that had been paid, before the War was announced.

It was of paramount importance that Barrow F.C. should not fade away completely, as their reconstitution after the hostilities may have proved impossible. It was therefore decided to help develop Junior players in the area, and under the heading of Barrow 'A', the club would have representation - mainly local men - in the North-western League, a competition that had first started in 1895. The League contained nine local teams, and in the first - representative - game a League XI was thrashed by eight unopposed goals. The League Cup was won - for the seventh time - at the end of the 1944/45 season, when Barrow Celtic were beaten in the final, by five goals, before 1,244 Holker Street fans - at this time a very healthy attendance.

On May the 29th 1945, the decision was made to continue Football at a professional level, and the Club re-entered the Third Division North for the coming season. John Commins was re-appointed as Manager, after a break from Barrow of over ten years, and immediately set about the unenviable task of trying to find men to play in the Football League, but which was made somewhat easier with the recruitment of seven pre-war Barrow players.

It was something of a desperate season both on and off the field. The first half finished with the team in a familiarly low table placing, second from bottom of the West Region of the Division, and rock bottom in the second half Third Division Cup. In the National Cup competition, a rare third round appearance was made after the beatings of Netherfield and Carlisle. The first leg in the next round was lost 2-6 at Manchester City, and four goals were shared in little more than an exhibition second leg, before a crowd of 7,377.

No fewer than 43 different players were used throughout the campaign. On the money front, things were once again looking bleak. £720 was the net loss over the War-time period - only a paltry £514 being taken in total gate receipts over the previous four years of junior football - which had to be added to the accumulated losses of over £6,000. However, at the Shareholders Meeting in July 1946, it was somewhat glibly announced that the Bank overdraft had been wiped off, and other large debts had been settled by the ever faithful Supporters Club!

The first post-war season of normalised football started with the Club having to rely to a large extent on local players, there may have been no debts, but there was also little spare cash. By Christmas 1947, the Club was located in a heady ninth in the table, then Mr. Commins dropped a bombshell by announcing that he was resigning - despite guiding the Club through this difficult transitional period. His reasons for leaving were related to disagreements, not only with the Board, but with the supporters themselves.

Despite the lack of a guiding hand for three months, the team maintained a reasonable League placing and finished the extended season (due to the severe winter) in an encouraging final ninth in the table. Even more gratifying were the gate receipts of £10,404, a new record. With the appointment in late March of the respected ex-Scottish International Andrew Beattie, the time appeared ripe for the Club at long last to achieve some real success. A revolution at Barrow was created with the players reporting for training a whole month before the season's start! The resultant new found team spirit paid dividends, and after the Boxing Day victory the supporters could savour, for just one day - for the first time ever - their team heading the table. The form was not maintained - even though they were not defeated in an away game until January the 24th - and at the end a position in the League of seventh had to suffice.

The period also had other highlights. In the F.A. Cup, Carlisle were beaten before an all-time record Holker Street crowd of 14,801, and in the third round the team were watched by another Barrow record attendance (for any game) of 44,336 at Stamford Bridge, where they lost by five unopposed goals. But at least goalkeeper Roxburgh saved a second half penalty, and the share of the £3,840 gate did not go amiss. A further attendance record - in a Football League game - was achieved, which numbered 11,644 for the Good Friday visit of Wrexham.

The Club and its supporters were devastated when on August the 6th 1948, Manager Andie Beattie tendered his resignation just two weeks before what was thought - but was subsequently disproved - could easily have been the best season ever for the team. Differences of opinion between Beattie and the club Chairman were given as the reason for this shock move, and after the Board refused to accept the letter, the Chairman and another Director resigned, upon which the Manager withdrew his action and opted to stay with Barrow. In the final event the 1948/9 season was far from a happy one. Whether the disharmony at Holker Street caused the team's failings is impossible to confirm, but the resultant start was another disaster.

It was twelve games before the first victory, and the sixth match before a striker struck. At least some ground was made up, for the team finished in thirteenth place in the Division. But there were two particularly disquieting effects. The team, by scoring only 41 goals (in 42 matches) recorded the lowest number in the Third Division North, and another low - that of the worst supported club in the whole Football League. At a time of plenty, Barrow lost out, with some 2,000 on average - below the break even figure. Beattie's restlessness had been solved when he left to take over the helm at Stockport at the end of March.

Another famous name took over in May, Jack Hacking a former International goalkeeper who had previously managed Accrington Stanley for fourteen years. Yet, another poor season was on the cards, for by January 1950 the team lay within the bottom four of the table. A somewhat drastic step was taken when one of the few 'stars' of the team, Stanley Mayhurst the goalkeeper, was transferred to Grimsby for £3,500, which at least provided money for team building in other departments. First Hannah from Preston was secured for a Barrow record £2,500, and shortly after this fee was exceeded when Scottish International McLaren, from Sheffield United, made the move to Holker Street.

Many had argued that if good players could be attracted to Barrow, then the support would follow likewise. This appeared to be borne out, for when the first match after the new record signing was played, 11,542 came to the derby game with Carlisle.

But the extras were no more than 'one-offs', for after losing this home game, the attendances did not even reach half that figure for the rest of the campaign. Even so, the final League placing of 15th was considered better than could have been anticipated a few months earlier.

But nothing better was in store for the team as a further downward move in the final League table showed, and with the local Rugby club on a high, Barrow F.C. were rapidly becoming not only a perennial 'Cinderella' club in the Football League, but also playing a similar role in their own area. Continuous operating losses were re-

Most clubs played prestigious Festival of Britain Friendlies.

FESTIVAL OF BRITAIN MATCH
BARROW
versus
Shamrock Rovers (Ireland)
Thursday, 17th MAY, 1951. Kick off 7-0 p.m.

ported - £4,767 announced in the year ending in July 1951 - which resulted in the necessity of selling promising players, to the frustration of all connected with the Club.

Halfway through the 1951/52 season, it really looked as if the team may mount a serious challenge for promotion, but a poor second half showing in which only 17 points from 46 possible were obtained, a final mid-table position had to finally suffice. The final run-in produced a loss of form, and on their travels (just one victory), points were often lost by not holding on to half-time leads. The season had seen the Club celebrating their half century, but in fifty years there had been precious little to celebrate!

Yet the season had started in a sensational way, with a five goal drubbing of Mansfield at the Field Mill. Latent support in Barrow was evident when nearly 10,000 attended the second League match, but a defeat - and a further three - resulted in the inevitable loss of support again. By October, despite the initial five goal blitz, there were only three teams in the Division with less credits, and none with less goals against. The decision to have a change of Manager was to have a tragic effect - directly or indirectly - for Mr. Hacking was retained until a replacement could be found, but he only just saw the season out before dying of a heart attack.

The team avoided another re-election application by one place - on goal average. It was a strange time for Barrow to achieve their one and only success in the Lancs. Senior Cup, when Oldham were defeated at Holker Street before 6,110 spectators.

The next three years produced little. Another mid-table League placing was the best in this period, and as the Club in effect stood still, the support didn't, for it left in increasing numbers. The only cause for joy was the team's rare appearance in the third round of the F.A. Cup, in January 1954. After an easy passage - victory over two non-League teams - the next match brought Second Division Swansea Town to Barrow. An all-time record attendance of 16,874 (receipts of £1,680) was attracted to Holker Street, but a drawn match was insufficient for progress onto the next round, and the team lost 2-4 in the replay.

A definite move in the final table was made in 1955-56, a downward one! The new Manager, Joe Harvey, had made his presence felt however, with several radical changes to Club policy. Amongst these innovations was the purchase of Club houses in order to attract players of the right calibre (no explanation was provided as to where the money came from!), the installation of training floodlights, an update in the Junior players set-up, and an overhaul in the Club's scouting system.

Three notable close season signings were made, including Tommy Cahill - a then current First Division player - from Newcastle, and a near 8,000 crowd greeted the team in the first game of the season - which ended in defeat. Only five points were obtained on foreign soil, and a bottom position in much of the first half of the campaign, was only partly relieved in the second, with a final finish two places higher. Despite this poor season, the team made another appearance in the third round of the F.A. Cup, but they were humbled at Brammall Lane with five goals from Sheffield

United in front of an attendance of 20,475. Despite the Club's poor form over the year, the attendances - helped by a charismatic Manager - were actually marginally up. By now the accumulated losses of the Club had reached £8,320, despite a massive donation of £3,096 (after tax) from the Development Branch.

The 1956/57 season included a post-war record run of eight successive League games without defeat, and an eighth place in the League by the dawn of 1957. But continued improvement was not to be, and a final - at least encouraging - tenth was the outcome. For the sixth consecutive season Billy Gordon was the leading goalscorer, this time with 27, and it was something of a wonder that the Club were not forced to part with his company; attendances however, were only slightly higher than the previous campaign.

Just when it looked as if the Manager may be able to produce something worthwhile for the Club, he left, on the 24th of June 1957 to join Workington. His successor, one month later, was the ex-Newcastle favourite, Norman Dodgin.

The 1957/58 season had a particular significance, for by finishing in the top half of the League, those Clubs would earn a place in the new Third Division. Things went well until New Year's Day, when the team were handily placed fourth, but with only two more victories, the final outcome was 18th, and so Founder-membership of the Fourth Division. Despite the severe stretching of the Club's resources, the old floodlights of Arsenal were purchased, with a starting donation of £331 from the Supporters Club. Although the Club's wages bill was by now one of the lowest in the Football League, after other expenses there was rarely anything left - either for new players or Ground improvements - and one can only admire the resourcefulness (which non-sympathisers could construe perhaps as stupidity) of the Club's Directors that allowed the Club to carry on.

Another change in Managership was made when Mr. Dodgin resigned - reputedly due to problems concerning the team selection and the retained list - with ex-Grimsby Captain, Bill Brown taking over. The Club lost several players, due partly to the low morale caused by the drop into the Fourth, and also the departure of Dodgin. The first season which was to show a sharp rise in travelling costs due to the sometimes enormous distances that would be required in the newly created, non-regionalised Division; e.g. to Exeter, Gillingham and Torquay.

On this far from happy note the 1958/59 season started, and until Christmas a mid-table position was, in the circumstances, reasonable. But just like a year earlier, their form dropped from January onwards, resulting in another re-election application through a second from bottom place in the League. Attendances had dropped even more, and it was only another run in the F.A.Cup that pulled them through another year. The third round draw brought Champions-elect of the Football League - Wolverhampton Wanderers - to Holker Street, and a near record gate of 16,340 was present. The match ran true to form, a 2-4 defeat for the homesters, but the fight they put up belied their lowly status. In February an appeal went out to the Barrow townspeople for money, it was reckoned that a minimum of £100 extra per week was necessary for solvency.

A bombshell was dropped in August 17th, four days before the first game of the season, when Mr. Brown resigned. It was not until October that the former England full-back, Staniforth, was appointed as the new Manager, by which time the team had played themselves into another re-election looming season. The faithful Supporters Club informed the parent Club that the fund raising for the installation of floodlights was not successful, and the Club itself certainly could not afford this relative luxury.

A very rare piece of luck came Barrow's way when the massive Vickers Armstrong Company made a donation of over £20,000 to the Club. It was a windfall that undoubtedly kept the Club going, for they were able to pay off many of their enormous debts, and actually had money left for such luxuries as summer wages, Ground improvements and transfer fees! The paltry gates, slightly up on a year earlier, were nowhere near enough to pay the Club's way, especially since in a little over ten years wages had nearly doubled, and some other expenses by now had increased several fold.

After a rise of five places over the previous season, and the financial position somewhat better, the 1960/61 season started with more hope. But the reality was somewhat different for a bottom four position required the Club's eighth re-election application. Barrow's 35 votes were only three more than Hartlepools, and the top outsiders, Oxford United, managed 19. The previous months had seen an injury ridden period, with no suitable reserve force.

The local Press chastised the Club, remarking that the team was the most half-hearted at Holker Street for years; and the fans showed their feelings, with average gates that had dropped by almost 1,000 per game. With the Players wages alone equalling nearly twice the gate proceeds, it was only donations of nearly £19,000 (over half from Vickers again) that allowed the Club to struggle on for another year.

Five new signings were made during the summer of 1961, and amongst them was George Darwin from Rotherham, for which a record fee was paid. Three of the newcomers made their debut for Barrow in the first match - a 3-0 home win - which augured well for the rest of the season. By Christmas, the team were in a similar place in the table as a year earlier, but on this occasion their winning ways did not slip, and although missing promotion, their eighth final position was only four points away from an upward move. The October signings, which balanced to a degree the later departure of Lowes for £6,000, gave not only the supporters something to cheer about - for a rare change - but also the Directors to declare an even rarer announcement, profit on the season. There was though an operating loss, however, with the help of Vickers again, and other donations, a net profit on the season of £6,621 was realised.

The 'crying wolf' of Barrow and several other Clubs in respect of possible obliteration due to the financial state of affairs, was proven to be no bluff so far as Accrington Stanley were concerned. They resigned from the Football League before completing their fixtures, and deducted were the three Barrow points gained from their home draw and 3-1 win at Peel Park.

The 1962/63 season was very much a repeat of the previous one, with a home win start, a generally consistent run throughout, (although on this occasion a mediocre patch followed the first game), and a final League placing of ninth. Despite this second bid for promotion, there were some poor away defeats, including 0-6 reverses at both Rochdale and Newport, and a five goal thrashing at promoted Mansfield. Two notable signings were made late in the campaign, viz. Thackerley from Blackburn and Tommy Thompson the former Stoke International player; both were to make their presence felt.

After two near misses, was the 1963/64 season to be the third time lucky? Far from success, the Club lapsed back into their familiar failure style! The one third reduction in playing staff - down to only 16 professionals - and the surprise non-retention of former leading goalscorer, Dixon, had without doubt a big effect on the team's sudden plunge down the Fourth Division. For their two nearest neighbours, Carlisle and Workington, the season ended with promotion. For Barrow it was the lowest position in the whole of the Football League - 92nd - and another re-election application. There had been just two away wins, at fellow strugglers Rochdale and York, while heavy defeats resulted at Bradford City (1-7) and 2-8 at Aldershot.

Attendances naturally took a plunge and for the last home game, versus Lincoln City, the Club's lowest Football League gate (to that time) of 1,741 was recorded. Match receipts had fallen by £400, but a cost cutting exercise to make up this shortfall was made with Barrow purchasing their own Motor Coach, which was used in lieu of hiring transport, or expensive train journeys. If it had not been Hartlepools fifth re-election application in succession, and the fact that there was no strong non-League contender for Football League membership, then, in view of their dismal past, Barrow might have not been retained in the League.

After five years as Manager, Staniforth, had had enough, and gave his reasons for resigning as not being given sufficient control in his department. This was a familiar cry at Barrow, but the Club Chairman's only retort was, in effect, that the man had left the badly floundering ship.

The Club were in a not unfamiliar desperate position. There were only ten players, including three new men; they had no Manager and the 1964/65 season was to commence in six weeks. Don McEvoy, the Coach at Halifax, was persuaded to come to Holker Street, and within one week of his arrival five more players were signed up. Barrow were hardly in a position to entice quality footballers to the Club, and this was shown in November, when the team were just one off the bottom of the League. November the 11th became a genuine crisis point, when the Club Secretary announced that after losing several hundreds of pounds per week, unless £3,500 was found very quickly, the Club - like the hapless Accrington team - would not last out the season.

On this occasion Vickers were not willing to help out. Over the previous six years, the company had advanced a total of £33,000 (two thirds of which was a donation, and the rest a loan). A certain degree of sympathy was felt in the town, for £1,200 was raised in further shares sales, and coupled with a three match F.A. Cup tussle with Grimsby this brought in extra revenue. A "Save Our Soccer Appeal" raised some cash, but not enough, and the new dateline by which the £3,500 must be raised, came and went, without the full amount being realised; yet the Club survived, but only just! Admission charges were raised by over 50% to 4 shillings (20p), and the gamble paid off; there was little point in appealing for more support, and as the support had reached such a low ebb, it was a fair bet that those remaining, were true supporters who would inevitably pay up! By now attendances were around an average of three thousand per home game, a slight increase on a year earlier.

The end of season record made dismal reading. The highest number of goals conceded throughout the League (105), fourth from bottom, and a new record number of re-election applications from any one Club - their eighth. Amazingly, but in fact as was almost always the case, the 'old pals act' operated at the re-election meeting, and yet again Barrow F.C. were almost overwhelmingly - and some would say undeservedly - welcomed to stay in the fold. It was ironic that at this, the lowest time of all in the Club's undistinguished history, and when their very existence was on a knife-edge, they were on the verge of entering their most successful - albeit short - period.

Four new signings before the start of the 1965/66 season, plus two more after it had commenced, raised the Club's morale and status in the Fourth Division. By the Christmas matches, the Club held a useful eighth position in the table, but inconsistencies were letting the team down. On December the 18th, after taking a one goal lead over middle of the table Barnsley, they ended up on the wrong end of a 1-5 defeat; whereas the holiday period saw them take three points out of four from table topping Doncaster Rovers. At the home match with the Rovers, Bob Knox created an unusual double record. During the first game he came on for the injured Barrow goalkeeper, and became the first substitute to save a penalty!

Fortunately donations and various fund-raising efforts kept the Club's head above water, and a final mid-table position in the Fourth Division, at least gave some hope for the future. At the A.G.M., the Chairman announced that, with good reason for such confidence, he was satisfied for the first time in five years; finances were healthier, gates were up, and the team was performing better on the field. The main room for improvement was consistency - after challenging for promotion, the last seven games had produced just three miserable points.

At the start of the 1966/67 season, there was a genuine air of optimism around the Club from its supporters. With the signing of four new players, it was felt that at last they had a real chance for promotion, a rise that had eluded them for nearly half a century. This confidence was rewarded, for by finishing in third place, they at last achieved their first ever step up into a higher division.

From the start the team broke various Club records. The away win at Barnsley on September the 30th put them at the top of the table - this time for three days, rather than the previous occasion in 1947, when this heady position lasted just 24 hours! Further victories on their travels, at Southend, York, Brentford and Tranmere, represented the first home defeats of each Club.

When a win was achieved at Exeter, it was their ninth away conquest of the season, a new Club record, and at the end - the twelve successes on foreign soil were the most in the whole of the Football League. In addition the Club paid a new record fee - £6,000 - for McGarry from Newcastle.

Tony Field steers the ball past Gordon Phillips—and that's the goal that brought victory over Brentford in Barrow's last match of the season and clinched promotion.

The end of the 1966/67 season,
and at last the fans had something to celebrate

After so many years in the doldrums, the Club were in jubilant mood. Over the season, the gate receipts were up by £12,000, yet amid all the joy, the Club could not overlook the fact that even over this past year, a loss was still made - only £1,236 -but the overall deficit of the Club had now climbed to over £32,000. The selling of George Smith to Portsmouth had a double edge to it.

The loss of the driving force in the defence would be difficult to replace, but conversely the £20,000 record fee received not only wiped off much of the Club's debts, but also allowed them to pay out a new record £7,000 for left-winger, David Storf.

Before the start of the 1967/68 season, the Club received a severe shock, when Manager McEvoy ended his three year reign to take over at Grimsby Town. His successor was Colin Appleton from Charlton Athletic, in a dual player/manager role. Amongst the 38 applicants for the job was a 72 year old weight-lifter, who was rejected, amongst other reasons no doubt for his inability to become a team member on the pitch!

With a basically unchanged team the Club set off in the heady heights of the Third Division. The Campaign turned out to be a hopeful one. The team, after an encouraging 2-1 away win at eventual runners-up Bury, maintained a top half of the table position throughout, and the final eighth place could have been seen as a good springboard for greater achievements. The Cup Competitions also proved fairly fruitful. In the League Cup, the team were not disgraced when they bowed out to, second in the First Division, Sheffield Wednesday by 1-3, after having one goal disallowed and conceding a late one. The F.A.Cup, third round, brought a rare appearance of First Division opponents - on this occasion Leicester City - to Holker Street. The crowd of 16,650, paying record receipts of £4,096, saw their local heroes lose out aided by a freak goal. In the second minute, an attempted interception by Arrowsmith, was badly sliced, and from fully 25 yards he scored for the visitors. Even so a fighting comeback resulted in a very creditable 1-2 defeat. Even the final of Lancashire Senior Cup was reached, but lost, to First Division Burnley.

The loss of several of the promotion winning combination, was to signal the start of the end for the Club - as far as the Football League was concerned. For several months it looked as if the only way was up, as the team reached a peak - seventh in the League - which was followed with a complete turnaround that nearly ended up as 'down'! After a point at Crewe in the last match of 1968, five straight defeats sent the team plunging down the League ladder, and only 14 points from the last 16 games prevented a relegation back to the Fourth, as they finished just two points clear of the drop position.

The revival coincided with the appointment of a new Manager, in place of Appleton, who had to relinquish his leading role in January 1969 due to ill-health. The 1969/70 season was an outright disaster. With virtually a new team from two years earlier, it took six away games before a goal was scored on foreign soil, and November before a point was taken on their travels - and only one home victory was achieved up to December. With a record such as this, the inevitable bottom slot was occupied up to Christmas, and by the season's end the only consolation was one place higher, but none the less - relegation.

With attendances well down, and the Board desperate to avoid relegation, The Manager - Norman Bodell, the youngest in the Football League - was sacked on February the 11th, and the hot seat was taken over, for the second time, by McEvoy. But his arrival was too late to achieve a miracle, and so the Club had to start back in the bottom Division, which after so many years they had only recently vacated. By the end of the season, the attendances had dropped to below 3,000, but the building of the Supporters "Bluebird Club", at a cost of £40,000, was to eventually reap financial dividends. But this lifeline proved to be too late to save the Football League career of Barrow F.C.

Things, it would seem, could not get worse after the end of the 1970/71 season, when the Club's downward move reached the ultimate bottom, yet again - 92nd in the Football League. Just seven wins were achieved and 22 points obtained. Gates were down, finance - as ever - became a critical factor once again, and morale was at its lowest ebb. The Club's recent exploits in a higher division virtually guaranteed them continued League membership, with the second highest number of votes. But one year later things were far different. By the 11th November 1972, Barrow had 'risen' to fourth from bottom, at which time McEvoy resigned, with Jock Crompton taking over one month later. The locals absented themselves from Holker Street to such an extent that the lowest Football League attendance at the Ground appeared on November the 27th, when a meagre 1,031 saw two goals shared with Cambridge United.

For a time it really looked as if Crompton may have pulled the team around, and a rise up the League table won him the Bell's 'Manager of the Month Award' (Fourth Division) in February. At one point the team even rose to around halfway in the table, but after a two goal home defeat (attendance 2,500) to Peterborough, they dropped to sixth from bottom. From then on victories were a very rare commodity, one being a two goal home success over Chester on March the 25th before a gate of 2,105. A four goal defeat at Bury on April Fool's Day was followed one week later with a single goal victory over Gillingham at Holker Street, which lifted the team to tenth above the bottom slot. It began to look once again as if the Club may avoid the dreaded bottom four, when on April the 15th fate stepped in and dealt a cruel blow.

Harry Thompson, the goalkeeper, reported ill for the game at Cambridge, and in this emergency, outfield player Bob Knox took over between the posts. Knox was only beaten once, but it was enough for the team to be defeated. Barrow were in dire straights, for they had no fit goalkeeper on the books, and despite a frantic search a suitable player could not be loaned to them. They had little choice but to retain Knox in goal, but his second appearance in that position resulted in him conceding four goals at home to Darlington. By now Stockport and Crewe were virtually booked into the bottom two positions in the League table, but avoidance of the other two re-election places was going to be a close run affair. After a two goal win over Workington - marked by crowd violence before and after the game - just two games were left.

The first of the final pair resulted in a three goal home defeat to promotion heading Brentford before an improved attendance of 2,666. The last game, at Exeter City on April the 29th, had to be won for a chance of finishing in a 'safe' position. A shock lead was taken by Barrow in the 5th minute through Eddie Garbett, but this was equalised by half-time. It appeared that Barrow were still in with a chance, then the flood gates opened in sensational fashion, and Exeter scored an incredible six goals in the second half, to equal their best win since 1926. The team for this, Barrow's last Football League match consisted of:- Thompson, Clarke, Knox, Calvert, Noble, Harrison, Garbett, Irvine, Rowlands, McDonald and Hollis. This was to be Barrow's eleventh and final re-election application. In the past years of failure - and a bottom placing - could have resulted not unreasonably in rejection, but on this occasion they had ended up only third from bottom. Just two years earlier they were playing in the Third Division, but it was their bad luck that those perennial candidates for re-election - Hartlepool - had avoided this fate this time, otherwise they may well have been the prime choice for the 'push'. Ambitious and successful Hereford United were the clear favourites for election (with them and Barrow obtaining equal votes for the final Football League place). A second poll gave Hereford 29 votes, and Barrow, 20. Fifty-one years of membership were over for Barrow F.C.

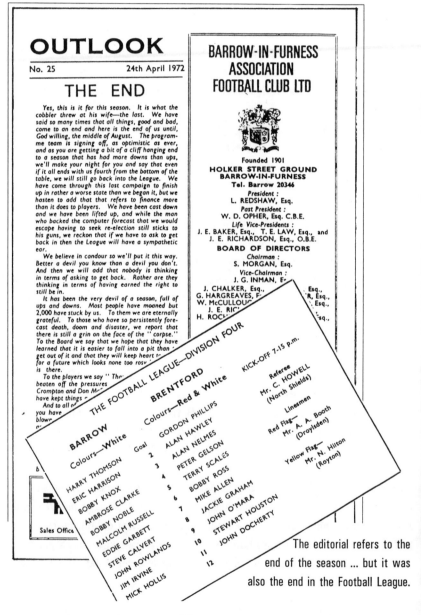

The editorial refers to the end of the season ... but it was also the end in the Football League.

The day after the Club's rejection, the town was full of indignant 'supporters', most of whom were noted absentees from Holker Street when their money and support was most needed. A town's identity is lost to a certain degree when a Club is rejected from the Football League. Unlike Accrington Stanley, Barrow were comparatively secure from a financial viewpoint, and so where able to carry on in non-League circles; but a new Manager was required, for Jack Crompton promptly resigned.

The Northern Premier League was the natural competition to move into, but the Bluebirds were to quickly find that their recent Football League status was no guarantee of success at a lower level. The first game was lost at Ellesmere Port by four unopposed goals on August the 12th, and was followed by a single goal home defeat to South Shields. The one reassuring aspect of the latter game, was the crowd of 1,358 which was not that many less than the latter days of the previous season. The scorer in this home game was Ian McDonald, and by now Billy Haydock had been appointed the Manager.

The first victory came on August the 26th at South Liverpool, but mediocre football ensured that the encouraging first game attendance was not repeated, and crowds soon slipped below four figures. No honours were won that season, total gate receipts were down to under 50% of a year earlier, and financial hardship was again of great concern.

Aided by the Bluebirds Club, the football team survived the 1970's without any major honours, although there was a home appearance in the first round of the F.A. Cup (lost to Goole Town) in 1976. A long wait for success came at the end of the 1979/80 season when a promotion of sorts came, with the Club becoming founder-members of the Alliance Premier League. Although this move was to dramatically increase travelling costs - as far, or even further than in the earlier Fourth Division days - the new League, it was hoped, could provide a realistic springboard into the Football League. Extra expenses were to a degree matched with increased support, for the late 1970's average crowds of a few hundred increased, to 873 in the 1979/80 season. This was followed by variable numbers of 669, 725 and 546 respectively during the next three years. During this period the record high was in the first campaign when 2,027 paid to see Yeovil Town as the opposition. Success was not forthcoming in the Alliance, for a best season of a final 8th in the League was achieved, and relegation soon followed, at the end of the 1982/83 season.

Barrow bounced straight back when they captured the Championship of the Northern Premier League and also won the League's Challenge Shield. This promotion season, saw the average gate nearly double over that of a year previously, the best since Football League days, and even on their travels the team excited interest - over 1,600 at Burton, and 1,700 for the Christmas derby match at Workington.

Once again the stay with the non-League elite was short, just two seasons, and the end of the 1985/86 period saw the Club footing the table, and they made another move back to the Northern Premier League. The late 1980's produced little in the way of honours other than runners-up medals in the League Cup in 1988, and notably a return to the non-League elite, now known as the GM Vauxhall Conference, one year later. This later promotion came as something of a surprise, for the 1986/87 season was one of the worst - so far as League matches since the Club's Football League days - since they finished 15th in the 22 team table.

The League Cup final appearance - they lost on penalties to Goole Town - plus four matches to settle their F.A.Trophy semi-final, helped to pile up their end of season fixtures, when for the last two weeks they were playing virtually every day. Therefore, overall it was one of the most successful season's for some years, despite the lack of silverware. The first leg of the Trophy semi-final attracted an enormous crowd of 6,002 to Holker Street, when they lost 2-1 to Enfield. A 1-0 victory in London ensured a replay (1-1 at Kidderminster), before finally bowing out by the only goal in the second replay which was staged at Stafford Rangers' ground. A final 5th place in the League provided the springboard for a return to the highest level in non-League football.

Despite this highly successful season, the gates only occasionally rose above 1,000 despite the team topping the table for much of the time. Now, with a realistic chance of regaining Football League status with (supposedly) automatic promotion from the Conference, the average gates rose to 1,292 (with a top crowd of 4,244 for Darlington's New Year's Day visit) during the 1989/90 season despite a below mid-table finish.

But some of this renewed interest can be attributed to the Club's first appearance at Wembley, when they easily overcame the challenge of Leek Town by 3-0 in the F.A.Trophy Final, which was played before a crowd of 19,011.

The following campaign gave reason for hope to the Club's fans, with a final placing of 9th in the Conference, an appearance in the Bob Lord Trophy Final (and a humiliating 5-0 second leg defeat to Sutton United), and an average attendance which rose by 10% to 1,427. But these hopes were soon dashed, for rather than capitalise on their successes, they were promptly relegated again in 1992. The 1992/93 season saw some an interesting group of teams in the Northern Premier League, Premier Division - Accrington Stanley, Barrow, Gainsborough Trinity, Southport and Stalybridge Celtic, all five at one in name being former Football League members.

As in the past, the team over the past twenty years or so have made little impact in the F.A.Cup, and apart from several 1st round appearances, their only noteworthy achievement was in the 1990/91 season when a fairly easy passage (first and second round victories over Bishop Auckland and Whitley Bay respectively), gave the team a rare third round showing, when they were narrowly beaten 1-0 at Bolton Wanderers.

Barrow are something of a 'sleeping giant' of the non-League world. With the Football League featuring prominently in their history, their name in these fixtures would not seem strange, and the Holker Street Ground has a major venue feel about it. Their sorties into the Vauxhall Conference and their rare Cup successes have shown that the potential is their to attract good support - despite their dismal crowd figures in the past - but to date they have not been able to translate that potential into reality.

For most of the ex-Football League Clubs, there is little hope that they will ever regain their lost status. Indeed for many, the Club no longer exists, and for others they have slipped well down the Pyramid (non-League ladder), and such a rise is extremely unlikely. Barrow F.C. fall into the minority category where there is real hope. Given the right occasion, the latent support is there, the Club has learned to live within its means, and the Bluebird Club has provided substantial revenue. There are just two major obstacles to overcome for the team to regain its Football League status. The Championship of the premier non-League competition is necessary, and Ground security of tenure, for the latter threat hangs over the Club while decisions are made on whether to develop the Holker Street venue, and if so where the Club will continue in its football endeavours. The latter problem appears to have resolved itself and the Club seem set to remain at their Stadium, although large sums of money will be required to build it up to the required standard.

THE GROUNDS

When Barrow F.C. were created in 1901, the provision of a suitable Ground was difficult. They would have liked to have played at the Stadium of Furness (Association) Football Club, who appeared to have folded at the time of Barrow's formation. This Stadium formed part of the local Athletic Ground, and could offer around its oval arena, two small seated Grandstands, seated but uncovered stands on two sides, and embankments elsewhere. But the Athletic Club, in collusion with the rival Rugby Club who also played within Cavendish Park, and whom presumably feared the threat that a rival 'Football' Club would pose, refused permission.

The Strawberry Hotel in 1991

Eventually the Strawberry Ground was chosen. This was located at the North-east boundary of the town, near the junction of Abbey Road and Strawberry Lane; the Strawberry Hotel which remains to this day, was used as changing rooms and headquarters for the Club. The field was located a short walk to the West of the road junction, and was later to become the home of the Barrow Rugby Union Club. It is doubtful if the Ground was any more than a levelled and fenced field, and its difficulty of access led to a centralised move to a venue in Ainslie Street, after three years.

The Club had been offered five different fields by the Furness Railway Company, but they chose Ainslie Street, despite the work needed to make it fit for Senior football. A group of supporters laboured during the close season, after their normal day's work, in order to remove a number of ridges which ran across the field, and they erected an enclosure fence and a large hut for use as a changing room (complete with bath). But their efforts were somewhat wasted, since a pronounced sideways slope to the pitch was present, pools of water formed in the middle during wet periods, and the venue proved to be generally unpopular with both teams and supporters.

The stay lasted for less than one season, for on the 18th of March, 1905, another move was made, this time to Little Park, Roose. Little Park was, like The Strawberry, of difficult access, but the pitch was a great improvement over Ainslie Street. Once again, this Ground offered little for spectators' comforts, just a reserved enclosure with possibly a small Grandstand, plus dressing rooms and turnstiles. For a short period Barrow Rugby Club leased the Ground after the football club's departure in 1909.

The Cavendish Park Athletic Ground has now long since disappeared, although on the raised, flat area, Football is still played. The Strawberry Ground, later became the home of the Furness Rugby Union Club. The field in Ainslie Street was no more than the title suggests, located adjacent to the school, whilst Little Park is now built over with housing, although Roose itself is still fairly rural.

A long term home was at last found, and first used in September 1909, when the Ground of Hindpool Athletic in Holker Street was taken over. Being once again more centrally located, and the rent at the same level as Little Park, the Club felt they has secured a much better Headquarters. A five year lease was obtained from the Steelworks Band, which caused some early problems, for the Band in fact were

Holker Street in 1987
East End looking North

only tenants as the enclosure was owned by the Furness Railway Company. But for Lancashire Combination level football, the venue was sadly lacking in many respects. It required a labour of love form Supporters and Directors alike to transform the former rubbish tip, bereft of grass, into a Football Ground. Picks, spades and rakes went into use to rid the playing pitch of broken pots and glass, and for many years such objects kept appearing on the surface, causing either injuries or the necessity to wear knee protective pads!

The Little Park fixtures and fittings were transported to Holker Street in sixteen lorry loads, and embankments were formed for improved viewing for supporters. Finally, attempts were made to fill in the clay hole which was located just outside the Ground, and which was prone to cause many delays due to lost footballs. Even after all their efforts, there was little if anything provided for spectators comfort, until the building of the seated Stand around 1912. The Stand later had wings added to each end, which gave a seating capacity for some 1,500 but after the Second World War, the structure was condemned! The need for demolition was avoided by repairs that were carried out, with the timber coming from a disused boat.

It was apparent that Holker Street was to become the Club's home Ground for the foreseeable future, and over the years, the enclosure was gradually built up into an acceptable location for Football League matches. A 'covered shelter', which extended for approximately the central half of the pitch, and opposite the seated stand, was built, with a strip of concrete terracing to all sides of the Ground in 1920 for £1,300. This was a shrewd move and gave the Club the confidence to develop the enclosure prior to and during their early Football League days. During the close season of 1920, volunteer workers helped to carry out improvements; the covered enclosure, on the South side, was dismantled and re-erected at the Steelworks (West) end, and in its place a new one was built of greater depth, with cover for some 4,000 spectators. This now gave the Ground a capacity for approximately 20,000, of whom 7,000 would be protected from the elements. These major improvements were completed with the installation of several turnstiles, the pitch being extended by a few yards, and the extension of the Players' dressing rooms.

There was little done to the Ground for nearly thirty years, until the perimeter wall on three sides of the Ground, was uniquely reinforced with thick concrete blocks that had been used by the Vickers Company to protect machines from enemy bombing during the War! And soon after, at the end of the relatively successful 1947/48 season, reconstruction of the concrete terracing was undertaken at a cost of £3,500.

In the mid-1950's, the turnstiles were renovated and it was probably at this time that a covered enclosure was erected on the (East) Holker Street side, and the old enclosure at the other end was replaced with a new one. These improvements provided cover and/or seating on at least parts of all four sides of the Ground. Floodlighting, but only for training purposes was also provided, but in 1963 a full secondhand system was purchased from Arsenal, even so it was four or five years before the costs were repaid. The 1969/70 season saw the 'Bluebirds Club' building erected at a cost of £40,000, and which is located behind the South side enclosure. The final development of note was the re-designing of the Steelworks end of the Ground. Even during the Club's brief heydays, attendances never approached the claimed capacity of around 20,000, and to realise some capital, the enclosure and terracing was removed and replaced with a new indoor sports centre.

PROGRAMMES

It is most likely that these were produced from the earliest of the Club's days, but few if any appear to have survived. Pre-war Football League issues are known to exist, but the 'unfashionable' nature (low gates) and ex-League status are likely to command higher than average prices for programmes of this era. Post-war programmes are relatively common, but once again the Club's ex-League label makes them a 'Collector's Item', particularly the last Football League season of 1971/72.

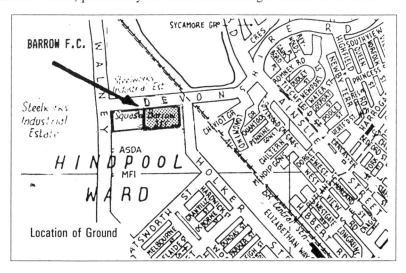

The Holker Street Ground (c.1960)

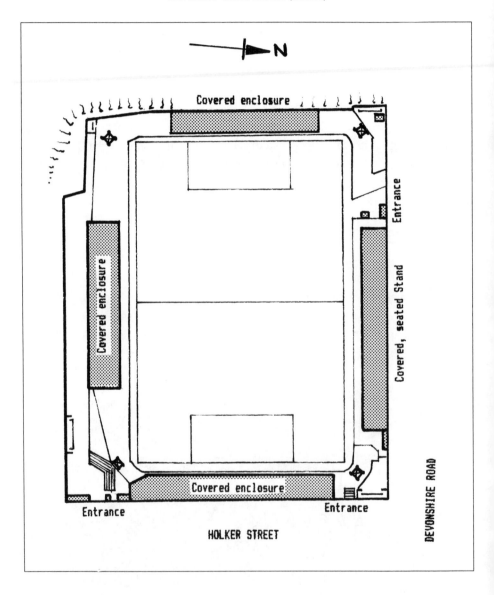

DARWEN F.C. 1879 (taken outside Alexandra Hotel)

(Standing at rear. Mr.Bromley, the Hotel's licensee).
Players:: (Back) Duxbury, Fish, Brindle, Broughton, Moorhouse.
(Middle) Marshall, Rostron, Dr.Gledhill, Holden, Kirkham, Bury. (Front) Suter.

DARWEN

Founded: 1870

Reformed: 1899

Football League: 1891-1899
****

1870	-	1889	*Friendly matches**
1889/90	-	1890/91	*Football Alliance*
1891/92	-		*Football League*
1892/3	-		*Football League Division 2 #*
1893/94	-		*Football League Division 1*
1894/95	-	1898/99	*Football League Division 2*
1899/00	-	1902/03	*Lancashire League*
1903/04	-	1908/09	*Lancashire Combination Div. 1*
1909/10	-	1914/15	*Lancashire Combination Div. 2*
1915/16	-	1919/20	*Ceased Activities*
1920/21	-	1938/39	*Lancashire Combination*
1939/40	-		*Lancashire Combination ***
1940/41	-	1945/46	*Ceased Activities*
1946/47	-		*Lancashire Combination*
1947/48	-	1962/63	*Lancashire Combination Div. 1*
1963/64	-	1965/66	*Lancashire Combination Div. 2*
1966/67	-		*Lancashire Combination Div. 1*
1967/68	-		*Lancashire Combination Div. 2*
1968/69	-	1974/75	*Lancashire Combination Div. 1*
1975/76	-	1977/78	*Cheshire County League*
1978/79	-	1981/82	*Cheshire County League Div. 1*
1982/83	-	1983/84	*North West Counties League Div. 1*
1984/85	-	1986/87	*North West Counties League Div. 2*
1987/88 - To date			*North West Counties League Div. 1*

\# *Founder-members*
* *1874 to 1876 played to Rugby rules.*
** *Three games were played before the League matches ceased. Entered Lancs. Combination East Division, but withdrew December 1939.*

Football League Record:-

	Played	W	D	L	F	A	Pts	Position	Av.Att.
1891/92	26	4	3	19	38	112	11	14th	4920
	Not re-elected to 1st Division but elected to new 2nd Division.								
1892/93	22	14	2	6	60	36	30	3rd	3500 *
	Promoted to 1st Division (via play-offs)								
1893/94	30	7	5	18	37	83	19	15th	3700
	Relegated to 2nd Division (via Play-offs)								
1894/95	30	16	4	10	74	43	36	6th	3650
1895/96	30	12	6	12	72	67	30	9th	2700
1896/97	30	14	0	16	67	61	28	11th	2350
1897/98	30	6	2	22	31	76	14	15th	2275
	Not re-elected, but were voted back in due to increase in Divisions.								
1898/99	34	2	5	27	22	141	9	18th	1225 **
	Did not seek re-election (became defunct).								

** Top ave. attend. of Division 2 teams. ** Lowest ave. attend. in Football League history*

Number of Football League matches played: 232 (plus 2 Test Matches).

SUMMARY OF FACTS

Grounds

1870-1874:   Lynwood, Darwen, Lancashire.
1874-1899:   Barley Bank.
1899 to date: Anchor Ground, Anchor Road.

Colours:

1879:   Narrow Black and White Hooped Shirts, White Shorts.
(May have changed in interim period)
(Football League)
1891/92-92/93:   Salmon and Pink Shirts, White Shorts.
1893/94-94/95:   Black and White Shirts, Dark Blue Shorts.
1895/96-97/98:   White Shirts, Dark Blue Shorts.
1898/99- :   Black and White Striped Shirts, Dark Blue Shorts.

Nickname: The Darreners.

Significant Matches:-
First League Game:
5th September, 1891. Versus Bolton Wanderers (Home). Lost 1-2. Attendance 7,000.

Last League Game:
April 22nd, 1899. Versus Newton Heath (Home) drew 1-1.

Record Attendances:
(Probable overall) 18th March, 1882 versus Blackburn Rovers (Friendly) approx. 14,000.
(During Football League career) 1st January, 1892 versus Preston North End (League): 8,000.
(Post Football League) 13th November, 1920 versus Fleetwood (Lancs-Cup) approx. 10,000.

MAIN ACHIEVEMENTS

International Players (England)
T. Brindle, T. Marshall (1880) J. Marsden (1891)

Promoted to 1st Division: 1893
First Club from North of England to reach F.A. Cup semi-finals.

F.A. Cup:
Semi-Finals: 1880/81
4th Round (Quarter Finals): 1878/79
2nd Round - 2nd series (Quarter Finals): 1886/87
3rd Round (Quarter Finals): 1892/93
4th Round (Last 14): 1881/82 (last 18): 1884/85
1st Round - 2nd series (last 16): 1887/88
2nd Round (Last 16): 1890/91. 1891/92
3rd Round (Last 32): 1882/83
1st Round (Last 32): 1893/94. 1894/95. 1895/96

(F.A.Cup contd.)
(As Post League, non-League Club):
3rd Round 1931/32
1st Round 1932/33. 1933/34. 1934/35. 1935/36

Lancashire Challenge Cup Winners: 1879/80. (Inaugural season)
Lancashire Challenge Trophy Winners:1932/33

Lancs. Combination Champions: 1930/31. 1931/32
Runners-up: 1905.06
Lancs. Combination Div. 2 Runners-up: 1967/68
Lancs. Combination Cup Winners: 1929/30. 1930.31. 1974/75

Lancashire League Champions: 1901/02
Runners-up: 1902/03

North-West Counties League Cup Winners: 1982/83

Best League Win: 1896/97, versus Walsall (home) 12-0

Worst League Defeat: 1891/92 versus West Bromwich Albion (away) 0-12
1898/99 (Last season): Three away defeats (Walsall, Manchester City, Loughborough) of 0-10
(away goal difference 6-109

All time League Record of goals conceded - 1898/99 season: 141 (34 games - average over 4 per game). The 112 conceded in the 1891/92 season remained the second worst concedant record until 1928.

All time record consecutive defeats - 18 in 1898/99 season.

Reputed to be the first team to include professional footballers (Fergie Suter and Jimmy Love in 1878/79 season).

'Play-up' cards that were produced c. 1890 to 1920.

Despite a Club that in modern times can only be regarded as of little consequence, Darwen F.C. have few equals, with their contribution to the final 'shape' of Football, when the sport was still in its infancy. The romance behind the Club extends further than their two notable F.A. Cup ties in 1879 and 53 years later.....

Football in Darwen in some form, can be traced back at least to the late 18th Century. By the 1820's there was a small degree of order to the game, as played then. The 'Ground' was usually the field between Union and Charles Streets. Most of the players were handloom weavers, and it was not unusual for a match to be 'upped' (kicked-off) at 12 noon, and continue into the night - even midnight at the time of the full moon! The Darwen 'team' were well nigh invincible, and could even beat off the challenge of a force from the combined area that lay between Bury, Bolton and Turton. 'The' match of the year was no amateur affair, for the sum of £2.50 was normally lodged by each team, with the Landlord of the Round Barn Public House, and played for on the day before Shrove Tuesday.

Each team contained twenty players, but there were no Referees or Umpires to ensure fair play. A neutral, the 'trundler-in', would start the game by throwing the ball between one row of 13 players from each side, the 'in-players'. The game was more serious than a mere Football match: *"... but some of the grosser brutality, for it mattered not if one man met an opponent where or how he hit him, as the sooner a few men were disabled the better. In some matches players would wear an iron clog on the right foot and a shoe on the left."*

Lines marked the ends of the pitch, and were drawn 15 yards from the boundaries of the fields - these outer areas being known as the 'Assholes'. Players could catch and run with the ball, throw it, or kick it from the ground, but not from their hands. The duration of a match was fixed by the time it took one team to have 'upped' the ball twice over their opponents fence, from outside the 15 yard line. In 1829, a second 'upped' goal by Darwen was disputed by the opposition; after a brief altercation, it then became a general stampede to the Round Barn to collect the stake money.

A replay was demanded by the losers (i.e. those who lost their money), and before an estimated crowd of five to six thousand, Darwen - distinguished by their 'team strip' of white stockings - became the winners.

The main qualification for a good player in those days was to be a good kicker, a swift runner and a desperate fighter! The play took place amongst a great deal of howling, hissing, cursing and swearing, and it was not unusual for pairs of opponents to be fighting on one part of the field, while the action with the ball was in another. The spectators would also endeavour to get into the action, stones being thrown in all directions plus blows made with sticks and staves. 1829 heralded probably the last match of this form played in the district, as on this occasion hammers and cleavers were also brought into use. One participant suffered a broken collar bone and others various injuries such as broken noses and dislocated joints!

In 1870, Darwen F.C. were founded, and although the rules of Football were rudimentary, matches were somewhat more controlled!

The Club was formed from two mill teams, with Mr. J.C. Ashton and the three sons of Nathaniel Walsh (owner of the Orchard Mill) being the prominent founders. The Walsh sons had attended the Public School at Harrow, and their interest no doubt stemmed from the games played there, while they were able to bring the game to the millworkers during their holidays. From this mixed background, but with plenty of enthusiasm, the Club first rented a field at Lynwood as a home Ground. The first match was played in 1870, and lost (1-3) against Brookhouse. The leading personality in the opponents' team being A.N.Hornby, who was later to achieve fame with Blackburn Rovers, and also the blameless central figure in a controversial match some ten years later.

Matches were played under Association Rules, for the Club chose to adhere to the rules of the London Football Association (an early match versus Turton was expressed as - *"being played according to the Association Rules as interpreted by the London Association"*), however, in 1874 - and for two years after - they played the Rugby game. At this time a move was made to Barley Bank, where the large Ground was used for both Cricket and the winter sport. As with so many teams of this period, the Club was a combined sports organisation, known as 'Darwen Cricket and Football Club', and in fact separate committees for the two interests were not introduced until 1884. The Committee at one time consisted of two local cotton manufacturers, two Bank Managers, two Solicitors, an Accountant and the Manager of the local Gas and Water Company. The Secretary Mr.T.Hindle, was a stalwart of the Club for many years.

Darwen soon became a leading Club in the North-west of England. In these formative days of the game, the initiative had come from the South, with the introduction of the F.A. Cup in 1871 - at which time there were no entries from Northern England. With their re-introduction of the 'round ball' rules, the Darreners quickly established their prowess in this version of the sport. Early in 1878, two prestigious hame matches were played against Sheffield in the F.A. Cup, and a Friendly with Partick, a leading Scottish Club. Darwen was the first Club from Lancashire, along with Manchester, to enter for the English Cup. Whilst the latter were beaten in the first round, Darwen's - in the 2nd - versus Sheffield was lost by a single (disputed) goal, before several hundred spectators. The match with the Scotsmen, was an even bigger attraction for around 3,000 enthusiasts - including many ladies - were present to see the homesters triumph. The degree of interest can be judged from the discomfort those spectators had to endure, ankle deep in mud and with no cover!

The last home game brought the Eagley team to Barley Bank on February the 9th, but the 2-2 draw had to be played on an adjacent field, as the regular pitch was a sea of mud. The last game but one had been played at Turton, probably the most formidable opposition at that time, for Darwen's opponents had not lost at home for seven years! Enormous interest was generated in the game, and aided by a special train, 1,000 away supporters were overjoyed to spoil Turton's long standing record with a single goal victory. After this success, Darwen were regarded as virtually invincible, having lost just two games all season - the reserves went one better and were undefeated in their eleven matches - and the local press could not sing the praises of the Darreners highly enough: " *Our team had done us splendidly during the past year, and have been a credit to the town..... Darwen was famous for football and envied by all the countryside thirty years ago.... we invariably play our own men instead of scouring the country for strangers to help us".* This noble philosophy in the last comment was soon to change!

The visit of the Partick team to Darwen on the first day of 1878 had repercussions that changed the face of Football, although if it had not been the team from the mill town it would doubtlessly have been another. The Club's actions at least hastened the process, and brought to Darwen the dubious honour of being the innovator of a radical change - the dawn of the Professional footballer. Two players in the Scottish team, Love and Suter, took a liking for the Darwen area, the latter writing to the

Club and informing them that he was to continue his craft as a Stonemason, and was taking up a position in the locality. In the final event he brought with him both a relative - an established goalkeeper and Love. It was initially denied by the Darwen Secretary, the respected Mr. Hindle, that these were paid players, but when Fergus Suter gave up his Stonemason's position (the stone being apparently harder to work than its Scottish counterpart!), it somewhat stretched the imagination to believe that he continued to play for the Club without payment, when he had no visible means of support!

Fergie Suter
Arguably the World's first (unofficial) professional football player. In 1880, he joined neighbours Blackburn Rovers.

The importation of the Scotsmen was not without precedent, for two players had made the move in 1878 to the Heeley Club, but there had been no suspicion of professionalism in this transfer. The payment of Players was such an innovation, that initially there was no Football Association rule to take account of it, but it was not long before such a move caused friction amongst the leading Clubs in Lancashire, and was for many years frowned upon by the righteous, true Amateurs of the South. Eventually rules were introduced, but were openly abused by the teams of the North, and it is no coincidence that despite the dominance of the Southern based Clubs in the major competitive tournament (the F.A. Cup), at the start of the Football League in 1888 there were no representatives further South than Birmingham.

The 1878-79 season was to become the most memorable for the Darwen Club, and provided an event that was to make the Club famous for all time.

In October, the Club initiated the forming of the Lancashire Football Association, and on the 28th of that month took part in one of the first ever matches lit by Floodlights. The game was played at Barley Bank, and played against a team from Blackburn that contained players from eight or nine teams.

It was a brilliant success in more ways than one, for the light - provided by two Magneto-electric engines - provided 36,000 candle power, *"clear, constant, steady and without blemish",* and attracted several thousand spectators. In an even game in which, not surprisingly, the Darreners produced better teamwork, the home Club ran out 3-0 winners.

The Club by now were really becoming virtually invincible, with wins which included an 11-0 rout over Blackburn Association and the strong Eagley side by 4-1 in a F.A. Cup 2nd round replay. The first tie had finished as a scoreless away draw, but the Darreners had played the whole match with only ten men. They arrived late for the second match on December the 23rd and with the kick-off delayed until 3.30p.m. they took a commanding four goal lead by half-time, with Love netting a hat-trick.

The first ever Lancashire team trial was played at Barley Bank on the 16th of December, and the strength of the Darwen Club was evidenced by their providing six of the twenty-two players.

On the first day of January 1879, the Darreners were shaken out of their complacency in no small way, when they lost at home to Glasgow by seven unopposed goals! The game attracted a £40 gate, and goalkeeper Booth was severely criticised for his play. Although it was a shock for their morale, the Club could look back with satisfaction that they had only been beaten, since reverting back to Association rules, by the Sheffield and Glasgow clubs. Three days later, Lancashire played North Wales in the first representative game for the County, at Barley Bank, and four Darwen players were included.

Interest then once again centred on the F.A. Cup, when the team were cast as 'no-hopers' against the ex-Public schoolboys club, the Remnants. Darwen had obtained a walkover in the first round, when the Birch Club from Manchester scratched, and in the 2nd Round Eagley were easily overcome by four (plus one disputed) goals to one. Darwen play the game with only ten men, for Manchester based Dr. J. Gledhill had alighted at the wrong train station and eventually arrived at the match just before the end! The Remnants match was to be a real test against a formidable amateur club from Slough in Buckinghamshire.

The game presented financial problems, for apart from Love and Fergus Suter - who were both regulars in the team by now - the rest of the players were undisputed Amateurs and were near impoverished millworkers; in addition the Club's finances were not as healthy as their team's ability. Collection boxes were set up at the Ground for donations for the team's train fare and expenses, and a Benefit Concert was held to raise funds. The game before the London visit, a 2-1 defeat to Sheffield at Attercliffe, hardly gave cause for optimism.

The Cup game was played at The Oval, on Thursday, January the 30th, and the Darwen line-up consisted of:- Duxbury, F. Suter, Briddle, Moorhouse, Knowles, Marshall, Love, Gledhill, W. Kirkham, Bury and R. Kirkham.

Despite the poor weather - snow - a good crowd had assembled by the time of Kick-off, at just after 3-00p.m. It came as no surprise when the experienced Remnants took an early lead, but by half-time the Darreners had equalised. Once again the visitors conceded a goal, but were rescued with an equaliser near the end of 90 minutes. The match went into extra-time, when the Darreners scored again, this time through Love, to bring off probably the first ever real 'Giant-killing' act of the F.A. Cup.

The next game, on February the 8th, at home to Accrington, drew a large crowd to the Ground to acknowledge their local heroes. But the minds of the Club and team were really on greater things, for in the next round of the F.A. Cup they had been drawn against the mighty Old Etonians. While this prospect was seen as undoubtedly the biggest match ever played by Darwen, or indeed any team from the whole of Lancashire, there were serious doubts over whether the Club should scratch from the tournament. The Darreners were already in debt, and the first trip to London had cost over £31. The money previously raised was insufficient to cover these expenses. Now, another visit to The Oval was necessary - at this time all matches from this stage through to and including the final were played at this venue. However, for the first time ever the meaning of 'Cup fever' became a reality, and once again the financial support of the town was prevailed upon. Collections were made at the Post Office, the Co-op, and the Mills plus the Pubs and Mines in the area. Individual contributions came from the Mayor, Aldermen, Councillors, Solicitors, Farmers, Butchers, and Plummers. Workers with the Manufacturers contributions included Entwhistle and Nutters men - 75p. Misses' Sutcliffe 25p.

Seth Harwood Joiners - 50p. Samuel Shorrock (London) 30p. Turncrofts middle pit - 42p. The Fund was first private but then became a public Fund.

With such support from the townsfolk, the team set off for the Capital once again, for the epic battle on Thursday the 13th of February; strong in spirit, but knowing that their chances of success were infinitesimal against the twice previous Finalists. Once again the match was cursed with poor conditions, a strong wind and a slippery pitch from earlier heavy rain, and on this occasion a paltry crowd of some 200. The Darwen team consisted of:- J. Duxbury, F. Suter, W. Brindle, W.H.Moorhouse, J. Knowles, T. Marshall, J. Love, J. Gledhill, W. Kirkham, T. Bury and R. Kirkham.

True to form the old Etonians completely dominated the Darwen players, who were tired from their long journey. Even so, the Southerners played below their normal form, and were prone to slicing the ball on many occasions. But the enormous throw-ins of Kinnaird were proving a problem for the Darreners, and from one of these throws Whitfield scored first, quickly followed by a second from Christian. Having won the toss the Old Etonians had chosen to play with the wind in the first half, and the tiring Darwen team conceded two more goals before the break.

None but a supreme Darwen optimist would have given the team a chance, especially when Goodhart completed his hat-trick early in the second period. Dispirited and without real hope, the Darreners surged upon the Old Etonians goal, en bloc, in an effort to at least show that they too could score, which they did. With just 15 minutes remaining there then followed what must be regarded as the greatest fight back ever in the F.A. Cup, and a performance that was to earn the millworkers from Lancashire their worthy place in the history of the game. With their confidence rising, despite the superior fitness and physique of their opponents, and following greater dominance by the Darreners, Weldon of the Old Etonians scored - an own goal! 2-5. Love, using his speed to good advantage, scored the third through a powerful header. 3-5. A scramble in front of the Old Boys goal resulted in the ball passing between the posts - disallowed; but after a strong protest from Darwen, the Official reversed his decision. 4-5. By now the Old Etonians were well shaken out of their complacency, and they had every reason to regret their probable easing of effort which had aided their opponents continuous onslaught. With the seconds ticking away, Love scored again. The final result 5-5.

The option was there, for extra time to be played. Darwen were in full agreement, the Old Etonians declined the invitation! Although this refusal hardly came as a surprise, it was something of a comedown for the likes of the Hon. A.F. Kinnaird, who had in the past stated to the effect that:- *"I can never understand players who complain of playing an extra match in midweek. Why, I think nothing of playing three hard games within one week, and even then expect to take a little exercise - to keep myself fit."* Sentiments no doubt normally echoed by his team-mates, but on this occasion noted for their reluctance!

The town of Darwen greeted the homecoming of the team as heroes from a War just won, but the battle was far from over. The Second trip to London had shown a surplus of £40 over and above the donations that had been given, but the Club were in total £200 in debt, and the replay had to be fought - once again in London! The hard-up Club tried desperately to get the Old Etonians to agree to play the game in Darwen, and offered them £40. Apart from not relishing another expensive and tiring trip to London the Darreners naturally reasoned that their chances would be better on home territory. Conversely the London team, although still odds-on favourites, could not risk the unthinkable, a defeat by a bunch of mill-workers! Their opposition probably went further than this though. As true Amateurs, they may well have been willing to give the other side their chance at home, but as Amateurs they abhorred the hint of professionalism attached to the Darwen team, and if the truth be known, probably flinched at the thought of having to play another match with this - in their eyes - sham team.

And so it was necessary for the Public Subscription from the town to be extended. The money came in willingly, with a final magnificent total of £175 in the Fund; for their part the Old Etonians had sportingly sent £5 and the Football Association - possibly with a twinge of guilt in their rules demanding the repeat venue - contributed £10. Three hundred townspeople gave the team a rousing send off at the station when they left in a specially comfortably equipped carriage, courtesy of the Great Northern train company.

The better weather and the prospects of an intriguing match enticed a large crowd to The Oval - in reality the Old Etonians' home ground - for the replay on Saturday the 8th of March. Darwen played an unchanged team, while the Old Boys recruited L. Bury (an England International), and two forward playing changes.

Showing more respect for their opponents on this occasion, and displaying far better skills than previously, the Old Etonians took the lead through Whitfield. But Darwen were not to be denied their undoubted ability and equalised through R. Kirkham, to produce an all square score at half-time.

The second half proved even more entertaining than the first, although once again the match was dominated by excellent defensive work from both sides. Once again the Old Etonians took the lead, only for it to be cancelled out by T. Bury. The four shared goals at full-time was not added to in the thirty minutes of extra time that both teams were amicably disposed towards, on this occasion!

The weary players came home again to a rousing welcome, and once again resigned themselves to another trip to London one week later. The Old Etonians were again asked to come to Darwen, but once again the request fell on deaf ears. By now the whole country was not only well aware of the mill town, but championing their cause. Many letters and opinions were printed in the newspapers, criticising the Old Etonians for their intransigence, although in fairness the repeated venue was not chosen by themselves, but more particularly the unfairness of the Football Association in such a blatantly South biased rule. Quite inadvertently Darwen could once again be shown to be responsible for a shift in football thinking, as from the next season onwards, early rounds were regionalised, which led to more entries - especially from the rapidly emerging Midlands and North.

For the third match in London, the Darwen team presented a jaded spectacle, tired from long working hours and now also from their frequent long distance train travel. McLachlin replaced the injured W. Kirkham in the Darreners line-up. Although the visitors had the best of the encounter for fifteen minutes, their tiredness coupled with an early injury to the Captain, Knowles, led to the Old Etonians eventually running out as easy 6-2 winners.

So for Darwen the excitement was all over. But they had learnt a lot, had caused a change in the rules of the Competition, and even taught the Old Boys a lesson. The Darwen play was influenced by the Scottish style, that of involving several of the team in passing the ball, rather than the cavalry charge down the field with one man dribbling his way through with the ball. By the third Cup match, the Old Etonians had evaluated and counteracted the Darwen style, and had introduced a degree of this element in their own play; another Darwen influence to change the thoughts of Football! The overall financial situation for Darwen, was a profit on the three matches of nearly £57; travelling expenditure amounting to £119 and the four London games, when the team had travelled a total of 1,760 miles.

Four matches against Blackburn teams in April followed. The Association Club (or Christ Church Football Club, based at Ewood) were first beaten by four unopposed goals, then a rare defeat - against the Rovers - followed by a £40 (near 2,000 crowd) gate for the 8-2 hammering of the 18 month-old Olympic team. The return at the Olympic's Ground in the next game was also won. The Rovers match had only produced receipts of £25, but the attraction of matches between the two Clubs was to shortly reach huge proportions.

On April the 26th, the first home game ever versus Turton was played, the venue being near the Anchor Inn, Lower Darwen (at or near the Club's future home) which attracted a crowd of over 1,500, but had a greater significance. The contest was an unprecedented Benefit game for Darwen's Love and Suter, a fact which provided fairly conclusive evidence that the two were professional players - a claim that had been consistently denied by the club.

In all just four matches of the 25 played ended in defeat, with a goal difference of 100 - 40. Although it had been a momentous season on the field, it had been unhealthy on the financial side. Only the profits from the Cup games having kept the Club's head above water.

The first game in the 1879/80 season was played with Darwen Grasshoppers, and won by 7-0, on September the 27th - this being the first match in the new Lancashire Cup. 1,500 turned up for the home friendly with Bolton - another seven goal victory - and 2,000 when Blackburn Olympic were beaten 4-2. It was expressed that, with the Darwen townspeople showing great interest in the game and with four figure attendances, the Club's debt would soon be cleared. A crowd of 'several thousand' at Barley Bank, witnessed a rare home defeat, by 3-1, to Nottingham Forest.

The Reds were a strong test for they had already made their mark in the F.A.Cup competition, and went on to the semi-finals for the second year running. The main events of the season, however, was the four tussles with the up and coming

Blackburn Rovers club. The first game, was a portend to the animosity that was to soon develop between the two Clubs as each battled to become the leading team in the area. There was a 5,000 crowd at Barley Bank on November the 8th, and by half-time the homesters were leading by a single goal. As the game wore on the rougher the tactics became, and in the second period, Darwen's goalkeeper - Duxbury - was injured. He gamely carried on, but a soft equaliser from the Rovers, compelled him to leave the field, and 1-1 was the final score.

The next meeting of the two teams, was in the F.A. Cup, and the match aroused tremendous interest. Over 5,000 packed into the Alexandra Meadows Ground - including a large contingent from Darwen. Despite the importance of the game, it was fought in a sporting manner, but the Darreners could not repeat their Cup success of a year earlier, and after many missed chances finally succumbed to a 1-3 scoreline.

But the interest of all previous games was outshone on March the 20th for the final of the Lancashire Cup, when the biggest ever attendance for a football match in Lancashire, of around 8,000, packed into Darwen's ground. One hour before the kick-off large crowds were already making their way to Barley Bank, and it was necessary to have six, match ticket-selling positions, to cope with the throng. Twelve lorries were commandeered as temporary seated stands on the North side of the ground, and these were soon filled to overflowing. Even team photographs were taken, and in the line-ups two future Internationals were on show; Marshall of Darwen and the Blackburn Captain Hargreaves.

Blackburn quickly established control of the game, but against the run of play Darwen went ahead, through Bury, which caused, *"Hats and sticks to fly up in all directions."* Darwen piled on the pressure in the second half, and ran out eventual easy winners by 3-0. The third goal was hotly disputed, and the two Umpires could not make a final decision; eventually the Referee had the final say - an amazing compromise, since such an action was not covered in the rules at that time! The season had been the first ever in competition for the Lancashire Cup, and was won, ironically for the only time, by the Darreners. The match was surrounded with more controversy though. The rules of the Competition required that players should reside within a certain distance of their clubs. In this instance there was one questionable player in each team.

The Rovers sought from the Association a ruling on the matter, and received the incredible reply, to the effect that, each could play their suspect player if they wished, Blackburn chose - in the circumstances - not to play their 'star' Hornby. Darwen meanwhile went ahead and fielded their 'foreigner', Kirkham.

The Darwen committee maintained that only Hornby was the questionable player, and saw no reason why their man should not play; additionally they created a smear campaign against their neighbours. With the Association's further controversial decision to hold the match at Darwen, the Rovers were not unreasonably somewhat riled at the disadvantage that they had suffered.

Darwen showed their overall superiority two weeks later, this time at Blackburn, where they ran out three goal winners once more. The second was scored on the stroke of half-time, and a further success in the second half, although the homesters came back very strongly. The Lancashire Cup matches had produced a staggering goal difference of 39 for and only 2 against! The early round games included a 12-1 hammering of Haslingden Association before a one thousand plus home crowd.

The previous two seasons had seen the Club rise in status, and they were by now one of the strongest Clubs in the North of England, but even more triumphs awaited them in the 1880/81 season. The first game, on the 25th of September, got off to a cracking start on Merseyside, with a thirteen goal demolition of Liverpool (not the later Football League team) at Newsham Park, Fairfield. This win was, however, overshadowed when a sensational 4-1 win was achieved over the famed Partick side, in front of 2,000 Scots. The overall power of the team continued with another 'cricket score', this time 14-1 over Preston North End, a team yet to rise in the Football World, and who until shortly before this time, had been playing to Rugby rules.

Poor old Haslingden were again at the wrong end of a big score, this time by nine goals, and once again in the Lancashire Cup. The winning ways were put to a stop when eight goals were shared before a 4,000 Barley Bank crowd, but it was no disgrace for the opponents were the well respected Nottingham Forest side. The first match for two years with Turton, was played and won by 5-2, before the F.A. Cup campaign got underway.

The first victims in the Cup were Brigg who were overwhelmed by eight unopposed goals, before Sheffield were hammered 5-1 at Brammall Lane. The 3rd round draw gave the Darreners a bye, and in the next match, another game with a Sheffield club was decreed. Although the weather was poor, the crowd, anticipating a repeat of the F.A. Cup excitement of two years earlier turned out in large numbers at Darwen. Another victory was achieved by the Lancashire Club, this time over the Wednesday, and again by 5-1.

Once again the Club had reached the quarter-final stage, but on this occasion they did not have to play the game at The Oval! But the luck of the draw was as bad, as fate required them to travel to the London area yet again, this time to Romford. Not relishing the thought of a long and tedious journey, Darwen managed to 'persuade' (a financial inducement) the Essex Club to come to Lancashire. The home team goalscorers ran riot, and created a record (at that time) goal winning margin in the Competition.

Rostrom scored first, followed by Mellor, and after 7 minutes the Darreners were three up. The fans had difficulty in keeping up with the score as the unfortunate Romford goal was bombarded with successful shots. By half-time the tally was 11-0, and although the pace slackened in the second period, the final score was 15-0. The Club had for the first time reached the semi-final stage in a no uncertain manner!

The match, against the Old Carthusians, did have to be played at The Oval, a ground which could almost be considered the Club's second home! But on this occasion, far from being the underdogs as was the case two years earlier, the Darwen team's fame and winning ways made them favourites to become the first Northern team to reach the Final. Just this one game was between them and another match with the Old Etonians - who had a bye at this penultimate stage. Although the Southern Amateur Clubs had completely monopolised the Competition to date, the rapid rise of the Northeners abilities produced the prospect of a fascinating, first ever, North versus South conflict on the football field.

The weather at The Oval was fine but cold, and a large crowd of 2,000 - matches in the South were not regarded as spectator attractions to the same degree as the North - attended. Despite winning the toss, Darwen chose to play into the sun in the first half, and Brindle got the game into motion. Several early chances were missed by the visitors, including two shots that hit the bar, before they took a one goal interval lead. Possibly Darwen became over confident in the second half, for their overall earlier superiority vanished as the Old Carthusians stormed back in the second half. After ninety minutes, the score showed a 1-4 defeat to Darwen. The Lancashire team had been unable to reproduce their fighting-back spirit, and the prospect of a classic confrontation in the Final was lost by a scoreline that somewhat flattered the Amateur team.

The Darwen streets were packed with people, all anxious to get word of the final result, and were shattered when they heard the news of the game that they hoped for, and expected, their favourites to win.

Between the F.A. Cup games, friendlies had continued. On Christmas Day, a hastily arranged fixture was surprisingly lost at Church (4-6) followed by another defeat, this time in Scotland. Dumbarton were the hosts, and the first half was played to 'Scotch' rules - which differed somewhat from the English rules - and Darwen were overshadowed in the 3-1 defeat. Earlier, on November the 27th, a friendly was played at Alexandra Meadows with Blackburn Rovers, and once again these two neighbours attracted unsurpassed interest.

This match, although only a friendly encounter, played between what were by now recognised as the two premier Clubs in Lancashire, attracted an interest that once again overshadowed all others. It was estimated that over 12,000 fanatics packed into the ground. The two sets of supporters excitement this time spilled over into violent confrontations that had threatened in previous matches.

Darwen opened the scoring in the first half, which let to a pitch invasion. The inadequate number of police present had difficulty in clearing the field of play, and the game was held up for seven minutes. The Darreners lead was shortlived and at half-time each team had scored once. In the second half of a rough and tough game, a serious confrontation occurred between Suter, who had by now transferred his allegiance to the Rovers, and Marshall. The ugly scene happened in front of a broken barrier (from the earlier pitch invasion), and a number of spectators joined in with the fighting. The Darwen News in an article featuring the match claimed that their contemporaries in Blackburn, had highly coloured their report, and exaggerated the friction as well as giving a one-sided account. The Darwen paper's opinion was that the Ground had been unsuitable for such an enormous crowd. The final result was a cooling down of the members on both teams, and although Marshall issued a general apology, Suter didn't!

Although increased admission charges were made at the Aston Villa ground on the 8th of January, a record attendance - *"The largest and most enthusiastic crowd of spectators ever brought together on the ground"* - 5,000, came to see their favourites play Darwen. The visitors, weakened by injury to several players, were a great disappointment and lost by four unopposed goals. This match was followed by another game with the Forest, this time in Nottingham. Despite their prowess, the Darreners had never beaten these opponents, and this record was kept intact with a three goal defeat!

More friction was created when the two top Lancashire Clubs met in March. The Lancashire Cup-tie between the pair had been scheduled for the 5th of March but had to be postponed due to Darwen's F.A. Cup commitments. The Rovers took this as a snub, and at the 'eleventh' hour called off the game which had been re-scheduled a week later - and played Nottingham Forest in a Friendly fixture instead. Meanwhile, Darwen - who had earlier arranged to play Partick, but who had to postpone this match because of the Lancashire Cup Tie - hastily arranged a game at Accrington. Such were the vagaries of the rules at this time, which allowed such arbitrary decisions. The antagonism between the two Clubs reached the point where both were thrown out of the Lancashire Cup Competition that season! There was little doubt that the infighting between these two teams, whilst including the natural competitive element and desire to win, was overshadowed by the importance of each to be the best! Securing the best (professional) players was the ultimate necessity and hence required high attendances to pay those players. The Football Records Book of 1881 stated:-

"... What an unwholesome prominence the gate occupies in the consideration of football clubs in the North. Indeed there is no need to disguise the speedy approach of a time when the subject of professional players will require the earnest attention of those on whom devolves the management of Association football." The time was fast approaching!

Despite the late notice, nearly 3,000 fans were present at the Accrington game, but Darwen were highly critical of their neighbour's pitch which was barely 50 yards wide. At the season's end, a match, *"to the benefit for the players composing the Darwen team"* (i.e. professionals), was played against Staveley on the 16th of April. Several cancelled games in April led to financial problems, which otherwise would have been a highly entertaining and profitable season.

The 1881/82 season proved that Darwen F.C. had lost their edge over their contemporaries. From a team that had carried virtually everything before them, they were to find that although far from being a poor combination, there were others reaching, and even passing their level. The previous four seasons had been the most successful for the Club, and were to prove to be superior to the future. In many aspects they had led the way and set the trends within the game. Meanwhile a whole host of Clubs from neighbouring towns were to reach and surpass the superiority previously shown by the Darreners.

The campaign started on September the 10th with a practise game against Lower Darwen. Two weeks later a trip to Scotland was made, and although starting well - a surprise since the changed team was very much experimental - they eventually succumbed to an embarrassing 0-6 defeat. October the 8th brought Turton to Barley Bank, but only a moderate attendance of 1,700 was present. Other early visitors were Nottingham Forest, and despite these attractive opponents, barely 2,000 were present to see the homesters go down by one goal.

On October the 29th, something like the past season's support was present - 3,000 to 4,000 - for Blackburn Olympic's F.A. Cup visit, although a large number of the crowd were from the nearby town. There was never any doubt which team was the best, and Darwen went on to the next round with a 3-1 victory. Although a high scoring 7-5 defeat was sustained at up and coming Accrington, the F.A.Cup match in late November saw a reversal of superiority, an attendance of nearly 4,000, and a 3-1 Darrener victory.

The thoughts of earlier Cup successes must have come to the fore, as the team continued to flourish in this Competition. December was the month when the next round was played, and won. On a frozen and therefore very slippery Barley Bank pitch, Turton were beaten 4-2, but before only 1,500 spectators. The 30th of January was the date for the next round, and what better opposition at this 4th round stage than Blackburn Rovers, on their new, recently opened Leamington Road ground. The past bad feelings between the two Clubs had by now subsided, and yet again interest in a match - especially the F.A. Cup - between these close rivals generated terrific interest. This new Ground was far better suited to Football, the previous home at Alexandra Meadows doubling up for Cricket during the summer.

At Leamington Road a sturdy barrier (two railed) to the pitch on all four sides contained the crowds whilst a purpose built seated Grandstand was in place. Spectators started arriving two and a half hours before the kick-off and with one hour left, the Ground was considered full with seven to eight thousand spectators inside. Although the match passed off trouble free, the Rovers proved themselves a force by now superior to the Darreners, and romped away with a 5-1 victory after a 4-0 scoreline at half-time. This result was shown to be no one-off event, as the Rovers went on to the Final, and so became the first team outside the - Amateur - South to reach this stage.

It must have come as severe blow to the once mighty Darwen to suffer such a defeat, and the next match - with Accrington - only raised an attendance of around 2,000. On March the 18th, a return game with Blackburn Rovers was arranged, but this time with nothing more than pride at stake. At Barley Bank the crowds came out again in great numbers, but to the homesters distress, another heavy defeat was sustained, with the same scoreline as two months earlier. The main reasons for such a poor result were put down to poor goalkeeping, bad luck, and the poor play of Cross; Cross was in fact a Welsh Druids player who had arrived at the game as the referee, but played for Darwen, substituting the injured Rostrum!

The season trailed off with some variable results. A 2-3 defeat at little known Staveley (attendance 1,000), a single goal victory but entertaining home match before 2,000 spectators versus Walsall Swifts, and a morale boosting 12-3 win at the year-old Preston North End club. Preston were to become another Lancashire Club who started as the pupil and quickly became the masters of Darwen F.C. The season had been one of mixed fortunes and an unsettled team. The final record, while not poor by normal standards, was none the less a discouraging 16 wins, 4 draws and 14 defeats.

The 1882/83 season started, and Darwen supporters now could only stand back and see their favourites take second place to several other Lancashire teams. Blackburn Rovers - the toast of the North after their Cup Final appearance - refused to play at Darwen unless their exorbitant demands for their gate money share were met! Bolton Wanderers, although formed in 1874 but as yet not very prominent, were able to attract an 'immense crowd' (approximately 8,000) when they held Darwen to a 2-2 home draw. Whilst at home less than 1,000 fans turned up for the Friendly home game with Sheffield Wednesday - which was abandoned after 65 minutes due to torrential rain.

Reduced support and successful neighbours provided the Darreners with the incentive to make a good show in the F.A. Cup, which they in part achieved. A poor first match in the competition, but none the less a 4-1 home win over Blackburn Park Road, was first accomplished. The 2nd round draw decreed that Darwen would yet again travel up the road to the Rovers of Blackburn. Once again a capacity crowd of between 8 to 10,000 was present, and although the visitors were given little chance against their opponents, they achieved a shock win. After a scoreless first half, the all important goal was scored in the second period. The end came in the next round, with a two goal defeat to Church, after a previously drawn encounter.

The next few years were to see Darwen - although still a major force - pass the mantle of greatness, to a greater degree, over to other town teams in the locality. The 1883/84 F.A. Cup adventure ended in the 1st round with a defeat to Blackburn Olympic. The Olympic went onto the semi-final, but nearby Rovers not only reached the Final again but this time won it by defeating Queen's Park of Glasgow. One year later it was a three goal defeat to Church after a bye in the 1st round. A further year on, (when 'those' Rovers won the Trophy for the third successive season), despite the appearance of six Lancashire and several other Northern Clubs in the Third Round, Darwen F.C. were not amongst them!

By 1887 football was beginning to stagnate! The demands for success led to increased professionalism, which in turn led to the necessity for good attendances for economic survival. Whilst the F.A. Cup - and to a lesser extent the County Cup and games with local rivals - could still arouse interest, something more was required; this came one year later with the formation of the Football League.

The twilight of 1886 had ended with a 1-2 defeat at the Rovers - who were still on a 'high' and attracted another 8,000 gate - followed by a single goal defeat at Bootle. On New Year's Day, Kilmarnock Athletic were the visitors, but the attendance was only 1,500 for a fixture which a few years earlier would have been a highlight.

But at least some headway was made in the F.A. Cup once again. Bolton were first overcome, followed by a bye in the newly designated 1st series - 4th round. The 2nd series - 1st round, required a journey to fresh fields. A party of only forty supporters accompanied the team to the village of Chirk in North Wales. Although coming away as the victors, the £6 share of a £17 gate from a record 2,000 attendance did little for the finances of the Darreners, as their expenses alone amounted to £20!

More rewarding, financially, was the next round trip to Aston Villa. Once again few fans made the trip - although their battles of a few years earlier required the laying on of special trains - but the 6,000 crowd was entertained by a thrilling match. A strong wind in their faces during the first period resulted in the visiting team being outplayed and three goals to the worse at the interval. The second half was a complete reversal as the Darraners stormed back and scored twice while a third effort was disallowed. Darwen had once again reached the quarter-final stage, but the Villa went on to claim the Cup for the first time, at a period when the still Amateur South were beginning to lose their dominance in the Competition. A Friendly, versus Blackburn Rovers - a 3-1 victory - only attracted a 4,000 gate, and near the season's end just 1,000 were present for Halliwell's visit, and even less when the attractive Blackburn Olympic put in an appearance. The final game of the season was lost at home by three unopposed goals, to the Rovers, in a Charity match which pulled in 3,000 spectators.

Although the likes of the Blackburn's (Rovers and Olympic) had become the dominant forces in the area, it had now reached the time when Preston North End would reign supreme for a spell. A few years earlier there had been a veritable proliferation of Darwen teams, but the number of Clubs with senior standing had dropped to just three, the Darreners (and their Reserves), the Wanderers and Rovers. Although the power of Darwen F.C. had continued to decline, they were still a force to be reckoned with, and the many Friendly matches that were played by the first team, seldom needed to include one of the other Clubs from the town.

The start of the 1887/88 season was one of mixed fortunes - a single goal defeat at Everton (attendance 5,000) followed by an excellent 5-2 home victory over the Olympic in the Lancashire Cup before a very large crowd. Whereas such a game could attract the fans, the same could not be said of the interminable friendly games with the same opponents, for which there was nothing at stake, save honour. Only £7 receipts were taken for the visit of Church F.C. (about 300 spectators) and the Halliwell match brought in only £20 - even this figure was barely enough to cover even basic expenses. It was apparent that something was needed to bring a 'bite' into the game, and stop the sport from stagnating.

But the F.A. Cup still captured the imagination, and a large attendance was present at Rawtenstall when the Darreners pulled off a 3-1 win. The next round attracted an unrecorded but, reported, 'immense crowd', when the little known Club, Witton, put in an appearance. The match finished up all square, and the replay attracted an unprecedented 6,000 crowd to the village of Witton, where, due to the unenclosed nature of the Ground, many gained free viewing. It was a beautiful December day, an entertaining match, and a 2-0 win for the visitors.

The following round brought a new team to Barley Bank - Notts. Rangers - but on a heavy pitch after prolonged rain, there was only a moderate crowd of some 3,000 present to witness the homesters 3-1 victory. Yet again Darwen had fought their way through to the last sixteen (2nd series - 1st round), but this was to be the end of the road. Blackburn Rovers were the victors by three unopposed goals, which added to their previous victory - a 6-3 result at the Leamington Ground over Christmas.

By the end of the season, the framework for forming a League in which Clubs would play set fixtures against teams on a par with themselves, on pre-arranged dates came to a positive conclusion. The formation of the Football League, was to radically change the whole face of the sport and attract attendances sufficient to pay expenses and the wages of professional players, which had finally been acknowledged and allowed by the Football Association in 1885. If this radical idea of a League containing the top clubs had been introduced ten years earlier, there is little doubt that Darwen F.C. would have been one of the prime members. But in the event they were not even invited to join, and had to take a back seat as twelve other clubs - some had not even been formed at the time of Darwen's greatness - led the way.

The 1888/89 campaign was far from successful for the Darreners. With Accrington, Blackburn Rovers, Bolton Wanderers, Burnley and Preston North End all being part of the elite twelve, there was little merit or interest in the local Friendly matches between these local teams. The Barley Bank fixtures with the League teams still aroused some passion, but when the same games were played away from home, the matches were lacking in enthusiasm and in numbers of spectators.

Unfortunately the F.A. Cup Competition did not even see the Darreners through to the last 32 Clubs. The Club looked further afield for their Friendly games, and although the plethora of new Clubs could rarely match Darwen's relative superiority - the first game with Birmingham Excelsior, for instance, resulting in a runaway 15-1 victory - a 1-6 home defeat to Blackburn Rovers highlighted the gulf that was now present between these two League and non-League Clubs.

Even so, Darwen were accepted willingly into the subsidiary competition, The Football Alliance, that was created the following season. On August the 31st 1889, Darwen played out an entertaining 2-2 Friendly before a 2,000 crowd at South Shore, followed seven days later with the Club's first ever match in a League. For their first visit to Barley Bank, Sunderland Albion drew a large crowd, but before the match there was controversy, as the visitors complained of the host's proposal to play the previously suspended Downes in the Darwen line-up. Under protest the Darreners substituted the player in contention with a reserve. The full team reading:- Holden, J. Marsden, Leach, Thornber, Owen, T. Marsden, Douglas, W.Marsden, Fish, Smith and Entwhistle.

There was no ideal start though as the Albion, after taking a two goal interval lead, managed to contain the Darreners in the second period, but without improving their own goal tally. Another good attendance was present, despite heavy rain, when the Club played their second League match at Birmingham St. George. But the weather didn't dampen the home team's enthusiasm or ability and they finished as 7-3 winners. Two matches and two defeats, was not an auspicious start for Darwen F.C. Worse was to come as this poor start to their first competitive season continued.

The first victory of the campaign did not come until the 5th of October - and that was only a friendly fixture at Witton (4-0), and there was, *"an immense concourse of spectators"*, for the 2-5 home defeat in another friendly fixture against the Rovers.

JOHN RALPH LEACH, left full back, is one of the oldest members of the Darwen team as at present constituted. He is two years the senior of his brother back, and by trade is a heald maker, succeeding to the business of his father not long ago. His abilities whilst with a junior club of the town soon brought him to the notice of the Darwen management, and he was not long in showing them they had made a wise choice. Being a man of few words and unassuming manner he is respected by all; and withal he is a player whom others would do well to imitate, for he looks to his condition, and it is seldom indeed that he is out of form. Many good and able judges consider him the better of the Darwen backs. Certainly he lacks nothing by comparison with Marsden. He is a good tackler and possesses rare judgment. It is not often he misses the object for which he goes. It is generally thought that on him the mantle of Elijah, or in other words, the captaincy of the Darwen team, will fall when Joe Marsden goes to Everton, and should he be chosen for that position next season, the selection would be immensely popular.

JIM HADDOW, the left half-back, is the junior member of the team, having been entrusted with his position very recently, consequent upon an injury sustained by T. Marsden, who has a bad toe. Haddow is a paper stainer, and is only 19 years of age, but he is possessed of both weight and pluck. He is, strictly speaking, a second team man, but on several occasions, both last season and this, he has assisted the premier team, and has generally justified the choice. He has always displayed good work when in the Darwen Reserve, and his selection gives satisfaction to the numerous body of Darwen supporters.

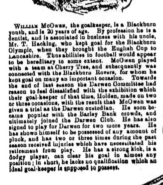

WILLIAM McOWEN, the goalkeeper, is a Blackburn youth, and is 20 years of age. By profession he is a dentist, and is associated in business with his uncle, Mr. T. Hacking, who kept goal for the Blackburn Olympic, when they brought the English Cup to Lancashire. Thus abilities in football would appear to be hereditary to some extent. McOwen played with a team at Cherry Tree, and subsequently was connected with the Blackburn Rovers, for whom he kept goal on many an important occasion. Towards the end of last season the Darwen Committee had reason to feel dissatisfied with the exhibition which their goal-keeper of that time, Holden, made on two or three occasions, with the result that McOwen was given a trial as the Darwen custodian. He soon became popular with the Barley Bank crowds, and ultimately joined the Darwen Club. He has also signed to play for Darwen for two more years. He has shown himself to be possessed of any amount of pluck, and has two or three times during the past season received injuries which have necessitated his retirement from play. He has a strong kick, is a dodgy player, can clear his goal in almost any position; in short, he lacks no qualification which an ideal goal-keeper is supposed to possess.

DAVID OWEN, the centre half-back of the team, is a slim-built player of some 26 summers. His occupation is that of a paper stainer. He was brought to Darwen when but a few weeks old, and he began at an early age to develop his football abilities, assisting St. John's for a few seasons. Gradually he improved, and eventually found himself installed a regular playing member of the premier town club. He has acted as captain of the team, and he always handled his men judiciously. He has been a thorn in the side of many a centre forward, and is very tricky; at times, too, he gets at the leather when it seems beyond his power to do so. At present he is vice-captain of the team, and when the "boss" is absent Davie somehow seems to feel his responsibility, and never fails to play one of his best games then.

JOSEPH MARSDEN, the captain of the team, is a weaver, and 22 years ago he first saw the light. The name "Marsden" is one familiar to Darwen people, and it may be presumed that the Darwen captain is a Darwener bred and born. It is said by those who ought to know that Joseph was an able exponent of the game of football before he could repeat his alphabet; at any rate, residents in Bolton-road district remember the white-haired lad who was always at the head of the teams of youngsters. He was connected with some junior teams in the town, and after playing with the Royal Blues, Hibernians, and Padiham, he became connected with the premier club, and took up his present place of right full back. He is not weighty, but he plays a fine game, and does not leave an opponent until either beaten (which is seldom) or he has managed to get the ball. He kicks very powerfully for one so light. He has represented both his county and country, and his admirers were disappointed that he was not among the eleven that met Scotland recently at Ewood. On this occasion, however, he was on the reserve.

RICHARD THORNBER is another of those players who have always known the ins and outs of the football game, in which he has taken a keen interest right from the cradle. He is the right half-back of the Darwen team and is by trade a broker's assistant. He is the liveliest member of the Darwen team. He is of a rollicking disposition, and enjoys a bit of real ding-dong play as well as anyone who does a jersey. "Dick" is then in his element. He is 24 years of age, and before joining Darwen he played with the Royal Blues and Hibernians. He and Joe Marsden understand each other well. He is a tough 'un to deal with, and he can bustle the opposing forwards to some tune when he likes. He feeds his forwards well in general, but sometimes he kicks rashly at goal when in a careless mood. He is a general favourite with the Barley Bank spectators, his style suiting them to a nicety. Purely scientific football is not in "Dick's" line, but the forwards in the best teams in the country invariably find it no easy matter to go against him. He is, we understand, registered as one of Darwen's players for the next two seasons.

JONATHAN ENTWISTLE, the outside left, is another who was originally a Darwen Rover, and is a plumber, or at least has served an apprenticeship to that trade. He is 25 years of age. After ceasing with the Rovers he joined a club at Haslingden (where he now resides), and the Accrington F.C. were not long in being on his track. Darwen induced him to join them at the end of last season, and he has done rare good service at outside left. He is very speedy and runs strongly; when once clear he is bad to get at, and he goes for goal with a vengeance, as the North End know. He has allied himself to Darwen for another term, and it is on the cards that he will take up his residence in his native town are long.

J. W. SMITH, the inside left, is a loomer, and is one of the players furnished to the Darwen Club by the Darwen Rovers. He is not a brilliant or individual man in the field, but he loses nothing in comparison with his companions, for he plods along from beginning to end. It has been difficult for him, for whilst at inside left he has had many men as partners, and this does not conduce to continuous good work. Nevertheless he is a tryer, and gets along neatly between W. Marsden and Entwistle. He first joined the Darwen team in 1887, when he partnered Jimmy Shorrock on the left wing. Inside left has been his usual position, although he has not been a fixture, sometimes playing on the outside of his wing and sometimes in the centre.

W. MARSDEN, the centre forward, is a younger brother of Joe, and when only 17 years of age he made his bow before the Darwen public on Barley Bank, having previously played for Darwen Reserve. He is now 19 years old, and, like the captain, he is a weaver. Formerly he played inside right, but now acts as centre forward, and possesses rare pluck and any quantity of "go." He is ever ready to tackle the biggest antagonist, and is well adapted to the Darwen style of forward play, of which he is an able exponent. Sometimes he cannot get going, but when in the humour he is a bad one to shake off. He holds his wings together well, and altogether is well qualified for the position which he holds.

R. SMITH is the inside right wing. His connection with the Darwen club dates from the commencement of the present season. His abilities were brought to the front by the Darwen Rovers, and on Fish retrograding in form Smith was given an opportunity among the Darwen forwards, and he has amply justified their choice. He is a self-actor minder; is 21 years of age, and partners Nightingale nicely, feeding him with conspicuous judgment.

JEMMY NIGHTINGALE, the outside right forward, is the patriarch of the eleven, being 27 years of age. He was a factory operative until recently, when he began the business of an insurance agent. He, like the majority of the team, was drafted from the ranks of a junior club, and began to play forward for Darwen. This was several years ago, but in 1886 a serious injury to his knee forced him to drop football for two or three years, and it was only last season that he again courageously took to the field. He is all but indispensable in the Darwen forward division. He is possessed of a turn of speed which at times is almost unequalled, and gets the ball along as a rule, while his centering is generally well-timed and pretty accurate. His shots at goal are also very troublesome. He commands the respect of his colleagues, for Nightingale is, above all, a gentlemanly player.

1890/91 Season:
The Lancashire Cup Final
Team members

But the locals were not impressed in general with the team's performances, for only a small crowd was present when Long Eaton Rangers came and won by 5-3, in the Club's third League game.

Some relief was felt when two important games were won, the first, an easy 7-2 away victory before 2,500 spectators over South Shore in the Lancashire Cup. On November the 9th the fourth League game was played, and the Darreners were comprehensively beaten at Bootle to put them firmly at the bottom place in the table. The second notable victory was achieved in the F.A. Cup - 4-1 at home to Halliwell - followed at last by the first League victory on November the 23rd. Walsall Town Swifts were the visitors at Barley Bank, and the homesters, on this occasion described as 'brilliant', won by 6-3.

The F.A. Cup aspirations came to an end when the third game of the season was played at South Shore; the weather was poor and there was little Darwen support in evidence. Fortunately by the season's end, although no honours were won, a moderate recovery was made to place the Club in a final 6th in the League (10 wins and the same number of losses, plus two drawn games) of 12 Clubs. Such were the vagaries of the rules at this time, that the first game - when Darwen decided against playing a dubious player - was ordered to be replayed! Significantly of these teams in this original season of the Alliance, most were to become eventual Football League members.

For a Club that had considered itself worthy of full Football League status, it had been a poor season, and an application for that competition was not even applied for on this occasion. At the final reckoning, the second outing in the Football Alliance was very similar to the first. An eventual 6th League placing, with again 10 victories, but this time only 9 defeats and 3 draws, and a goal difference of 64-59. However, financially the situation was somewhat grim, for in January it was announced that the Club was over £250 in debt. The bank balance was slightly bolstered with an appearance in the final of the Lancashire Cup, which was played at Everton, and contested with Bolton Wanderers. The opposition's team contained no fewer than seven Scottish players (plus two Welshmen), and it triumphed over the Darreners with a 3-1 scoreline. Earlier, excellent victories by the Darwen team in this competition, had included victories over Accrington, Burnley and Preston.

The F.A. Cup sorties also had their rewards, at least on the field. On January the 17th a large crowd was present to see a 3-1 victory over Kidderminster, but following a protest the match was ordered to be replayed. The crowd only numbered some 1,000 for the second game, but those who stayed away missed a treat, for the opposition were hammered 13-0 - one of the biggest F.A. Cup scores on record. The 2nd round (last 16) saw the Darreners go out 0-2, rather lamely, at Sunderland on the last day of January.

After a few years of somewhat indifferent performances and interest in the Club, excitement mounted as the 1891/92 season drew near. For the Football League had been increased with the addition of two extra places and Darwen had secured one of them. As the Darreners had not excelled in the Football Alliance, it was rather surprising perhaps that they were afforded this elevation. Along with the four Clubs applying for re-election, there were six newcomers trying their luck, and of them Sunderland Albion would have appeared, on paper, to have been more readily accepted. In the event Darwen secured the third most votes for the six elected while the Albion were given a firm rebuff. Ironically, of the other refused hopefuls, Nottingham Forest and Newton Heath (later Manchester United) became Champions and Runners-up respectively in May 1892, in what became the last season of the Alliance, and both were elected into the further expanded First Division of the Football League.

The prospects of action with the elite, stirred the locals, and at the Public practice matches up to 5,000 crowds packed into Barley Bank. The Club had made several new signings, including Slater and Duckworth, but were somewhat dismayed to be ordered to change their first choice colours, as their Black and White were the same as fellow Leaguers, Notts. County! The choice was made and Salmon Shirts and Indigo Shorts were chosen.

Improvements were carried out at the Ground. The dressing rooms were dispensed with - presumably located a long distance fro the football pitch - and dressing tents at the Clough end of the Ground were provided instead, and in addition to the permanent Grandstand, a temporary one was erected on the Clough side.

In preparation for the big day, a Friendly match was played at Blackpool, and on September the 5th Bolton Wanderers came to Darwen for the home Club's first ever

Football League match. A special train had brought a contingent of visitors who helped to swell the crowd to an impressive 7,000. The kick-off was delayed by ten minutes, due to the late arrival of the Referee! But things did not go well for the Club and the Wanderers took a two goal lead, before Entwhistle reduced the lead to 1-2 by the interval. There was no further scoring, and so Darwen - as with their first initiation into League football two years earlier - had suffered a defeat in their first game. The team consisted of:- McOwen, Leach, Simmons, Thornber, Owen, Haddow, Alexander, Heap, Smith, Carty and Entwhistle.

Two days later a high scoring game went against the Darreners when they were defeated 3-5 at Everton. The misery piled up for the newcomers, for despite playing well in the away game at Bolton on the 12th of September, an exciting game saw them go down by a single goal. This put the team in bottom place in the table, and although the first win came on September the 18th (5-2 at home to Accrington), and another good victory over fellow-strugglers Stoke (an amazing 9-3 scoreline - the biggest at that time recorded in the Football League) on the 3rd of October, by November things were looking bleak.

The question was asked: *"In what position will the Darwen Club be at the end of the season.... week after week the Darreners are beaten, but none the less the Committee do not get good men."* How often were those sentiments to be repeated by other Clubs in the years to follow! Significantly the team generally consisted of ten English players and only one Scot. This led to several disputes between the Committee and those Players, as the former searched for suitable replacements from over the border.

The season had started with good attendances, but as the Club's fortunes dropped so did the interest in attending matches, not helped by the 6d. (2½p) entrance money mow imposed. If the home record was poor, the results on foreign soil were even worse. Four goals shared at Wolverhampton in late September, and another draw - at Accrington - constituted the only points picked up on the teams travels throughout the season. Apart from a surprise 3-1 home victory over the current Champions, Everton, on November the 14th, the run-up to the year end produced such defeats as those at Derby, Sunderland and Aston Villa - all to the tune of seven unopposed goals!

The second half of the season became a nightmare when every match was lost except a 1-1 draw with West Bromwich Albion. Amongst the defeats was a nine goal thrashing at Burnley, and an even worse 0-12 defeat at - surprisingly - West Bromwich! The end of the season showed the appalling record of 4 wins, 3 draws and 19 defeats, with an awful goal difference of 38 - 112, this represented the conceding on average over four goals per game! Darwen had finished bottom of the League. In general the attendances had slumped, but even so the local derby matches - aided by plenty of travelling support - attracted good crowds, and on the 1st of January - with Championship challenging Preston's visit - the crowd of 8,000 represented probably the Club's record attendance during their spell in the Football League.

In the F.A. Cup, and exit was made in the 2nd Round with a two goal defeat to Aston Villa - which should have been won - and in the County Cup, the Darreners went down 2-3 at the semi-final stage, at home to Blackburn Rovers before a 6,000 attendance. At the Club's A.G.M., the Chairman was scathing in his remarks about the players. He stated that he believed drink was the reason for the team losing matches (it should be added that he had opposed having any Publicans on the Committee). The Players, he considered, were not training sufficiently but spending their time in Pubs from morning till night!

With the final legalising of professional football in Scotland in 1892, the Club (in common with others) found those Scots that they had managed to secure were 'defecting' back to their homeland. Three of the four bottom Clubs had to seek re-election. West Bromwich by winning the F.A. Cup were re-elected automatically, Accrington and Stoke scraped home, but Darwen were rejected and along with an influx of other Clubs helped to become the founder-members of the newly created Second Division. For a team in the doldrums, Darwen started the season in a surprising and successful fashion. After a pre-season 'warm-up' game at Blackburn Rovers, a 2-1 win, it was immediately obvious that with a number of changes, the Club now had a better team than a year earlier.

This was confirmed when the first League game was won at Walsall Town Swifts. Doubts were cast when the second match was lost at home to Burton Swifts, but this was only a temporary set-back for the next four games ended in victory, and by mid-October the team were riding high on the top of the table. This run included a 3-1 home victory over Ardwick, which displaced the visitors from their number one position. Two defeats were suffered on their travels, but an excellent record at Barley Bank - just one game was lost throughout the season - returned them back on top by December the 10th. The game on that dismal winter's day was to prove to be one of the best games ever seen at the Ground. High-flying Small Heath - eventual Champions - were the visitors, who straight from the kick-off swept into the lead. The goal was vigorously protested as being offside, and insult was added to injury when two Darwen efforts were disallowed! One extra goal was scored by each team by the interval, and so the Darreners went in 1-2 behind. Despite Darwen having the aid of the wind in the second period, Small Heath scored again. But, perhaps with memories of the Old Etonians clash many years earlier, the homesters swept back. After pulling back two goals, the winner was scored 12 minutes from the end to give the team a highly exciting and entertaining 4-3 victory.

Although the top place in the League was held until the New Year, the indifferent away form that followed was to displace them, and by the season's end a final third place had to suffice. This position gave the Club a chance of promotion in the play-offs which were introduced in the early years when elevation for the higher teams was not automatic. A 3-2 victory over First Division Notts. County on April the 22nd ensured that the two teams would change Divisions.

This move back to the First Division was Darwen's greatest achievement of the season, but even the F.A. Cup had its rewards. The 1st round decreed that the Darreners would play host to Aston Villa, a leading 1st Division team who had defeated them in the Cup a year earlier. Villa wanted the venue reversed, but would not succumb to Darwen's somewhat exorbitant demand of £300! The money was badly needed, for despite their current successful season, the crowds were not present in great numbers at home matches. This was born out at the Cup matches, when despite such attractive opposition, only 5,000 turned up - which produced a gate of less than £150.

Against all predictions, the homesters won an exciting game by 5-4, with Entwhistle scoring the winner. Villa's defeat had some repercussions back home, where the Birmingham team were severely criticised for their defeat, and demands were made to the Management that they reorganise the Club! The second round was also won, by two goals, over Grimsby in a poor game. This put the team into the quarter-finals once more, and special training was undertaken for the forthcoming visit to 1st Division Club Wolverhampton Wanderers. After their previous exploits, they must have considered their chances favourable, but the match turned out to be a fiasco. After a goalless first half, the Darreners collapsed in the second and finished on the wrong end of a five goal defeat!

Between F.A. Cup games, the team made an exit from the Lancashire Cup at the hands of Liverpool, despite the protest which was overruled, that the Merseyside team had played two ineligible players.

A Scottish Junior International team was entertained with a view to reducing the Darreners debt, followed by a Friendly with Preston, which attracted well over 2,000 spectators. A number of non-competitive matches were played during the season to make up for free weeks, and these spare Saturdays led to talk about extending the numbers of Football League Clubs. *"There is no mistake about it, nothing but Cup-Ties and League games are worth playing."* Was voiced by a local scribe. How well Darwen knew this, to their cost!

By the start of the 1893/94 season on September the 2nd - now back in the First Division - the Club announced that they were £500 in the 'Red'. The 3-2 first League game home defeat to near neighbours Blackburn provided no comfort! The 2-1 loss at Sheffield United, was no better, for the standard of the team's play in both games - despite the narrow scorelines - was very poor.

Fortunately the third match was won, but the aftermath of the game on the following Monday, the 18th of September, was to leave the Club looking very foolish. It is apparent, from the frequent references relating to football during this period, that in many cases the standard of refereeing left much to be desired. But after the match in question (a 3-1 defeat at Wolverhampton), Darwen reported the Official, Mr. Jeffreys, for 'general incompetence', and worse. They also claimed that he had been biased and that he was under the influence of alcohol! The latter point was subsequently withdrawn, but after a long discussion at the next Football League Management meeting, the Committee could not substantiate any of the points raised. Darwen F.C. were ordered to publicly apologise to Mr. Jeffreys, and the Club's actions in this matter did little to endear them to the League, its Officials or the Clubs themselves.

The Club's losing ways continued and kept them in the basement area of the League table, and by the end of November a drop to the lowest spot. Generally the many defeats were fairly close affairs, but there were exceptions; 8-1 at Everton, and no cheer at Christmas with an awful 9-0 reverse on Boxing Day at Aston Villa - the future Champions. It was one long season of gloom, with no highlights, that placed the team one off the bottom of the table at the finish. It came as no surprise, when in the play-offs, a defeat was sustained to Small Heath, which produced a resultant change of divisions for the two.

There was to be no return for the Darreners, as they became - at first - a 'middle of the table' Second Division outfit, and at the last a complete failure. For a while, the 1894/95 season looked reasonably bright - at the end of March they lay in 4th place in the table - but a poor away record put paid to any hopes of the end of season test matches. Inevitably, as their successful neighbours prospered, the financial fortunes of the Club plummeted. The New Year crowd of over 4,000 on New Year's Day at Barley Bank for Woolwich Arsenal's visit, was by now exceptionally high. Even the reserves - who had operated with some success in the North-East Lancashire Combination - were unable to financially justify their existence, and at one stage produced 11 games running at a monetary loss.

A special meeting regarding finances was called for in mid-April, when a number of members supported the idea of forming the Club into a Limited Company, but the motion at this time was not carried. The end of season accounts made dismal reading; gate receipts totalled £1,630, wages paid amounted to £1,427 and a heavy loss on the season of £240 was made. Running two fully professional teams - the last Amateurs with the Club were Shorrock and Dimmock who left in 1888 - was a drain on resources that could not last, and didn't.

With new players in the team - including the former International, Forrest, from Blackburn - a good display was shown in the pre-season (1895/96) Friendly versus Blackburn, but even a crowd of around 2,000 was by now reasonable for this fixture which, fifteen years earlier, would have guaranteed a full house. Attendances of around 2,000 were to become the norm for the season, and could have easily been less, but for a year of exceptionally good home results. Just two Barley Bank fixtures were lost, and the successes were often most emphatic; 8-2 over Burslem Port Vale, 6-1 versus Crewe, five unopposed goals against Lincoln and on January the 13th, a 10-2 crushing of Rotherham Town. The away record was indifferent, a mid-table placing ensued and a notable 67-30 goal difference was amassed.

The team's performances became of secondary importance, when, at the end of February it was publicly expressed that the Club was close to extinction. The question of becoming a Limited Company was again raised, and defeated, and it became questionable if the Club could fulfil the rest of their fixtures. There was an irony in the fact that after being the first Club ever to pay players for their services, there were now doubts as to whether the team's wages could be paid! One of the main concerns had been the reluctance of Club members to renew their subscriptions, even though the cost was only 33p, or 50p which also included free admission to the Grandstand.

The following Campaign showed little financial improvement, and now on their last legs, they at last succumbed to a reformation into a Limited Company. Initially things went happily with revived interest in the Club, and with the shares selling well. It was, however, a moderate season so far as the team was concerned, and a ninth final position in the League resulted. The one outstanding match occurred on Boxing Day, when the Club's highest ever Football League score was recorded. Walsall, another team with problems were the visitors, and were thrashed 12-0 after a four goal half-time score; the supporters were delighted, although the visitors played the game throughout with only eight men!

But it was not long before the Darreners fortunes, on and off the field, took a turn for the worse yet again. The 1897/98 season resulted in disaster for the team as well as at the money at the gate, with an eventual second from bottom placing in the League, and a re-election application as the outcome. Darwen only escaped expulsion by a hairline, as they were voted out of the League, and only the extending of each Division by two Clubs brought them back into the fold with another vote, and also ensured that neighbours, Blackburn, were not relegated from the top Division.

Morale had been at an all time low, and at one point Earnshaw was suspended for 'insubordination'. He had demanded more money, which he eventually received, and in this way nailed yet another nail into the Club's coffin!

After the record of the past season, wholesale changes were made to the team for the coming 1898/99 campaign. But any hopes of an improvement in the Club's fortunes were soon dashed, and the coming months were to prove a nightmare and an unmitigated disaster that was to finally finish off the Darreners. Even so, things started deceptively well, with a Friendly visit of Second Division newcomers, New Brighton Tower. With a 2-0 win and a gate of £70 (over 2,000), hopes were high but were very soon dashed.

Warning bells sounded with the first game on September the 10th, a two goal defeat at mediocre Lincoln City, and rang loud and clear when the next game was lost by 4-1 at home to Woolwich Arsenal. These defeats this were followed by an 8-1 hammering at Luton. In the latter of these defeats, the team were described as: *"Fagged and worn out, suggesting players hadn't gone to bed the previous night."* But the defeats were also blamed largely on goalkeeping errors, and a replacement - Whittaker between the sticks - two weeks later, and a three goal win over Leicester, gave new reason for hope. But the team had flattered only to deceive, for it was an unprecedented run of 29 games before another victory ensued - in the last but one home game of the season.

Defeat followed defeat as the months passed by, and the manner of these reverses was unprecedented in the Club's history: 6-0 at Barnsley and Blackpool, 7-0 at New Brighton, scoreless in the eight goal thrashing at Small Heath, and to cap it all a 9-0 demolition at Newton Heath on Boxing Day. Several players had gone on strike before the latter match, due to non-payment of wages, and the Club could only raise the entrance charges.

Naturally enough the gate receipts dropped lower and lower, eventually to levels never before experienced; barely 1,500 spectators present for Manchester City's visit on October the 22nd, and half this number (producing £16) on Loughborough's appearance in early December. At this point, the Reserve Team was disbanded, to date that season the expenses for the second string had been £80, whilst total receipts were just £15. There was no doubt that the Club was on the point of extinction, but somehow they carried on. The Barley Bank owners gave the Club three days to find the rent that was owing, and miraculously the money was raised by the departure of Barnes to Bolton for £40.

Bleak days for Darwen
in the 1898/99 season.

The programme cover and line-ups
for the 10-0 defeat at Manchester
City (February 18th).......

...... and 9-0 at Newton Heath
(line-ups above) on Christmas Eve, by 9-0

During the period to Christmas, just one point was picked up at home, although the Barley Bank defeats were not so emphatic as those on the team's travels. The 4-2 home defeat to New Brighton on December the 31st was considered a near victory for these were the first goals scored for weeks by a near complete new team, due to the non-appearance of the regulars; suspension of these errant players followed.

On the first day of the New Year, Burslem Port Vale were entertained (an inevitable defeat - by 3-1), and in view of all the circumstances, and the poor weather, the attendance of around 400 (receipts of £10) was not that bad. Three days earlier with the New Brighton visit, there had been barely half that number present. The problems were never ending! An early F.A. Cup exit was made, 4-1 at home to non-League Wigan County (also the previous season's victors), which was accompanied by derision from the few remaining Barley Bank faithful, and a five goal defeat exit from the Lancashire Cup was made at Newton Heath.

By now the team was placed in the virtually unshakeable position at the bottom of the League, and there they remained. But there were still to come some highly embarrassing scorelines, including two more 6-0 defeats, and no less than three losses by ten unopposed goals each - at Manchester City, Walsall and Lough-borough. The latter defeat was perhaps the worse, for the Luffs managed only six victories all season, and finished only one place higher than the Darreners!

At the beginning of the year, the plight of the Club did not go completely unnoticed. With the past terrible problems of fielding a full and capable team in mind, Derby County generously offered two of their players. In the next match, on January the 7th, at home to Lincoln City, there was initially a new spirit in the team. With only 20 minutes remaining, Darwen were leading by one goal, but their joy turned to despair when two goals were then scored by the visitors.

By now the finances were in a hopeless state, the Lincoln gate had brought in only £14, and there were serious doubts as to whether enough cash would be forthcoming for the long trip to Woolwich, let alone paying the Players their wages. Due to the bad weather, two home games were then postponed, and hence no benefit from the - albeit - pitiful gate receipts. Aston Villa stepped in and offered £100 for Whitley - one of the few players left who could command a transfer fee - with £50 down (which was used to pay the team some wages) and the balance if the player proved to be suitable. At home to Glossop at the end of February another gate of only £10 was received, and for the match one week later at Walsall, it was doubtful once again, if even a full team could be raised.

The final straw came when a former Player all but brought the Club to its final end. Grier, who had not played for Darwen since the disbanding of the Reserves, was given a free transfer, upon which, the player - not unreasonably - demanded his back pay. There was nothing in the kitty to give, whereupon Grier called in the Bailiffs in an effort to raise some money from the Club. An Auctioneer was appointed to conduct the sale of the Club's assets. He found that there was virtually nothing to dispose of! The proposed Auction was postponed and an attempt made to make an amicable settlement with the player. When this failed, Grier pursued his somewhat fruitless attempt to recover that owing to him. Eventually an Auction was held, and the few pathetic possessions of Darwen F.C. - the football kit, dressing tents, and even the railings to the pitch - were sold. After legal expenses, there was little left for Grier; an action in which all parties were the losers, except the Auctioneer and the Solicitors!

The final, and second win of the season - 4-1 at home to Luton Town - was a quite amazing feat in the circumstances. A Shareholders meeting was held in mid-April to consider the following season, but by now it was apparent that there wasn't to be another one for Darwen F.C. The last ever game for the Club was played on April the 22nd at home to Newton Heath. It was a spirited performance by a hopeless team as they earned a point in a 1-1 draw, the second consecutive home game without a defeat! The team on that sorry day consisted of:- McIvor, Woolfall, Cawthorne, Moore, Liversey, Ratcliffe, Wilson, Bleasdale, Pilkington, plus Collinson - notably just ten names!

After this last match, the Books were audited, the Club shown to be bankrupt, and the few pounds in hand were given to the Secretary as part payment of wages. There was no option for the Club but to cease operations, and at the Football League meeting which considered re-elections, Darwen did not bother to apply for continued membership.

As has happened on many occasions, the Phoenix of a new team arose from the ashes of the old. In a matter of days - on May the 3rd 1899 - a Public Meeting was held to consider the formation of a new Club. The attendance initially consisted of a few enthusiasts, but eventually became packed, and those attending included, by invitation, Mr. Duckworth - the Landlord of Barley Bank. The suggestion that the new Club, which would not be a Limited Company, could continue to make use of the former Club's Ground, was immediately quashed by the Landlord. Even with assurances that the back rent of the former Darwen F.C. would be paid, that the initial lease need only be for one year (at the same rental of £40), and that the new organisation would re-erect fencing, were not accepted. Not surprisingly in the circumstances, Mr. Duckworth no doubt had had his fill of an unstable Football Club!

The creators of the new Club were ambitious, for they intended that the new team would play in the highly rated Lancashire League. For this - and in order to present a truly representative 'Town' team - a proper enclosure would be required. Reasonably the promoters argued that to leave the re-formation for one year, while Ground problems were sorted out, would probably result in a loss of impetus.

The problem was solved by the new Darwen Football Club in effect taking over the successful Junior team of Darwen Woodfold (from the Heyfold district) who had been renting a field, which was known as the Anchor Ground, located to the North, in Lower Darwen. Now equipped with a home venue, it became necessary for the 'Woodfold' to be dropped from the Club's name; the Lancashire League insisted on this change as they considered that without the omission, the Club did not sound like a true, senior, representative organisation. With the hope and expectations that the Club could attract subscriptions of £300, and attendances of between one and two thousand - with travelling costs of only £1-50 for each game - the new Professional team was born.

On September the 2nd, the new Darwen F.C. got off to a rousing start with a victory at Earlestown, and completed the 'double' one week later. Within a short time a new Stand was nearing completion. Entrance to the Ground was fixed at 4d. (under 2p.) and to the enclosure - 7d. Success at the sport which had been all but forgotten in Darwen was revived as the team headed the table after a few matches, and later played through to the 4th qualifying round of the F.A. Cup. The euphoria was shortlived, however, for it was a generally poor end of season run, that finally placed the Club 4th in the League table.

Early days for the reformed Darreners - an 'away' programme of the 1904/05 season

For several years the Club flourished. An early highlight being their F.A. Cup run through to the supplementary round (pre-first), when on the 5th of January 1901, old foes in the shape of Woolwich Arsenal were again visitors to Darwen. An attendance of over 6,000 (receipts of £131) was attracted to the match, but the Darreners could not pull off a shock result and went down by two goals. The next year saw the Championship of the Lancashire League achieved in an unbeaten run, and runners-up one year later, the last season of the Lancashire League.

But a turning point came in the 1907/08 season when relegation to the Second Division of the Lancashire Combination - which was entered in 1903 - was narrowly avoided. Finances once again became a prominent feature, and the Reserve team had already been disbanded. One year later the drop could not be avoided, but even so reasonable support was there with home attendances often reaching 2,000, far more than in the latter days of the Football League.

The First World War brought an end to the Club, but on their reassembly in 1920, the enthusiasm was quite phenomenal. 7,000 were present for the first game on the 28th of August, when Accrington Stanley spoilt the party with a 3-1 defeat. But the fans faith was rewarded with an extended Lancashire Cup run, including an unbelievable record crowd of nearly 10,000 for the appearance of Fleetwood on the 13th of November. Darwen enjoyed ten years in the single division Lancashire Combination, during which time support peaked, with attendances often around the 5,000 mark. Two Championship winning seasons followed, and in the latter campaign their exploits captured the imagination of the whole of England - much as their predecessors had some fifty years previously.

Following a run through to the first round proper of the F.A. Cup, and subsequent conquests over Peterborough and Chester, their opponents for the third round were the dream of every lesser Club - the mighty Arsenal at Highbury. The 'old' Darwen had of course met the London Club on a number of occasions, but now the Club's respective roles were somewhat different. Arsenal, the current Football League Champions at the start of a period of dominance that had never been matched to that time - versus - a non-League team, with Darwen cherishing little more than recent success at their own level and memories of memorable contests eons ago.

Many words of confidence emulated from the Mill town, words which were, it was perhaps hoped, to promote a slight lack of confidence in the Gunners and bolster the spirit of the no-hopers. The town turned up in force to cheer their team off on their journey to the Capital, with 700 supporters also making the trip to London. In the days when sport truly fulfilled its definition, the crowd of 37,486 gave the men from the North a warm welcome as the teams ran onto the pitch, but the Londoners gave little more! The early exchanges presented the Darreners with a real chance of causing a sensation by going ahead, but the opportunity was missed. From then on it was all one way traffic, until half-time when the Arsenal had built up a more than comfortable eight goal lead! Arsenal slackened the pace in the second half, but none-the-less when Dale reduced the arrears, from a corner, the Darwen team could at least claim a moral victory of sorts. The 1-11 reversal was not seen as a total defeat, the £25 team from Lancashire had scored against the £40,000 Londoners. The first Darwen home game after 'the' match attracted 3,000 fans, who gave their heroes a rousing reception.

The season had started with the Club holding both the League and League Cup awards, had ended with another title win, plus the distinction of having progressed further in the F.A. Cup than any other Lancashire Combination team to that time.

As the Second World War approached, the club again found themselves in financial difficulties. The late 1930's had produced a fall in prominence, a corresponding reduction in support, and by early 1939, a familiar cry from yesteryear: *"How long will the Club struggle on?"* The Club announced at the start of the 1939/40 season, that unless the receipts at each game produced £35 (a few months earlier they had dropped as low as £13), Darwen F.C. would be, *"waging a losing struggle, and would finally pass out of existence"*. The League Champions, South Liverpool, visited the Anchor Ground for the first League match - and the homesters won 3-2 - producing healthy receipts of £53. But after the third game - at Bacup on September the 2nd - War intervened, and on September the 8th the Club announced that until further notice the Anchor Ground would be closed.

This declaration was shortlived, for by the end of the month they were playing in the newly arranged Lancashire Combination - East Division, with nine other teams. Following the match versus Rochdale on December the 22nd, the Directors announced that they would be withdrawing from the League. With gates now averaging £10, and the difficulty in fielding a full team each week, commonsense prevailed, rather than the dogged determination and eventual complete failure experienced forty years earlier.

From the re-forming of the Club in 1946, sixteen unremarkable years followed - although the early period often attracted attendances of around 4,000 to the Anchor Ground - but culminated in relegation to the Lancashire Combination Division 2 at the completion of the 1962/63 season. Several years spent between the two Divisions finished with the club establishing themselves in the top group in the late 1960's. There was a revival of former heydays, with the Championship of the Combination being won in 1973 and 1975.

A short flirtation in the concluding years with the Cheshire County League, were followed with the Club becoming founder-members of the North-West Counties League for the start of the 1982/83 season. Although commencing in the 1st Division, after just two years the struggle proved too great, and relegation to the 2nd

Division was suffered in 1984. Three years later they were back in the top Division, where they have remained. Even so relegation again has always been a strong possibility, with a best final placing of 5th (in 1989), but conversely several seasons well in the bottom half of the table.

Geographically, Darwen the town is somewhat off the beaten track, and its Football team is now just another also-ran. But the town which in many ways has retained its old world flavour of a century ago, may recall the days when its sports fans could rejoice at their prominence and of having one of the top teams in the newly organised pastime, called Football!

BARLEY BANK

The first Ground of the Club, Lynwood, was located just to the North-West of Barley Bank. The 'Ground' was probably no more than an open field, and was only used for a short time before a permanent move was made to Barley Bank. This was the venue of the Darwen Cricket Ground - for several years the teams of both sports were run as one Club - and therefore Darwen, in common with many other Clubs of that era, groundshared. Although inevitably covering a large area, it had limited facilities for spectators. There was one, covered and seated Grandstand that held approximately 1,200 and some raised banking at one end of the stand. Presumably the rest of the standing areas were flat, and although there was the room to accommodate the claimed record attendance of around 14,000, many of the spectators must have had a very poor view! On a few occasions, in the early days, forms from schools were placed on lorries and used as temporary Grandstands. But on the Club's admission into the Football League, a more permanent structure was erected, which none the less was still referred to as being temporary and probably had to be dismantled during the Cricket Season. This was located on the 'Clough' side (no doubt opposite the main Stand) and the dressing tents which were also introduced in 1891 were at the 'Clough' end - behind the South-east goal, i.e. the Pavilion End where doubtless the dressing rooms (which the tents replaced) were also positioned

The condition of the pitch often left a lot to be desired. Several matches were played in deep mud, and for one game in 1896, so much water lay on the surface that a new pitch (either within or outside the Ground) had to be hastily set-out.

(Top) The Barley Bank Ground in c.1878 (The goalposts can just be seen, plus the top of the barrel-roofed Stand, nearside of pitch). (Below) Photograph from the same vantage point taken in 1988. Although there is now no trace of the Ground, the (now extended) terraces of houses remain.

The main entrance would have been at the junction of Barley Bank and Hindle Streets, whilst another entrance was probably located at the end of Bright Street. After the Club moved to the Anchor Ground at their re-formation in 1899, Barley Bank remained for several years - at least until 1904, when a pre-season trial was played (the Anchor Ground lease had not been signed) but was developed soon after, into, as now - mainly rows of terraced houses and a school. Nothing of Barley Bank remains save its namesake, the street at what was the Pavilion End of the Ground. However with the aid of a photograph of the site - when it was still the football Ground - and a current view taken from the same viewpoint, the outline of the Ground can quite easily be imagined.

The Anchor Ground which has been the Club's home venue since 1899, initially had a small seated and covered Stand, flanked each side probably with uncovered seating. Within a few years another covered enclosure was erected on the opposite side, and by 1931 there was a small building, possibly a Pavilion in the North-west corner. Over the years there have been many changes. The main Stand was replaced with another at the South-west end of that side with a long covered enclosure opposite, and there was the addition of a covered enclosure behind the South goal.

PROGRAMMES

It is very likely that these were issued from around the 1890's and up to the present, but needless to say should any have survived from those early days, they would be extremely valuable collector's items.

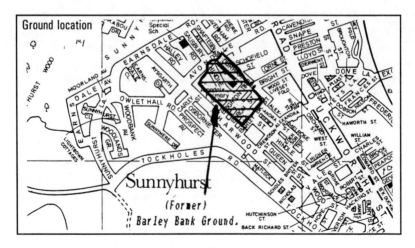

172

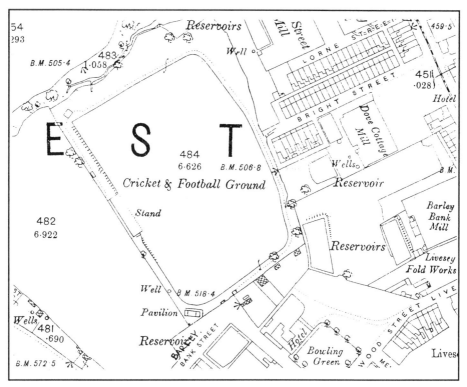

(Top) c.1890 map of Ground (prior to terrace house on South-west side).
(Below) The original Stand c.1902, that was moved from Barley Bank to the Anchor Road Ground.

LEEDS CITY 1905/06 Season (First in Football League)

(Back) Directors - R.Younger & R.Kirk, Morgan, Whittaker (Dir.),
Dooley, MacDonald, Austin, Walker, Singleton, R.Dow (Dir.), G.Swift (Trainer).
(Middle) G.Gillies(Sec/Manager),Parnell,Watson,Hargraves,Ray,Morris,Clay, O.Tordorf (Dir)
(Front) The 'City Dog', Stringfellow, Drain, Henderson

LEEDS CITY

1904 - 1919

1904/05 -	West Yorkshire League
1905/06 - 1914/15	Football League Division 2
1915/16 - 1918/19	(Wartime) Midland Section Tournaments
1919/20 -	Football League Division 2 *

* Did not complete fixtures, record expunged.

Football League Record:

	Played	W	D	L	F	A	Pts	Posn.	Ave.Att.
1905/06	38	17	9	12	59	47	43	6	10,025
1906/07	38	13	10	15	55	63	36	10	9,965
1907/08	38	12	8	18	53	65	32	12	10,780
1908/09	38	14	7	17	43	53	35	12	11,055
1909/10	38	10	6	20	46	80	27	17	7,245
1910/11	38	15	7	16	58	56	37	11	9,295
1911/12	38	10	8	20	50	78	28	19	7,885
Successfully re-elected									
1912/13	38	15	10	13	70	64	40	6	13,405
1913/14	38	20	7	11	76	46	47	4	15,845
1914/15	38	14	4	20	65	64	32	15	6,835
1919/20 *	8	4	2	2	17	10	10	-	-

* Fixtures not completed.

Number of Football League matches played: 388 (including those in 1919/20 season)

SUMMARY OF FACTS:-

Ground: Elland Road, Leeds.
Colours: Blue and Gold striped Shirts, White Shorts.
The Nickname: The City or The Peacocks.

Significant matches:
First League Game: 2nd September 1905 versus Bradford City (Away) lost 1-0.
Last League Game: 8th October 1919 versus Wolverhampton Wanderers (Away) won 4-2.
Record Attendances:
('West - East' Pitch): 30 December 1905 versus Bradford City (Football League) 22,000
(Overall): 1 February 1907 versus Bradford City (Football League) 35,000

MAIN ACHIEVEMENTS:

F.A.Cup: 2nd Round - 1908/09, 1911/12, 1913/14, 1914/15
(Wartime) Midland Section Principal Tournament Champions: 1916/17, 1917/18,
(Wartime) Midland Section Subsidiary (North Division) Tournament Champions: 1915/16
Best Football League Win:
1913/14 versus Nottingham Forest (Home): 8-0
Worst Football League Defeat:
1908/09 versus Oldham Athletic (Away) and 1912/13 versus Stockport County (away): 6-0

It is quite surprising that the town of Leeds should host such a -generally - successful, and fervently supported football team, for in the late 19th century - at a time when the game was flourishing countrywide - the local populace refused to join in!

The late 1870's produced a period when - quite unashamedly - representatives of the different football codes (i.e. Rugby and Soccer) would do their upmost to promote 'their' football. Such demonstrations were particularly prominent in large northern towns and cities where support for the alternative versions was particularly sought. Soccer tended to be the more aggressive of the two codes, the rugby men tending to accept the status quo; if soccer was the dominant game in a particular town - so be it - whereas the round ball enthusiasts would use all means to swing the pendulum in their favour.

Earlier, in 1864, when the first football club in Leeds was formed, under the name of 'Leeds Athletic', the formation did not escape the notice of Sheffield F.C. who invited the newcomers to a match in their town. With no nationwide rules at this time, those used by the Leeds team were akin to rugby, and consequently they lost heavily to the men from the steel town who favoured the 'other' football.

Several further attempts to persuade the sportsmen of Leeds to favour the dribbling code were made, not least Sheffield (again), who - on Boxing Day 1877 - supplied not only two teams of players, but the umpires and goalposts as well, and played an exhibition match at Holbeck Recreation Ground (located off Top Moor Side and Brown Lane) - a venue used principally for Cricket, including County matches (the site is now built over). Apparently, whilst the experiment was well received, it made no lasting impression.

The 1880's saw the town still dominated by the handling code, although a brief attempt at the dribbling method was again made with the formation of the Leeds Association Football Club. Despite playing such prestigious Friendlies as those against the likes of Blackburn Rovers and Preston North End, the Club soon faded and folded in 1886. The next serious attempt was in October 1894, when another Leeds A.F.C. came upon the scene. They made an immediate impact, joining - and winning - the first West Yorkshire League in its first season. This club changed grounds on several occasions, finishing at Headingley, the home of Leeds Rugby Club. Unable to attract sufficient support they folded in 1898.

Meanwhile in one part of the City, Hunslet F.C. (who were formed in 1889) were making progress. 'The Twinklers', as they were known, became a formidable amateur club (twice reaching the quarter-finals of the F.A.Amateur Cup), and in 1895 they moved from their Wellington Ground in Low Road, to groundshare with Hunslet Rugby Club at Parkside. Within a few years they were in effect driven out and went the way of the other round ball clubs in Leeds. However, on this occasion their demise led directly to the formation of a soccer club that was to eventually take their place in the Football League - Leeds City.

With a firm conviction that the handling code could support a Senior Club in the City, the committee and supporters of the former Hunslet F.C. reformed as Leeds City, gained entry to the West Yorkshire League for the 1904/05 season, and set about finding for themselves a permanent ground, a factor which had generally been a stumbling block of the earlier teams in Leeds. Holbeck Rugby Club, 'The Imps', were members of the Second Division of the Northern Rugby League and their home was at Elland Road. Previously they too had played at Holbeck Recreation Ground, but in 1896, after becoming a Limited Company, they purchased the formerly namcd Old Peacock Ground - which was named after a public house opposite - for £1,100. This Club finished the 1903/04 season as joint runners-up in their division, but lost out on promotion following a play-off match with St.Helens. Not relishing another season in the lower division, there was a great deal of disagreement in the camp, with many of the members arguing for a switch to Association rules. Such disagreement led to the Club disbanding during the Summer of 1904, leaving the way clear for Leeds City to adopt the Elland Road enclosure as their home Ground, at a rent of £75 per annum, in October 1904. Elland Road was in fact first used for football (soccer) by Hunslet F.C., when they beat Harrogate 1-0 in the Final of the West Yorkshire Cup on the 23rd April 1898.

The committee of Leeds City were determined to succeed where others had failed, and in an effort to raise their game, a number of Friendly matches were arranged during the season with Football League clubs. The Club's confidence rose, and in April 1905, Leeds City became a Limited Company with a share capital of 10,000 being offered in £1 shares. At last headway was being made in the largest City in the country without representation in the Football League. The club adopted the nickname 'The Peacocks', which was taken from the former name of the Elland Road Ground.

The City's debut season started somewhat hesitantly, for after a fortunate 2-2 draw in their initial League match - on September 1st at Scratcherd Lane, Morley - they then lost the next two matches. The first 'home' game (played at the Wellington Ground, Low Road, Hunslet) was lost 2-1 to Altofts and on September 10th another defeat by the same score was recorded at Elland Ramdonians. It wasn't until the 19th November that the first true home match was played - by which time the Club were in occupation of the Elland Road enclosure - when a 3-0 defeat to Heckmondwike was the disappointing result. By this time 8 League games had been played, and only 2 victories plus one draw had been achieved. By the season's end The Peacocks had recovered sufficiently to finish just below mid-table, with a final record of 7 wins, 7 draws and 10 defeats, and a goal difference of 33-47.

Fred Spiksley
England International and played
for City in first season

The Club entered for the F.A.Cup, but lost 3-1 to Rockingham Colliery in the qualifying round, and their other cup exploits saw them lose to Bradford City reserves in the West Yorkshire Cup, and bow out of the Leeds Hospital Cup in the 3rd round. Of particular note were the many Friendly games which were played mostly against Football League teams, and which were considered of prime importance. Of the 16 matches played, 13 were against strong League teams, and although the record was far from impressive; won 2 (Burton United by 7-2 and Barnsley) - lost 11, no doubt the experience gained put them in good stead.

The Club's obsession with these Friendly matches led to a farcical situation, and it is amazing that the West Yorkshire League Officials allowed it! League matches were frequently cancelled if a more prestigious friendly had been arranged, and if not called off then a Reserve Eleven played the fixture; usually the competitive match was a home fixture (in view of the early run of away games played), but the match was played at the City's opponents Ground in order that Elland Road could be used for the Friendly game. The situation led to a backlog of League fixtures, and three were never played (despite two games played in one day on a few occasions). On the 5th of June 1905, the Club officially became a limited liability company. Norris Hepworth was the first Chairman, and two other local men made up the majority shareholders - Ralph Younger (landlord of the Old Peacock Hotel) and a prominent Yorkshire Evening Post journalist, A.W.Pullin ('Old Ebor').

It happened that the Football League extended its membership in the Summer of 1905 by four, and this gave Leeds City a rapid and somewhat surprising lift into the elite of the football world. Or was it so surprising? Around this period, the Football League never disguised the fact that they wished to see Senior representation in all major Cities, and particularly in Leeds where Rugby League had easily held sway over the local populace. At least Leeds City were an established club - albeit just of one season, and their experience gained in only a minor league - but this was not necessarily a pre-requisite. Two years before, Bradford City had stormed into the League, capturing the most votes, yet at that time they had not even kicked a ball in anger! Formerly Manningham Rugby Club, the Football League jumped at the chance of welcoming them to the fold when the Club reformed as a round ball outfit. Similarly Chelsea were welcomed with open arms in 1905, for the Ground was already there - Stamford Bridge - and with only one team from the capital (Woolwich Arsenal) further representation from London was gladly welcomed, despite the fact that Chelsea had also never served their apprenticeship in the non-League world. Clapton Orient were another Club from London - but already established - that were voted in, in 1905, but the method used was somewhat bizarre.

Although the League intended to propose to increase its membership by four, strict protocol dictated that firstly the re-election procedure should take place. On this vote of the three re-election candidates Burton United and Doncaster Rovers lost their place, but Port Vale (21 votes) kept theirs. Also elected were Leeds City - who topped the polling with 25 votes and Chelsea. The proposal to increase the membership was then carried, and immediately a new vote was taken, when Hull City (another soccer outpost town), Burton United, Stockport County and Clapton Orient were given the seal of approval.

And so, barely a year since their formation, Leeds City took their place in the Football League. Frank Jarvis's post as secretary was taken over by Gilbert Gillies, the Chesterfield manager, who was enticed to Elland Road, and with a greatly reinforced squad, The Peacocks kicked off with a 1-0 defeat at Bradford City. Newcomers included Henry Bromage (goalkeeper from Burton United - who was near ever-present for the season), John MacDonald who joined the Club from Blackburn Rovers, Dick Ray from Chesterfield, Harry Stringfellow, the ex-Everton and Swindon Town centre-half, right-winger Fred Parnell (from Derby County), Dickie Morris (Welsh International from Liverpool) and Harry Singleton from Queens Park Rangers. The full line-up for this historic match consisted of: Bromage, MacDonald, Ray, Morgan, Stringfellow, Henderson, Parnell, Watson, Hargrave, R.Morris and Singleton.

One week later the City entertained West Bromwich Albion, and before what must have been a very disappointing crowd - only 6,802 - they lost again this by 2-0. The visit of Lincoln City the next Monday at least produced the first point for the newcomers, with Drain scoring both goals, but the crowd numbered only around 3,000. At last the

J. HENDERSON,   S. CUBBERLEY.

Both played in City's First League match

team got on its winning ways, for three victories followed, and the second of this trio - versus Hull City - produced a worthy attendance numbering 13,654 for the all Yorkshire clash. The Club maintained fairly good form throughout the season, although never seriously threatening the leaders, and finished in 6th position, from 17 victories, 9 draws and 12 defeats. The crowds varied enormously from a low of only 2,000 for Chesterfield's February visit, to an enormous 22,000 - a record attendance - for the local derby with Bradford City on the 30th December 1905, which produced record takings of £487. Whilst the Football League team's crowd varied, the local Rugby Club's took a definite tumble, the average on the season dropping to around 5,500 from 9,000 a year earlier.

On paper the Club had a good F.A.Cup run after playing six matches. However, these started in the 1st qualifying round - in which Morley were beaten (11-0), followed by three attempts before Mexborough were overcome. They lost out to Hull City in a home replay, but as this was only the 3rd qualifying round, their exploits in the competition are put in true perspective.

The Peacocks started the 1906/07 season with substantially the same team, and for the first game (a 1-1 draw with Bradford City at Elland Road before 20,000), included in the line-up were Andy Clark from Plymouth and Jimmy Kennedy - a Scot who had arrived from Brighton. It wasn't until the seventh match before the first win was recorded, when Burton United were beaten 3-0 at Peel Croft, and two more victories followed. But the team then hit another bad patch, and by December, after five straight defeats, they were languishing in trouble near the foot of the table. Indifferent results continued until mid-February, and a final run-in which produced 6 victories, 3 draws and only two defeats, which ensured a rise up the table, to a final 10th place. Despite a less successful season, the gates held up well and only dropped on average to just below 10,000 from just above, one season earlier. The F.A.Cup was best forgotten, for their first round match was lost 4-1 at Bristol City! One year later the situation was just as grim, for on this occasion they lost 2-1 at Oldham.

The start of the 1907/08 season saw a number of new faces, although throughout the campaign, only 22 different players were used. Yet despite their lack of any honours again - they finished in the lower half of the final table (at 12th) - committed support became a feature with the crowds averaging nearly 11,000. An all-time record crowd was present for local rivals Bradford City's visit on the 1st of February, when an enormous attendance of 35,000 was present. The result of the match, on the 1st February, was a 1-0 defeat, the third in a trio of such losing matches. The League season again passed by unremarkably, but at least with more consistency.

The Club's fourth season in the Football League saw them having settled in as an average Second Division team - neither looking like promotion candidates, nor exposing themselves to any risk of re-election. Even so the average attendances at home games continued to rise, albeit only marginally this time, to just over 11,000, although the numbers at different matches were not so remarkable with figures generally between 8,000 and 14,000. Things could have turned out so much better if it had not been for a terrible run starting in mid-December, when seven consecutive matches were lost. At the end of the season, the Club lay 12th in the League again, but worse was to come. The 1909/10 season started with an encouraging three goal home defeat of Lincoln City, but before a poor crowd of 6,000. After six matches, only a moderate start was made (2 victories and one draw), but this was followed with a run of 11 matches when the only two points obtained were from a 3-2 home victory over Blackpool. More players were brought in to try to raise the City above its lowly League placing - 28 different ones were used by the season's end - and eventually some more wins were produced. A lowly position of 17th in the Second Division was reflected in the attendances which dipped dramatically, and culminated in only 2,000 being present for the 1-1 draw with Leicester City at Elland Road on April 30th.

The first serious financial doubts came to the fore during the Summer, when additional money was asked of the Club's shareholders - together with £8,000 guarantees from the Directors - in an attempt to shore up the ailing Club, and provide additional revenue for team improvements. Manager Gillies moved on around this time, and was replaced with Frank Scott-Walford in the combined post of secretary/manager, but his time only lasted for around two years.

The team rarely posed a threat to any opponents in the F.A.Cup, for throughout their brief existence, their best run only carried them through to a second round replay. In 1909, after first disposing of Oldham Athletic 2-0 in an Elland Road replay, they then met West Ham United. Drawn at home to the non-League team from London, the match created enormous local interest, and before an attendance of 31,471, the City could only manage a 1-1 draw. The replay finished in a somewhat embarrassing 2-1 extra time defeat. The next F.A.Cup win came on 1st January 1911, when fellow second Division team Glossop was overcome by a single goal at Elland Road (before a crowd of 21,000), with defeat in the next round to First Division West Bromwich Albion. The Albion were also the victors two years later - but only due to both the opposition's two goals being scored in the last two minutes - after The Peacocks had beaten Gainsborough Trinity (who had departed from the League two years earlier) in the 1st round. This match attracted a record attendance of 14,000 to the Northolme Ground when the Lincolnshire club entertained their high-flying League opponents. But two goals from Jackson, and one each for Law and McLeod ensured a 4-2 victory to the visitors. The Club's only other second round appearance came one year later when Derby County were first beaten, before the City's single goal defeat at Queen's Park Rangers.

Meanwhile back in the Second Division things improved somewhat from the disappointing finish in 1910, before turning for the worse again! Four straight defeats at the start of the following campaign saw the Club bottom of the League, and they only rose slightly in the weeks leading up to the New Year. However, a much improved second half of the season saw the team finish in a respectable 11th final position. The best home attendance came on Boxing Day, when six goals were shared with Chelsea before 18,000, but the Londoners dwarfed these numbers in the return match in April. Chelsea, battling for promotion alongside West Bromwich and Bolton attracted 50,000 to Stamford Bridge, and won the match 4-1 (Chelsea finished third that season).

The 1911/12 season was little short of disastrous. A poor start was again made, and after the Christmas games only five victories had been obtained from the 20 matches played. But this season there was to be no respite, and the number of winning matches had only been doubled by the season's end. One win in the last eleven games - a surprising 4-3 victory at Barnsley - doomed the City to a re-election application, their 'reward' for finishing 19th (second from bottom). Leeds City's continued membership was never seriously in doubt, and they gained 33 votes, the highest number. Gainsborough Trinity, the other re-election candidates were not so lucky, in fact their treatment seemed very harsh, for despite this being only their second re-election bid, they were firmly rebuffed. Lincoln City were re-admitted, with 27 votes, whereas poor old Trinity received only 9. The season took its toll on manager Scott-Walford who resigned at the end of the season; the pressures of trying to keep a top club going on limited resources affected his health.

Financially the Club had reached its nadir. It was revealed that the Chairman, Norris Hepworth, had already ploughed the enormous sum of £15,000 of his own money into the Club. An extraordinary general meeting was convened when the full extent of the problems were exposed. The Club's liabilities came to nearly £16,000, with £11,321 being lost over the years since the City's formation. With assets standing at only £7,084, the bank had announced that it was to call in the overdraft that stood at £7,000. Such a move would have effectively finished Leeds City F.C., and the meeting agreed that they should be wound up. Hepworth generously provided more money, and a receiver was appointed - Mr Tom Coombes. Ironically Leeds Cricket, Football and Athletic Club made an offer around this time to take over the affairs of the Club, and use Headingley as a home ground, but no serious moves were made in this direction.

Before the Football League re-election meeting a new manager was appointed, a name that was to rise to the top during the following twenty plus years - Herbert Chapman. Chapman had already achieved a great deal of success at the then little known Southern League club Northampton Town, and despite his indiscretions and years of little success at Ell-

Herbert Chapman

-and Road, he later became arguably the greatest manager of all time, from his spells with Huddersfield Town and Arsenal. Quite innocently Chapman soon fell foul of the League authorities, when it was discovered that after the arrival of three new signings (Scott, Law and Lintott) they were each paid a full year's wage of £208, despite two months having elapsed.

It was discovered that the Club had transgressed the rules, which only allowed a maximum weekly payment of £4. Realising this error the Club reported the facts to the Football League, and were 'rewarded' with a fine of £125 and expenses (which they could ill-afford to pay), and the players were penalised by having to pay back their extra payments.

A final placing of 6th in the next campaign was a vast improvement, despite an opening defeat of 4-0 at Fulham. But this shaky start was followed with three victories and two drawn games, and the crowds started returning to Elland Road, with 15,000 present for the encounter with Stockport County. This game finished 2-1 in Leeds' favour, but the return match - in mid-February - saw the team crash to a 6-0 defeat, their all-time worse League defeat. Although only in a mid-table position at the time, this result was something of a shock, for Stockport had a poor season, and at the end had to seek re-election. The rest of the fixtures that season saw the City defeated in only two more matches, but their late successful burst - just one last game defeat in eight - was too late for any possibility of promotion.

But the Club had shown that they could capture the imagination of the local sportsmen with a generally successful team, for their average home attendance - the highest up to then - of 13,405, was the second best in the Division. On only two occasions did the number fall below five figures, and a dramatic contrast was made regarding support in early March. For the home game versus Hull City a joint best crowd of 20,000 was present at Elland Road, yet seven days later a paltry 2,000 turned up for their encounter at Glossop. This upturn at the gate had its effect in the Club's coffers, for they reported a £400 profit on the season.

The 1913/14 season was to become the Club's best ever. A good start was made which saw only 2 defeats and one draw in the opening 13 matches, and culminated on the 29th November with their record League victory, 8-0 over a struggling Nottingham Forest. 14,000 were present at Elland Road to see the prolific goalscorer McLeod hit four, aided by a brace from Price and single successes from Hampson and Spiers.

Billy McLeod was without doubt the City's most prolific goalscorer, netting 171 League goals in 289 appearances. He arrived at Leeds in November 1906 for a £350 fee (plus the gate money from a friendly match), from Lincoln, where in three months he made 13 appearances in the Second Division and scored 8 goals. The 21 year-old Hebburn born two footed centre-forward soon became a favourite with the Elland Road crowd, becoming the Club's leading goalscorer in all his nine Football League seasons with them. He finally moved on to Notts County in 1919 when Leeds City folded, and was regarded as one of the best uncapped players of the period, although he was once the named reserve for the England team. McLeod netted 27 goals during the 1913/14 season as the team made its first serious bid for promotion. Their main downfall was in early 1914, when three defeats were suffered in succession and five in seven games, and this setback proved too big to redeem. The final six games produced no defeats, but only three victories, and at the final count the team trailed runners-up and third place Bradford Park Avenue and Arsenal respectively by just two points. But there was no doubting that this was the Club's best ever season, and this was reflected in the average crowds which topped 15,000 at Elland Road.

From a near 'down and out' club, the City had re-emerged, and new interest in their success came from different quarters. In August a syndicate, which was led by the President of the West Riding F.A., offered Coombes (the Club's receiver) £1,000 plus an annual rent of £250 for the Elland Road Ground, which was accepted.

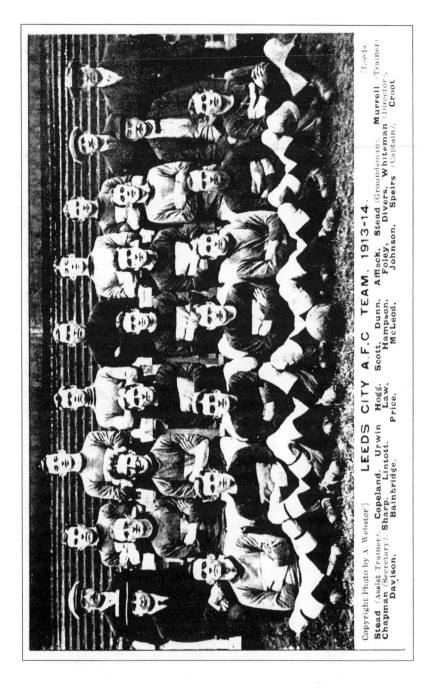

Copyright Photo by A. Webster]　　　LEEDS CITY A.F.C TEAM. 1913-14.　　　[Leeds.

Stead (Assist Trainer), **Copeland.** **Urwin** **Hogg.** **Scott.** **Dunn.** **Affleck.** **Stead** (Groundsman). **Murrell** (Trainer)
Chapman (Secretary). **Sharp.** **Lintott.** **Law.** **Hampson.** **Foley.** **Divers.** **Whiteman** (Director).
Davison. **Bainbridge.** **Price.** **McLeod.** **Johnson.** **Speirs** (Captain). **Croot**

The 1914/15 season was no doubt affected by the onslaught of War which was to adversely affect all Clubs, not least Leeds City. After such an encouraging year high hopes were expressed in the Summer when the team was expected to carry on where they left off. But just the reverse was the outcome, and the campaign got off disastrously, for the first four matches were lost, City were bottom in the table, and both home matches had produced attendances of only 8,000 each.

A moderate recovery had been made by the end of the year, to around mid-table, by which time seven victories had been achieved. The season to that point was one of peculiar contrasts, for despite a majority of defeats (nine), the worst was a 6-3 setback at Birmingham. Yet the victories produced some emphatic scorelines - 5-0 and 7-2 at home to Grimsby and Leicester respectively, 6-2 in the Club's all-time record Football League away win (at Hull), and the double over Glossop, both matches ending 3-0.

High scores continued to be a feature of this indifferent season, although the rest were generally reverses, and by the end of April the team finished in a very disappointing 15th in the table. But of particular concern was the support at the Elland Road turnstiles. In common with virtually every Club, the worry and threat of war had seen the crowds take a tumble, but at Leeds this was particularly noticeable, with an average of under 7,000 this represented a drop in excess of 50%.

Many clubs, including Leeds City, continued playing during the years of the First World War. Such action was generally frowned upon countrywide, when opinions were voiced regarding the many young men who were giving up their lives in Flanders and the like, whilst others were staying at home and playing and watching football. A more reasonable assessment was made just over twenty years later, when it was recognised during the Second World War, that the majority of those still in Britain were either incapacitated or following important protected occupations, and the sport was providing a degree of morale boosting, plus fund-raising for the war effort.

A localised War-time competition was organised in the Midlands during the four seasons from 1915/16 to 1918/19. During these years many players were used - up to 40 per season - and many were 'guesting' for different clubs, particularly City who were represented by a number of international players. Attendances were naturally well below peacetime numbers, five figure crowds being rare, and around 4,000 to 6,000 being the norm.

Each War-time season was split into two separate tournaments (in effect two mini 'seasons'), due to the low numbers of participating clubs. Leeds City had a successful time during these years, becoming Champions in two of the four Principal Tournaments, and once topping the lesser Subsidiary Tournament.

By 1919, the War was over and during the Summer that year preparations got underway throughout the country, for the return of a full programme of football. The War years had taken their toll on the Leeds City playing staff, and there were only 5 players in the opening game of the season that had played in the League for the Club in 1914/15. A 4-2 defeat at Blackpool provided a poor start, but the troubles on the horizon would far surpass this setback.

The first home match, on September 3rd brought Coventry City to Elland Road, and an 8,000 crowd went home happy with the comprehensive 3-0 - McLeod scoring a brace - City victory. Three days later Blackpool were beaten 1-0 in the return League fixture, when the crowd had increased by 25%. McLeod again scored twice against Coventry when The Peacocks completed the double over The Bantams, in their 4-0 victory at Highfield Road. On the 13th of September, the Club's hopes received a jolt, for they were defeated by Hull City 2-1 at home, although a week later in the return match, Edmonsen secured a point for the Leeds team in the 1-1 draw.

A crowd of 12,000 was present for the next match, at home to Wolverhampton Wanderers on the 27th September. The fans must have been in a fairly happy mood, for the early season table saw their team at least in the top half. The game finished 1-1, the Leeds goal being scored by Price, and nobody present could surely have realised that this would be the Club's last ever home match. Seven days later the journey was made to Molineux. The team line-up for this last Leeds City match consisted of: Walker, Millership, Affleck, Lamph, Hampson, Price, Lounds, Kirton, Edmondson, McLeod and Goodwin. Goalkeeper Willis Walker had played in the second half of the last pre-War season, and together with six other players was an ever-present in the eight matches played in 1919. Affleck, Kirton (who had signed for the Club six months earlier) and Goodwin, were ironically each making their Leeds City debut - and therefore their only appearance for the Club. It was perhaps fitting that McLeod signed off on a high, by scoring a hat-trick (aided by Lamph's goal) in The Peacocks 4-2 victory.

Affleck and Kirton both played in Leeds City's last match

Many Clubs have disappeared over the 100 plus years of the Football League. The majority have been 'rejected', i.e. not re-elected, a few have voluntarily resigned their status, and a handful have

fallen before completing their fixtures. But arguably none have been so badly treated as was the lot of Leeds City F.C. In those days when the Football Authorities held such unchallenged power of their member clubs, when aggressive Chairman and clever lawyers did not enter into the reckoning, the Club were expelled, without the right of appeal. Although, to a degree, they had brought it upon themselves, in the eyes of many their expulsion was unjust. The allegations against the Club and their subsequent ejection from the League must have come as a bombshell to the Club's supporters, and the full details were not revealed in full - by the *Yorkshire Evening Post* - until after the event.

Additional payments made to guest players during the War years, by many clubs, were an open secret, and so widespread that the powers that be turned a blind eye towards them. However, the start of Leeds City's downfall came to a head when right-back Charlie Copeland, who had joined the Club in August 1912, reported such payments following his acrimonious disagreement with them after they refused to award him a pay rise. On this notification the Football League and the Football Association had little option but to investigate the claims and act accordingly.

Yet the real problems started earlier in the War when manager Herbert Chapman chose to help the War effort by working for the local Munitions factory. Managers of Football clubs at this time also usually acted as the Club secretary and general factotum - even more so during the war years - and he suggested his assistant at Elland Road, schoolteacher George Cripps - take charge of the secretarial duties, while the Chairman Joseph Connor and fellow director J.C. Whiteman dealt with team selections.

At a period of very limited resources many duties either had to be left to volunteers, or alternatively close the Club down - a possibility which at one time was seriously considered. However, it was not long before Connor accused Cripps of incompetence, and the situation became so bad that Connor threatened to resign unless the stand-in was removed from the secretarial duties.

In 1917, an accountant's clerk was employed to take over the bookkeeping - which Connor alleged was in a complete mess - and Cripps, who's health was failing, would just take care of the team and correspondence. But Cripps was found to be just as unpopular with the players, so much so that the team threatened to go on strike, in early 1918, if Cripps continued to travel with them to away matches. Such an action would have been the death blow for the Club, and the players were persuaded to grin and bear it.

As the War ground to a halt and normality returned, Chapman returned as manager, and Cripps once again as his assistant. But this upset Cripps who supposedly threatened to claim £400 damages for wrongful dismissal, telling his solicitor (James Bromley, a former Club Director) that the Club were also guilty of paying improper expenses to players. Connor claimed that a settlement was reached in January 1919, whereby Cripps would hand over all documents relating to the Club (plus Cripps' own cheque book and pass book) and also any correspondence from the players addressed to Connor and Whiteman. These items would be sealed in a strongbox and kept by Alderman Clarke, the Club's solicitor. In addition Cripps supposedly gave a written promise not to disclose any of the Club's affairs and further swore to deny any knowledge of the documents that were under lock and key. In return the Club paid him £55, a somewhat lower amount than originally asked for.

However this version differed from that stated by Bromley (Copeland's solicitor), who said that he had handed over to his counterpart Clarke, a parcel given to him by Cripps, and that it was to held in trust, and the contents not divulged unless agreed to by both Cripps and Connor. In exchange £50 was to be donated by the Leeds City Directors to the Leeds Infirmary. Bromley claimed that he later asked for a receipt for this donation, but Connor refused to discuss further the affairs of the Club with him. Whatever the true situation, it was apparent that there had been underhand dealings, but at this time it seemed that the various grievances had been resolved.

The Summer of 1919 saw the Club assemble their playing staff for the return to peacetime football, and the question of the player Copeland's renewal of contract was raised. During the pre-war days he was paid £3 per week, with a £1 increase for first team appearances (he made 45 in total), and he was now offered £3.50 as a reserve player, and a large increase if he was picked for the first team. Alternatively he was offered a free transfer.

Copeland was not satisfied with this arrangement, and demanded £6 per week - the maximum post-war wage had been raised by 50% - or he threatened to report the Club to the Football authorities for the illegal payments made to players during the war. Leeds City refused to give in to this blackmail, called his bluff, and transferred him to Coventry City during the close season. Copeland had evidence regarding the alleged payments and carried out his threat, reporting the Club in July 1919. Copeland later denied this later involvement, although since Bromley was also his solicitor, the necessary information could easily have come from this source.

In his defence Copeland had remained faithful to the Club during the war years, had been promised a rise when peacetime returned, and the apparent increase - but with no Summer wage - in effect meant a reduction over the year. He claimed that he resorted to consulting Bromley since the City board refused to meet him to discuss the affair. On the day of the Club's last match, there was a rail strike, and on the team's return from Wolverhampton, they picked up several travellers in their charabanc who were heading North, one of these was Charlie Copeland!

The Football League and the Football Association set up a joint enquiry, and Alderman Clarke represented the Club in Manchester on 26th September 1919 to answer the charges. Clarke was asked to present the City's books to the enquiry in advance, but the Club stunned the Commission by refusing. The Club were told in no uncertain terms to comply by 6th October. The Club stuck to their guns, and when the deadline date passed, the Commission postponed the team's next fixture - versus South Shields - and following a meeting of the enquiry team at the Russell Hotel in London, Leeds City were expelled from the Football League, and disbanded. John McKenna, the League Chairman stated: *" The authorities of the game intend to keep it absolutely clean. We will have no nonsense. The football stable must be cleansed and further breakages of the law regarding payments will be dealt with in such a severe manner that I now give warning that clubs and players must not expect the slightest leniency."*

The irony was of course that the Club's guilt had never been proven, although of course their silence - to either protect themselves or the players - left little doubt regarding the truth of the charges. *"After the repeated warnings of the President and Committee they regard this violation of the financial regulations and the failure to produce documents vital to full and complete enquiry so serious that expulsion from the League can be the only fitting punishment."*

The fans, the Club and the City of Leeds could not believe the fate of the Club. The Lord Mayor of Leeds offered to take over the Club, but the members of the Commission would not alter their decision. Five Leeds City officials were given life bans - the directors Connor, Whiteman, Glover and Sykes plus - to everybody's surprise - the manager/secretary Herbert Chapman; on appeal Chapman's ban was lifted since he pointed out that he was not involved as he was working in the munitions factory at the time.

Burslem Port Vale were allowed to take over the Leeds City fixtures, and there were suggestions they had encouraged the Commission to act so drastically in order to further their own cause. Ironically Port Vale themselves were expelled from the League (but immediately voted back in) in 1968, for irregularities which they eventually admitted, after first remaining silent.

Despite this being the end of the Club their affairs had to be sorted out, and Bob Hewison (a war-time City guest player) acted as secretary, helped by Alderman Henry and a local accountant, W.H.Platts. The most difficult arrangements to be sorted were the players' futures, and this was solved by a somewhat unseemly, and humiliating auction, which took place at the Metropole Hotel in Leeds on the 17th October.

Thirty bidding clubs were represented, and between them they paid £10,150 for the entire playing staff at prices that ranged between £100 and £1,250 each. Billy McLeod was the top purchase at £1,250 - he went to Notts County - and the next most expensive players - who each realised £1,000 - were Simpson Bainbridge to Preston, John Hampson to Aston Villa and Harold Millership who joined Rotherham County. In all 22 players came under the hammer.

Four men - Kirton (who scored the winning goal in the 1920 F.A. Cup Final), Ashurst, Pease and Stephenson, all went on to play for England.

Before the dust had settled moves were already afoot to replace Leeds City. A meeting was called by Leeds solicitor Alf Masser, and a new club was formed. Within a month Leeds United, having been accepted by the Midland League on the 31st October, played their first fixture, having taken over those of Leeds City reserves. Despite only finishing in a mid-table position, they were elected into the Football League for the 1920/21 season, with apparent ease despite their lack of a worthy playing record etc. This may have been due to pity, or it may have been due to the power that a large City - and a proven hotbed of football - could exert.

The Elland Road Ground:

The Ground was formerly named 'The Old Peacock Ground' after the Public House that was once on the other side of Elland Road. The Ground was bought by Holbeck Rugby Club for £1,100 from Bentley's Brewery in 1896. Leeds City took over the lease of Elland Road in 1904, after the demise of Holbeck Rugby Club.

The Ground encompassed 4.2 acres, and at that time the pitch lay in a West to East direction. After just one year, and after the City's election to the Football League, extensive work was carried out. Two Stands (one on each side of the pitch) that had been erected by Holbeck were demolished. On the South (Elland Road) side, a new ¾ pitch length covered Stand, 35 feet wide, was built.

The Stand which held 4 to 5,000, and included some seating, also incorporated a commodious press box. The structure, built by H.Barrett and Sons (from Bradford) cost £1,060. There was the intention to erect a cover over the West end, but this was never built. On the other side, and the two ends, there were only rudimentary terraces, and these twenty steps were reinforced with creosoted battens to form more substantial risers. The pitch was in a poor state, nearly devoid of grass, and this was raised about 14 inches (25 cms.), drainage introduced and then re-turfed.

However, little over one year later further major works were undertaken, when a scheme proposed by Architect and City Director Douglas Whitaker was adopted. An extra five acres of land was purchased on the North side of the site from Monks Bridge Iron Works, and the Ground was turned at 90 degrees, which 'relocated' the Stand from the side to behind the South goal. On the West side, a 90 yard long double barrel-roofed Stand was introduced that held 8,000. The pitch now measured 125 x

85 yards (previously 115 x 73), and the capacity was raised from 22,000 to 45,000. These further improvements cost nearly £5,000 and probably explains why the Club for much of their time had difficulty in making ends meet!

On the demise of Leeds City F.C. there was talk of the Ground being demolished and using the clay that underlay the site, but this never proceeded. For a short period the Amateur team, Northern Nomads, made use of the enclosure, before the new club, Leeds United moved in.

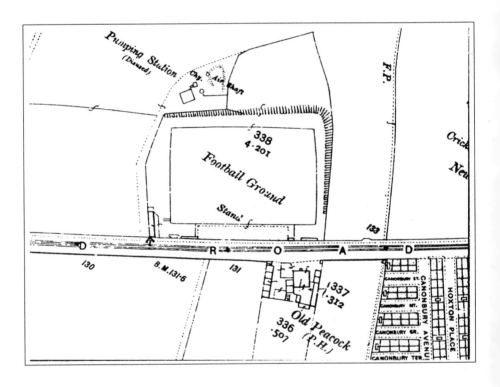

Elland Road as it looked in 1908.
At this time the pitch was aligned East to West.

SATURDAY, MARCH 26th, 1910.

LEEDS CITY
A.F.C.

SEASON 1909-10,

Members of the Football Association.   The Football League.   West
Yorkshire Association, and Midland League.

OFFICIAL PROGRAMME
PRICE ONE PENNY.

EMPIRE
AT 7 AND AT 9
TO-NIGHT.

RHODES & SONS, PRINTERS, LEEDS.

The staging of the F.A.Cup Semi-final between Everton and Barnsley (a 0-0 draw)
at Elland Road was controversial since the state of the Ground was questioned.

Merthyr Town A.F.C. Season 1925-1926.

MERTHYR TOWN F.C.
Un-named team groups from (Top) 1912
and (Below) 1925/26 season.

MERTHYR

1908/09	*Rhymney Valley League*
1909/10 - 1911/12	*Southern League Division 2**
1912/13 - 1913/14	*Southern League Division 1*
1914/15	*Southern League Division 2*
1915/16	*Friendly Matches***
1916/17 - 1918/19	*Ceased Activities*
1919/20	*Southern League Division 1*
1920/21 - 1919/30	*Football League Division 3*
1921/22 - 1929/30	*Football League Division 3 South*
1930/31 - 1933/34	*Southern League Western Section*
1945/46	*Welsh League Division 1*
1946/47 - 1957/58	*Southern League*
1958/59	*Southern League North-West Zone*
1959/60 - 1961/62	*Southern League First Division*
1962/63 - 1963/64	*Southern League Premier Division*
1964/65 - 1970/71	*Southern League First Division*
1971/72	*Southern League Premier Division*
1972/73 - 1978/79	*Southern League Northern Division*
1979/80 - 1987/88	*Southern League Midland Division*
1988/89	*Southern League Premier Division*
1989/90 - to date	*Vauxhall Conference.*

* First Team also in Western League
** As an Amateur team, several matches played before the cessation of activity.

Football League Record:-

	P	W	D	L	F	A	Pts	Pos.	Ave.Att.
1920/21	*42*	*15*	*15*	*12*	*60*	*49*	*45*	*8th*	*12300*
1921/22	*42*	*17*	*6*	*19*	*45*	*56*	*40*	*11th*	*8985*
1922/23	*42*	*11*	*14*	*17*	*39*	*48*	*36*	*17th*	*5265*
1923/24	*42*	*11*	*16*	*15*	*45*	*65*	*38*	*13th*	*6925*
1924/25	*42*	*8*	*5*	*29*	*35*	*77*	*21*	*22nd*	*4200*
Successfully re-elected									
1925/26	*42*	*14*	*11*	*17*	*69*	*75*	*39*	*14th*	*5910*
1926/27	*42*	*13*	*9*	*20*	*63*	*80*	*35*	*17th*	*3170*
1927/28	*42*	*9*	*13*	*20*	*53*	*91*	*31*	*21st*	*2745*
Successfully re-elected									
1928/29	*42*	*11*	*8*	*23*	*55*	*103*	*30*	*20th*	*3154*
1929/30	*42*	*6*	*9*	*27*	*60*	*135*	*21*	*22nd*	*2503 **

* Lowest average attendance in Football League

****

Number of Football League matches played 420.

SUMMARY OF FACTS:

Ground:
Penydarren Park

Colours Football League: 1920/21 - 1924/25: Red shirts, Green trim, White Shorts.
1925/26 - 1929-30: Red and Green Stripes, White Shorts.

Nickname: The Martyrs

First League Game: 28th August, 1920 versus Crystal Palace (Home) Won 2-1. Attendance approx 10,000.

Last League Game: 26th April, 1930 versus Gillingham (Away) Lost 0-6.

Record Attendance: 27th December, 1921 versus Millwall (League). 21,686 (Receipts £1,286)
Main Achievements:
Best Football League Win: 8-2 versus Swindon Town (Home) 1927/28
7-1 versus Exeter City (Home) 1920/21
6-0 versus Brentford (Home) 1925/26

Worst Football League Defeat: 0-10 versus Newport County (Away) 1929/30.

European Cup Winners Cup Entrants: 1987/88.

F.A. Cup:
(Pre League)   1st Round (Modern Equivalent 3rd Round): 1913/14
1914/15
(As a Football League Club) 1st Round (3rd Round equivalent): 1922/23
(Post Football League) 2nd Round: 1946/47; 1954/55, 1973/74, 1979/80, 1989/90, 1990/91.
1st Round: 1930/31; 1932/33, 1947/48, 1951/52, 1958/59, 1965/66,
1978/79, 1987/88, 1988/89, 1992/93.
Southern League Champions:
1947/48; 1949/50, 1950/51, 1951/52, 1953/54.
Runners-up: 1952/53.
Premier Div. Champions: 1988/89
First Div. Champions: 1987/88
Runners-up: 1970/71
North Div. Runners-up: 1978/79
League Cup Winners: 1947/48; 1950/51.
Southern League 2nd Division Champions: 1911/12
Welsh Cup Winners: 1948/49; 1950/51, 1986/87,
Runners-up: 1923/24; 1946/47, 1951/52.

R. Williams (1920-1922) whilst with Merthyr was capped twice for Wales.

September 1922 to September 1925: Football League record number of games (61) without an Away Win.
1929/30: Record Number of goals conceded in 3rd Division South (135)
1924/25: record number of defeats in 3rd Division South (29 of 42 games).

Until around the dawn of the 20th Century, Wales was split very much into a North/South divide as regards Football. In the North, the sport had taken a hold from the earliest days, and indeed the Welsh F.A. Cup was inaugurated back in 1877, just six years after the very first such competition in the World - in England. But the National Welsh competition was totally dominated by these Clubs in the North, and it wasn't until 1903 that the South made any impression on the competition, at which time Aberaman reached the Final. Around this time the Coal dominated Southern area was at last waking up to the Association version of football, having until then been very much a Rugby stronghold.

The 'new' sport spread rapidly, with Cardiff City formed in 1899, and Swansea Town one year later, being the earlier innovators that rose to become leaders in the area. The original Aberdare Club was formed in 1893 (the later Football League Club from that town did not appear until 1920), and nearby Merthyr was first noticed when their representatives - Merthyr Vale - won the Second Division of the South Wales League in its first season of 1902/03. But this Club made little impact overall, and it wasn't until 1908, that this Rhondda Valley town made a serious bid to form a Football Club with ambition.

It was during the summer of that year that a Football Club was formed as am offshoot of the Merthyr Athletic Club. By June the 20th, a Secretary/Manager had been appointed, Mr. D.T. Mantle, a man who had been previously associated with the Ton Pentre Club. The ambitions of the new Club came immediately to the fore when they applied for membership of both the Western and South Wales Leagues, but in the case of the former, it was to be a year before this materialised, and the Club had to content themselves by becoming members of the Rhymney Valley League. Although this competition was of a local nature, it none the less contained several teams of some standing, including Aberdare and Mardy, with several Clubs playing their first teams in two separate Leagues.

Players were signed on during the summer months, and on the 5th of September the first match of the new team was played at Penydarren Park. On that day in fact two games were played, firstly a practise game followed by the main event, a friendly match with Swansea Town. The inexperience of the locals was shown with their 1-2 defeat, and although the game was lacking in thrills, both Carrier and Humphries played well, with Owen marking his place in history as the first ever goalscorer for

Merthyr Town. Although defeated, the team was not overwhelmed, and it was thought that with more games, and playing as a team, the future looked bright.

With only seven teams forming the Valley League, a number of other Friendly matches were necessary to make up a full fixture list. On September the 12th, Merthyr were hosts once again, this time to Barry Cocks Albions. Playing far better as a combination, the homesters ran out as 2-1 winners. Although the Players had shown better understanding, the rules of the game were still something of a mystery to many of the spectators, some of whom could not understand the true role of the goalkeeper, and inevitably the perennial puzzle of the offside rule bemused a great number!

The first Rhymney Valley League match was played one week later, at Aberdare, where a comprehensive four goal defeat ensued. Apart from their opponents greater experience, the Merthyr team were missing two notable players - Hugh and Clarke - who had returned to their native Wrexham. But the interest in this first derby match was evident with an attendance that numbered approximately 3,000. However, this initial setback did little to quell the newcomers enthusiasm, and by the season's end there had been two notable encounters.

Their venture into the South Wales Senior Cup saw them win through to the Final, after turning the tables on the Swansea team with a four goal quarter-final victory, and a 2-1 win over former winners Treharris. The final was played at the Mid-Rhondda Athletic Ground at Tonypandy, and Merthyr were well represented with supporters who had made the journey on April the 5th, and had helped to swell the crowd to 8,000. But the cheers of those wearing the red and green of their favourites were insufficient to wrest the Cup away from Ton Pentre - their second of three successive victories in the competition - and the Town lost by two second-half goals.

A crowd-puller was arranged when the redoubtable Manchester City from the First Division of the Football League played a friendly match at Penydarren. This was not only the highlight of the Club's season, but also a great sporting event for the town. After being met at the station by the Mayor, together with several Councillors and the Football Club's Officials, the visiting team were escorted to the ground, where, despite the rain, over 7,000 fans gave their guests an enthusiastic greeting. True to form the homesters were outplayed in the first half, and by the interval trailed by four goals. In the second period, Merthyr, less overawed by their worthy opponents set about reducing the lead. Brookes scored twice, and at the end the 2-4 scoreline was seen as a reasonable achievement.

The 1909/10 season saw the Club playing in a much higher level of football, with their acceptance into both the Southern and Western Leagues. Although there had been many defections from the Western League at the end of the previous season, the - by now - single division combination contained 13 teams of proven capability - the Reserves of the Rovers and City from Bristol, Bath City, Ton Pentre and Treharris included. Despite this select company, the Merthyr team acquitted themselves well, and by the season's end finished in fifth place, but ten points behind the all-conquering Treharris team. The team also proved itself in the Southern League, for although only one of six teams in the Second Division, Section 'A', a final third place was achieved. The expenses of this venture could well have spelt the end of the Club had it not been for the enthusiastic support that they could command, for the teams competing in the Southern League were from incredibly diverse locations; former Football League teams Stoke (later prefixed 'City') and Burton United (both from the Midlands), plus Salisbury City, and fellow Welsh representatives in Ton Pentre and Aberdare.

Once again several friendly matches had to supplement the fixture list, and the most notable of such opponents was Southampton from the Southern League. This October match was something of a revelation, for the Welsh team completely dominated their opponents and ran out as four goal winners. This scoreline could have been greater if it had not have been for the visitors custodian Burrows' fine display.

The fragmented divisions of the Southern League were re-organised for the 1910/11 season, and Merthyr Town became members of the twelve team Second Division. On this occasion they exceeded their supporters hopes with another final third placing (only two points behind the Champions), but this time there were much stronger additional opponents such as Reading, Walsall, Cardiff City and the ill-fated Croydon Common. Along with Cardiff City and an eighteen strong mixed bag of other hopefuls, the Club made a somewhat surprising bid for membership of a new additional Division of the Football League that was being considered at that time. But the idea was eventually rejected, and Merthyr's application was not looked at in a favourable light by the Management Committee of the Southern League, since this organisation was also in conflict with the Football League over this same issue, i.e. the formation of a Third Division.

'Kruger'

The Merthyr Town mascot in 1910

Success followed success, and the next season the Club captured the Divisional Championship - on goal average - from Portsmouth, with 19 victories and only 4 defeats in their 26 games. This was not their only achievement, for the South Wales and Monmouthshire Cup was captured for the first time. There was an earlier round victory over Cardiff City.

In March 1912, an estimated 16,000 crowd was present at Ninian Park, of whom over 3,000 had made the journey from the Valleys. The result (2-1 to Merthyr) was seen as a yardstick to the unofficial title of 'South Wales' top team, although at this time the Club had not even reached its fourth birthday.

One of the earliest of Merthyr Town programmes (1911/12 season)

The close season in 1912 saw big changes in the Club's constitution, for they became a Limited Company, with Tom Elias at the helm, and Albert Fisher as Secretary/Manager. By the season's end, the Management's hopes were reasonably fulfilled with the Club's twelfth place in the twenty strong First Division of the Southern League that they had been promoted to. The League had become the unofficial 'Third Division', and indeed most of Merthyr's nineteen opponents that season were to become Football League members in the not too distant future. The Club by now could show how well established they were for they had on their books no less than 26 Players (most of whom were professional), and included several with Football League experience, notably S. Beaumont (Preston North End), J. Jeffrey from Aston Villa and one time Arsenal player D. Deave.

The following for the football team had reached unimagined proportions by now, despite such a short time since their formation, and even a Town Council Meeting in September was reduced to only twelve minutes, in order that the Councillors could attend a Southern League Charity Cup game at Penydarren! But all good things must come to an end, and after their rapid rise in the Football World, the Club came firmly back to earth at the end of the 1913-14 season, when they finished second from bottom in the Southern League, just two points above tail-enders Coventry City. This lack of success resulted in a drop back down into the Second Division of the League for the forthcoming campaign.

However, there was one highlight during the season, for Merthyr won through to the first round proper of the F.A. Cup for the first time. But they then met their match at Swansea when the locals triumphed by two unopposed goals. Such a result may not seem a shock now, but at the time it was the Merthyr team who were the favourites, as Swansea were then only a Southern League Second Division team!

The team's relegation at least provided them with a host of new opponents in the 13 strong lower division. Another strange 'bedfellow' was the Stalybridge Celtic team, who had made a peculiar geographical choice (the town is near Manchester) in their effort to gain credibility for election into the Football League. Additionally Stoke were also met again, a Club that for a few years hovered between the two divisions and were also very misplaced from a location point of view. The bulk of the League was made up with teams from South Wales - eight in number - plus Brentford, and Coventry.

By the dawn of 1915, the Club lay 4th in the League, and from then until the end of the season hovered between that position and second. Even so an embarrassing defeat was suffered on March the 27th at Ebbw Vale to the tune of 7-0. But once again the Club showed itself to be too good to remain in the lower reaches and finally finished in third place (behind the two Northern Clubs). The last fixture was drawn 1-1 at home to Stalybridge on April the 17th. Once again the real highlight of the season occurred in the F.A.Cup when the first round proper was reached for the second time. This time the draw had given the Welshmen a home tie to the - destined to be - mighty Woolwich Arsenal team. The local fans relished the thought of a shot at Football League opposition, albeit only Second Division - but were much aggrieved when the Merthyr Directors decided for financial reasons to play the game in London. This decision was to remain a point of bitter controversy with many of the Club's supporters for a long time, since the venue would now give the minnows very little chance of progressing further.

Ironically the attendance at Highbury - still a fairly new and humble Ground - was only a moderate 6,000, a crowd that would probably had been exceeded if the match had been played at Penydarren! The first half saw little from Merthyr, apart from a good work rate, and the Gunners went in with a two goal interval lead. Playing with confidence in the second period, Merthyr threatened to reduce the lead, while Arsenal were reduced to relying on breakaway efforts, but the Merthyr goalkeeper - Gibbon - thwarted their efforts until near the end when the homesters added a third goal to their total.

Every effort was made to try to regain the team's First Division Southern League status, even their probable appearance in the Welsh Senior Cup Semi-Final was sacrificed; the quarter-final tie with Llanelly clashed with an important and attractive home League match with Newport County, and the Club chose to play their first team in the latter game. This encounter was won 2-1, and the cup-tie lost by 9-1!

On the 20th September 1915, it was announced that although the team had originally intended to carry on playing during the War, they had now decided to cancel all matches - except those over Christmas and Easter - since the Management did not wish to encourage the colliers in the town to leave work early to attend games. Then, just five days later a match was played and drawn at home to Barry!

By now most of the Club's players had departed for the War in Europe - just three were left - and this match and others were played under the guise of an amateur team. A few more Friendly games were undertaken, but eventually the Club honoured their previous commitment and there were no more matches for nearly four years.

By the War's end in 1919, the coal-mining oriented town of Merthyr could boast a population of 150,000, and after the austere years, the area was ripe for a reformed Senior football team. Under the President, Mr. H. Seymour, and with the aid of local businessmen a sum of £3,000 was quickly raised. The enthusiasm and potential of Merthyr Town did not go unnoticed for the 1919/20 season saw the Club re-elected into the Southern League Division 1. The impetus was maintained with the Share Capital of the Club being increased to the vary large figure of £10,000. Dr. Alex Duncan was elected as Chairman, and under the Manager, Harry Hadley (ex-West Bromwich Albion), plus the services of Jack Garland as Trainer, a worthy team was assembled.

The first game was played on August the 30th, and although a two goal defeat resulted at the hands of Millwall Athletic at Penydarren, the attendance of over 10,000 bode well for the future. The team with an average age of under 22 years then shared two goals with Brighton before a 6,000 crowd. But although the results generally went against the Welshmen, there was little to complain about with respect to support; 8,000 versus Northampton (1-1 draw), and 10,000 for the last game in 1919 when Exeter were overcome - 2-1 after a 1-1 half-time scoreline - were fairly representative. When Southampton were the visitors, the £367 receipts from a 5,000 attendance were considered quite poor.

A moderate F.A. Cup run was made though to the final qualifying round, at which stage the team lost at Newport County by a single goal. The attendance at the start of the game was a mere 5,000 due to the early kick-off, but this increased rapidly as the game wore on.

A goalless draw was played at Millwall at the year-end, before a massive 15,000 crowd, and by the time the leaders, Portsmouth, had beaten Merthyr by two goals in the New Year, the Welsh team were languishing well in the bottom half of the table. An embarrassing 8-1 defeat at Southampton put the Club fourth from bottom in the table, and a final defeat on May Day at Exeter by three unopposed goals left them finally one place above the wooden-spoonists. Financially thing had gone well, while off the field it had been a different matter, but the Club were to find that fortune was to smile on them the next season.

The Club's return to the Southern League top division could not have come at a more opportune time. For at the end of the 1919/20 season the member teams, en-bloc, were to form the new Third Division of the Football League, a long held ambition of the Southern League that was to be at last fulfilled. And there were to be no relegations or promotions at the end of this season, therefore Merthyr Town and its supporters were able to look forward to a considerable rise in status for the coming campaign.

The big day arrived on August the 28th, when Crystal Palace were entertained at Penydarren. It was fortunate that the kick-off was delayed for one hour as the crowds were still packing into the Ground at the stated time. On a hot day, before an attendance of around 10,000, the homesters triumphed by 2-1. Merthyr took a first half lead through Walker, but in the 46th minute the lead was cancelled out. Then much to the large crowd's joy, their favourites later scored a second goal. The team consisted of:- Lindon; Copeland, Clarke, Brown, Jennings, Crowe, Williams, Barbour, Walker, Chasser and Nicholas.

Made his debut in the first Football League match

The return one week later in London was far from successful, for the Welsh team lost by three goals before a near 12,000 crowd. Even so a good overall start to the season saw the team in 4th place after four games, the last of the quartet producing a crushing 6-1 (2-0 half-time) away win over eventual wooden-spoonists Gillingham, before another five figure attendance. Moderate results from the first eight games, after beating Watford on the 9th of October, produced a mid-table placing with three games each, ending in defeats and victories.

By November the 6th, when Northampton were overcome by the only goal of the game, the Martyrs (as they were by now popularly called) had fought their way up to 5th place. The locals showed their appreciation by turning up in large numbers, and the receipts for this game amounted to £600, representing an attendance of some 13,000.

Next week another point was taken off the Cobblers before 8,000 fans. On November the 20th, a record attendance was recorded at Newport County for the South Wales F.A. Cup derby. The gates had been opened at noon for the eventual 18,000 crowd, and although the Martyrs were the superior team the game ended goalless. The replay was duly won, by four unopposed goals, which resulted in a final qualifying round home match with non-League Bath City. Before a surprisingly poor attendance of only 5,000, a minor shock produced another scoreless draw, which was followed by a single goal defeat for the Welshmen in the replay at the Spa town.

Between the Cup matches, Southend were beaten at home in a poor and unsavoury game. Crowe scored shortly before the end, but with five minutes to go, the home player Fairclough was sent off, which resulted in crowd disturbances and the Police being called in to quell the disquiet. But no-score draws became common as Christmas approached, for the same results were obtained at Portsmouth (attendance of 13,000) and at Penydarren with Plymouth as the visitors. The locals at least proved that they were willing to come and see Football League matches, for another 10,000 crowd (£437 receipts) was present at the match versus Argyle. By Christmas, the Club lay in fourth place in the table, just 4 points behind the leaders - and eventual runners-up - Southampton.

A lower point scoring rate ensued in the second half of the campaign, and at the end an eighth place was realised. Although better things were hoped for during the season, this top half of table placing represented a good debut in the Football League. Despite the earlier five figure gates, towards the season's end these had shrunk considerably, and for Brentford's visit on the 30th of April there were no more than 4,000 present to see the homesters lose 1-3.

Goalkeeper A.B. Lindon (who had been signed from Coventry City) was the only ever-present in the Football League team, and W.B. Walker was the leading goalscorer with seventeen from his 38 appearances. During the season, the Club were honoured with the selection of R. Williams who played for Wales in two Internationals matches; he later moved on to Sheffield Wednesday and further honours.

The 1921/22 season started off in fine style, with the best players being retained by Manager Harry Hadley, and with the notable addition of Fred Lea from West Bromwich Albion. After three games and two home victories plus one away win, the

Martyrs headed the table. The attendances had also partly recovered, but only to around 6,000 for these early home games. The team was soon brought back down to earth when on the 7th of September they lost by five unopposed goals at Reading. The match in Berkshire had seen Merthyr's Ferrans sent off, and from this game onwards the Club's fortunes dipped. It was the away games that let the side down, for in 21 such matches, just twelve goals were scored and only three victories were achieved; heavy defeats were also conceded at Gillingham (5-0) and by 4-0 at Millwall. But the return match with the Londoners over Christmas, attracted for the Club (and Ground) the all time record attendance of 21,686.

As the season progressed, just two more away victories were achieved, by two goals at Newport back in November and on the 4th of February by 2-1 at Brighton. Fortunately a generally good home record provided the Club with a final mid-table placing, of 11th. Twenty-three different players had been used in League encounters, and H.W. Turner was the leading goalscorer, but with just 13 successes. There was little progress made in the F.A. Cup, when the team lost in a final qualifying round replay at Darlington after extra time, following a goalless home match. The season had been something of a disappointment, and better things were hoped for, however, one year later the situation was worse.

The team coach of the 1920's...
No video, or even a roof!

The season started off with two 1-1 draws, away to Swansea and at home to Swindon two days later, and were followed by a run of generally good results - three home and one away victories (plus two defeats on their travels) during September. But a high placing in the League did not continue, for the home record became shaky - including a two goal defeat to close rivals Aberdare on Boxing Day - and a very poor away record that did not produce any more wins than the solitary victory at Charlton on September the 30th. Inevitably the crowds dropped again, to below 5,000. Seventeenth in the table was the final placing. E. Turner was an ever-present in the side and also the leading scorer with 12 goals to his credit.

Fortunately the F.A. Cup at least produced some excitement. The Club battled through to the 1st Round proper, after beating Swansea in a replay, and Brentford at Griffin Park before a 12,000 crowd. On the 13th of January, the Welsh Club entertained Second Division Wolverhampton Wanderers. The tie attracted great excitement in the town, and on the day support came from all directions including many who had walked over the mountain from Aberdare. The crowd of 13,000 who had paid £723 were all hoping for a giant-killing act, but as so often happens the day became an anti-climax. The Wanderers played well above their lowly League placing, and even when reduced to only ten men after a thirty minute injury to right back Baugh, they still showed their overall superiority. The Martyrs played well, but were beaten by a single goal, although there had been an outstanding display by their opponent's goalkeeper, George.

Although the Martyr's record in the Football League was far from impressive, they none the less were still able to attract at least reasonable attendances overall, and financial problems at this time were not a major concern. Even though only a moderate start was made to the 1923/24 season, the visit to Penydarren of Swansea on November the 3rd - a scoreless draw - attracted a gate of 15,000, and receipts of £703. But yet again it was to be a poor season, although the only heavy defeats were encountered at Millwall by six unopposed goals, and by four goals each at Swansea and Watford. A bottom half of the table position - 13th - was again the final result. Whereas no progress was made in the F.A. Cup (a 1-3 defeat at Llanelly), in the Welsh Cup the team battled through to the final for the first time ever. But a 2-2 draw at Pontypridd followed by a single goal defeat at their opponent's - Wrexham - Ground put paid to any hopes of lifting this trophy. No fewer than 27 players were tried in Football League matches in an attempt to form a winning combination, and once again Turner was the leading marksman, with 15 goals.

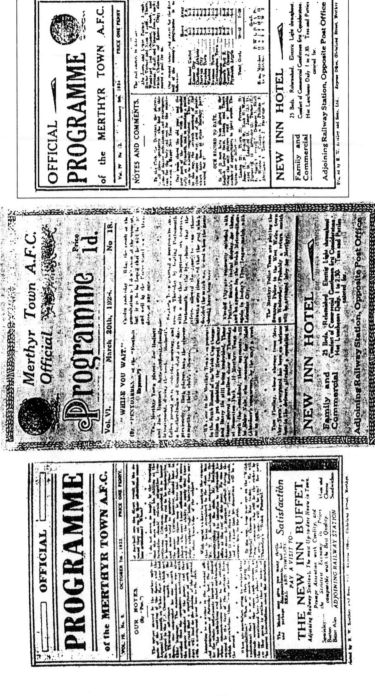

Programmes from the 1920's which produced mixed fortunes for the Martyrs.
Versus: Watford 1922/23 season (3-2 defeat), Plymouth 1923/24 season (1-0 win), and Luton 1923/24 season (scoreless draw)

The 1924-25 season was a disaster. Once again there were few bad defeats - by six goals at Luton and 1-5 in both matches with Swindon. But after the season had got underway in a poor manner - five away games before a point was obtained (following an opening victory over Southend), and an indifferent home record - the Club never looked like improving from their lowly position. During this season only eight victories and five draws were recorded, and the Martyrs finished bottom of the League. With 29 defeats this was to represent not only the most by the team during their days in the Football League, but also an all-time record number in the Third Division South of the Football League. With few goals to the team's credit, Arblaster was the leading scorer with just nine.

But along with Brentford, Merthyr received the maximum votes for re-election, leaving the hopeful Mid-Rhondda Club with none. One year later the situation had improved somewhat, with a rise up the table to fourteenth. This campaign had seen some high scoring victories in the Club's home matches; 6-0 versus Brentford, by four goals over Crystal Palace, and 5-1 against Southend United in the last game of the season. But by now the supporters in the town were becoming somewhat impatient, for there were only 5,000 present for the opening game against Luton Town. There was undoubtedly latent support in the town for a successful team, although by now crowds of mare than 4,000 were the exception rather than the rule, and near neighbours Aberdare were doing no better.

There was not even any solace to be gained from the F.A. Cup with a three goal reverse at Bournemouth. Apart from their first round (modern day equivalent to the third) appearance in 1923, this stage was never again reached during the Club's history. However, on the 19th of September a notable event occurred. On that day, the team won their match by 2-0 at Swindon, this being their first away victory since the 30th of September, 1922, an incredible three year period which embraced no less than 61 away matches without a win - an all time Football League record. A more settled team was resolved during the season, with only 21 different players being used, and with eleven of those appearing on more than twenty occasions, although these lower numbers were no doubt influenced by financial restrictions which were now taking effect.

The 1926/27 season proved to be another struggle, for although in customary style the first game was won, the team struggled throughout the season, and in fact only recorded one away victory - against Aberdare on October the 30th. This solitary win was only the second that the Martyrs ever achieved in twelve Football League matches against their fellow Welshmen. Fortunately the overall home record was reasonably respectable, with two very good wins, by 5-1 over eventual runners-up Plymouth Argyle and by four unopposed goals versus Queens Park Rangers. The final placing of 17th left a lot to be desired, and Aberdare's non re-election at the end of the season showed the Directors that continued membership of the Football League was not guaranteed in a re-election battle, for this was only the second application by the Athletic. J. Phillips had become indispensable as a goalscorer for Merthyr with his 29 in 41 appearances; the next highest were Pither and Sunderland with six each!

Merthyr Town depended almost exclusively upon support from the coalminers from the local pits. But as the 1920's drew to a close the Industrial situation in such areas was such that unemployment became rife, which in turn left little money for such pleasures as watching professional football. For three more seasons the Club struggled on in the Football League, accompanied with falling gates and poor performances.

At the end of the 1927/28 season, another re-election application was necessary when the team finished next to bottom, just one point above tail-enders Torquay United, but the rest of the League kept faith with both clubs, and the two were comfortably re-elected.

The F.A. Cup produced an early retirement for the Martyrs, when they lost at Charlton by two goals, in a replay. The departure of Phillips was a blow to the Club, and his goalscoring prowess was sadly missed; newcomer A.W. Mays headed the charts with 13 in 34 appearances.

There were three notable departures in 1928. Club stalwart, Albert Lindon - who played for the Club a record number 254 games between 1922 and 1928 - the Club's Player/Manager Godfrey, who after three years went to Charlton Athletic in the same dual role, and J. (Dai) Astley who after just three goals - a hat-trick against Brentford - also moved on. Charlton captured this seventeen year old, and after a further move to Aston Villa, he went on to win thirteen Welsh Caps.

One year later, and with just one point more than Exeter City, the Club finished in 20th place in the League. Another re-election application would have almost certainly doomed the team, as in fact it did twelve months later. It was only a fairly good home record once again that gave the Club some respectability. Just two points, from drawn games, were obtained on their travels, and some heavy defeats in the others; 8-0 at Queens Park Rangers, 6-1 at both Coventry and Newport, and further defeats of 5-0, 6-2, 5-1 and three by 4-0. It was little wonder that they recorded their worst goal difference to that time, with 55 for and 103 against. By now the playing staff had been drastically changed from a year earlier, for only six of the 28 players that were used in League games had appeared for the Club previously.

The 1929/30 season was to be the last ever for the Martyrs. The campaign started well with four goals shared at Coventry on the 31st of August, followed by a single goal home win over Northampton two days later. But from then on it was all downhill, in fact their next victory did not come until Boxing Day when Watford were beaten by the odd goal in five - the Martyrs first away win for two years! Whereas in the past the team could at least rely on a reasonable home record, this time it was not to be, and the reverses included a 5-1 thrashing by Norwich before the Year's End.

1930 began with the team languishing at the bottom of the League table and with no signs of a second half recovery. The signing of a new goalkeeper in Ben Lewis - the position on the field that had given the team one of its greatest problems - did little to alleviate their awful goals against record. By now the Club's finances were in dire straits along with the team's playing record. Gate receipts were down to £50 per match (representing little more than an attendance of 1,000), whilst the weekly wages bill amounted to £110; clearly the Club were not paying their way. Much of the poor attendance problem was put down to early kick-offs (during the winter) but this would have been a perennial difficulty. More to the point was the bad weather and the poor standard of football on display, not withstanding the continuing poor employment situation in the area. Inevitably the Martyrs had to sell players to keep afloat; Gibbons (the son of the then current Chairman, Samuel Gibbons) the team's leading goalscorer in the 1927/28 season, realised £200 when he moved to Fulham, and a similar fee was received for Sam Langford when he moved to Swansea (and subsequently on to Charlton).

The New Year started with the team seven points adrift at the bottom of the table, with the dismal record of 2 victories, 6 draws and 12 defeats. Just one point was obtained in January, and then on February the 1st, the most embarrassing result of the season occurred. At Penydarren, on a wet and windy day, Brighton were entertained, and the visitors completely outclassed and outplayed the homesters. After taking a five minute lead, the Sussex team went in at half-time with a 5-1 scoreline, and after a near repeat performance in the second period finally ended up as 8-2 winners. One week later there was a brief respite when Merthyr obtained a 3-3 draw with Swindon, after a last minute equaliser, but on the 15th of February the third consecutive home game was lost, by three unopposed goals to Plymouth.

Defeat followed upon defeat, including a six goal hammering on March the 1st at Southend, by which time the financial situation had become critical, when the Club failed to pay the players their wages. With a £1,650 deficit over the past year it was difficult to see where the money could come from; the last home game (a two goal defeat to Exeter) had realised only £30 after expenses. The immediate money problem was resolved with the team accepting half pay for two weeks, and the free transfers of Smith and Dransfield at least reduced the outgoings.

On March the 3rd, Queens Park Rangers were the attractive visitors to Merthyr, yet the match receipts dropped to an all time low of £20 after expenses.

The last month of the season produced greatly contrasting results. It started with a 3-4 home reverse to Fulham, and continued with the worst ever defeat for the team in the Football League, when lowly Newport County demolished the Martyrs by ten goals to nil. Two days later the team lost 5-1 at Norwich. They then startled their few remaining supporters with a point at home to Coventry, which was followed by two consecutive home victories over Easter - by 5-2 and 3-0! The Coventry game had produced a new low for the Club in match receipts, with Coventry's share being the princely sum of 18 shillings and four pence - 92p.!

But on their travels things were just as bleak, for between the two surprise wins, a four goal defeat was recorded at struggling Torquay. The three goal victory over Crystal Palace was the team's last ever home game in the Football League, and was followed by the last match on April the 26th, at Gillingham. Doomed already to bottom place, the Martyrs were humbled with a six goal reverse, after a four goal half-time deficit. The team for this inauspicious last League game consisted of:- Lewis, Carlton, Scott, Smith, Hargreaves, Creighton, Cruikshank, Sugarman, Parker, Fletcher and Slack.

The last season in the Football League, this match (4th January 1930) ended as a 1-0 defeat.

With a final goal record of 60 for and 135 against, this was a record number conceded in the Third Division South, and just one less than the all time record in either of the Third Divisions (Nelson with 136 in the 1927-28 season). The 21 points obtained equalled, along with the 1924/25 season, the Club's lowest tally. A total of 27 different players were used during the season, with Slack being the only ever present, and Parker's 13 goals representing the Club's highest scorer.

The Local Press in a highly optimistic statement were confident that the Club would, *"no doubt be re-elected"*. With two previous re-election applications, and the earlier fate of their fellow Welshmen, it really could have been no surprise when Merthyr Town were firmly rejected. The Club received just 14 votes, and were easily overtaken by the successful, but ill-conceived confidence shown for the Thames Association F.C., with their 20 votes. To finally cap the worst ever season for the Club, the Reserves finished 5 points clear at the bottom of the Western Section of the Southern League.

The 1930/31 season saw the Club competing in the Southern League - Western Division (where the Reserves had played in the previous season) and the Welsh League. The first game was played at home to Ebbw Vale, followed by a journey to play the Reserves of Plymouth Argyle. A reasonable start was made, including a 5-1 home win over Torquay United reserves, and by the season's end the team finished in a very respectable 3rd place. The first round of the F.A. Cup was reached after disposing of Swindon Victoria by 6-1, but ended in a 4-1 defeat at Bristol Rovers. On the field things were reasonable, the Championship of the Welsh League was even won, but financially the desperate situation continued. Home crowds remained at a low level, not only due to the Club's reduced status, but also caused by the continuing bleak Industrial situation in the area which prevented many miners having the money to attend matches.

The next two seasons produced not only a worsening money crisis, but a fall in the team's playing ability. Unable to strengthen the team due to financial restraints - even now the Club were losing approximately £500 per year - 8th of 13 teams in 1931/32 and 9th in 11 one year later, were the outcomes. The 1933/34 season, and the last for Merthyr Town, saw a reconstitution of the Southern League. Three sections - Eastern, Central and Western - of nine, ten and eleven teams respectively, saw the Martyrs playing in the latter. At the end of the season the team finished in 7th place, but there was to be no salvation for the Club.

Despite their plight and indifferent performances on the field, the Club had made - doomed to failure - re-election applications for the Football League on three occasions, but it must have come as no surprise when they were virtually unsupported; two votes twice, and just one in their final attempt at the end of the 1932/33 seasons.

Public Meetings had already been held to try to save the Club and to generate interest among the town's business community, but to no avail. Although the weekly wage bill was only £30, this figure equalled the highest gate (barely four figures), and attendances often dropped to a pitiful £4 gate or less, i.e. under 200. Although the Directors blamed the Club's drop in status for the lack of interest, with 12,000 unemployed in the town, supporting the local football club was hardly high on the list of priorities of the local workforce. Entrance money at one time was drastically cut to 2d. (1p.) but the Welsh F.A. instructed that the minimum should be 6d.

At the end of June 1934, the Club's Secretary announced that:-
"Merthyr Town is finished. Much as my Directors regret it, they feel they have no alternative but to close down. It is impossible for them to go on running at a loss".
The accumulated losses of £2,000 were borne by the Directors themselves.

The Merthyr Express stated that it would be a long time before local spectators will have another opportunity of seeing first class soccer in the Borough. And so it was, for another 11 years were to pass before such an event took place.

As the Second World War drew to a close, and although several more years of hardship were required, it also brought the dawn of a new age and a sense of freedom, plus the return of Britain's menfolk. The previous dark years opened the way for people to enjoy themselves, and for many this meant a return to the National sport of Football. In Merthyr Tydfil such an occupation was very limited, they had lost their own football identity when the 'Town' had sunk over ten years earlier. But this did not prevent a band of enthusiasts rekindling the interest, and from this group was born the new Club Merthyr Tydfil F.C.

The trio who instigated the new Club consisted of Major Frank Crago - a Director of the Rotax Company, D.J. Davis - another Businessman - and a school Headmaster, Eddie Rowlands. A trial match was arranged at the still available Penydarren Ground, and two teams competed against each other, one principally being composed of Rotax players, and the other of men and youths from the town. But who would have forecast that this gentle awakening could have such an immediate effect on the previously slumbering football public in this town in the Valleys.

An immediate entry for the 1945/46 season was made into the Welsh League, and under the Managership of Jock McNeil, the Martyrs took no time in making their presence felt. The first game - in September - was played at Nantymoel, and the Merthyr team surpassed itself by scoring four goals in an eight goal thriller. But seldom could a new Club impress itself more on its public than the Martyrs did in their next game, when at Penydarren in the return with Nantymoel they not only won, but with the "cricket score" of 11-1! The Club's centre-forward - Bill Hullett, previously of Manchester United - who became the star of the team, soon made himself known by scoring six of the goals. Under their Player/Manager, the team swept all before them, and in League games reached a century of goals scarcely halfway through the season. When Tredomen came to Penydarren, along with a crowd of 6,000, the visitors held an undefeated record that stretched back several games, yet Merthyr contemptuously cast them aside, and passed the hundred goals mark with their 9-2 win!

Unfortunately it was not all a smooth passage, as the fierce partisanship behind the new team was to have a dramatic effect in another direction. Away to Troedyrhiw, the Merthyr hero Hullett was sent off in a controversial incident. Both captains pleaded with the Referee to change his mind, but he wouldn't, and as Hullett reached the sidelines, he was immediately surrounded by a throng of people from the 3,000 strong crowd.

But it was not to attack the player that they surged forward, but to raise him shoulder high, as a salute to his ability and to show their continued support despite his unfair dismissal. Meanwhile another section of the crowd set upon the referee, and the Official had little option but to abandon the game. Seven days later the same two teams played at Penydarren, and the homesters lost by the odd goal in three, a surprise defeat perhaps, but even so it was regarded as one of the best games of the season, and watched by an incredible attendance of approximately 10,000.

If football entertainment can be measured on the basis of the number of goals scored, then Merthyr must surely have been the all conquering Champions that season and for several to come. In 36 League games, they scored an unbelievable 187 - an average of over five per game, having won 27, drawn 3 and lost only 6 matches. Yet they did not win the League! This honour went to Lovell's Athletic who beat the Martyrs into second place, with no fewer than 8 points more.

It came as no surprise that Merthyr Tydfil were readily accepted into the Southern League for the 1946/47 season, with Lovell's following one year later. But the Martyrs had no intention of just consolidating their position in this, the generally recognised most Senior group of clubs outside the Football League, for they just continued from where they had left off in the Welsh League, and carried most before them. The team were now under the leadership of the 1920's former Merthyr Town Player/Manager Albert Lindon, following the departure of McNeil.

Although they lost their first game, 2-4 on the Huish slope at Yeovil, a few days later before a home crowd of nearly 9,000, they demolished Gloucester City to the tune of 9-4 - Hullett completing his hat-trick well before half-time. By the season's end, the Welshmen attained third place in the table, just two points behind Champions Gillingham (some additional points had to be awarded to several teams, due to Millwall not completing their fixtures). Even in the F.A. Cup, the footballing fraternity had to sit up and recognise the name of Merthyr Tydfil. For the first time in 16 years, a Football League team came to Penydarren to compete in a competitive match, when Bristol Rovers were sent home smarting from a 3-1 defeat in the First Round of The Cup. Reading were the Martyrs next opponents, and despite a tremendous fighting spirit, the homesters ended up on the wrong end of the same scoreline; the attendance at Penydarren was 19,500 an all time record for the new Club. As if such accomplishments were not enough the Club even reached the final of the Welsh Cup, a feat only equalled once by the former 'Town' Club, when they were members of the Football League.

Merthyr were one of 27 Clubs - a record number - who made a bid for entry into the Football League, just two years after their formation, but all the aspiring teams were unlucky as the Clubs for re-election were each voted back in.

Merthyr Tydfil reached the pinnacle of success in the 1947/48 season when they 'walked' the Southern League, with six points more than nearest challengers Gillingham - and belatedly completed the double a year later with their five goal win over Colchester United in the League Cup. The team's achievements had not gone unnoticed, for both Hullett and Howarth moved on to Cardiff City and Aston Villa respectively - with the Martyrs receiving record fees for a non-League Club.

The loss of their two prominent attacking players proved a slight set-back to Merthyr for at the end of the 1948/49 season they finished third in the League - but had scored 133 goals in the process - two points behind the Champions. Compensation was however received with their first ever capture of the Welsh Cup, beating both Cardiff City and Swansea Town on their way, and the Reserves were hailed as Welsh League Champions. The final of the Cup was played at Ninian Park before a record (for the final) attendance of 35,000, 7,000 of whom had come to the Capital from Merthyr. Once again though their bid for Football League status failed when they received no votes at the election meeting.

In May 1950, the Welshmen won the Southern League again, on goal average (143 for and 62 against) from Colchester United in a cliff-hanger finish. The Club's success was aided in no small way by the return of Hullett as Player/Manager in January. With the Football League being extended by two teams in each Third Division, they felt that their chances were good for a re-entry, but the period of more recent and prolonged success counted, and both Colchester (runners-up) and fifth placed Gillingham were elected. With occasional five figure crowds and a consistently good team to match, the Martyrs had the right credentials for the Football League, but 1950 was to prove to be their only real chance of regaining Football League status.

1950 was the start for Merthyr Tydfil of an unprecedented run by a Club in the Southern League that was to eventually stretch over five seasons. During this period, the Martyrs were Champions on four occasions - once by a clear nine points - and Runners-up on the fifth, and then only on goal average from Headington (later Oxford) United.

The 1950/51 campaign saw the Club produce even greater goal-scoring feats, and beat the previous season's new Southern League record, this time recording 156 successes. Hullett was yet again the man in the limelight, and when in February the team crushed Bedford Town by ten unopposed goals, his final tally of five was his fourth hat-trick in five games! One year later, the title was won with Weymouth trailing by three points, and the goals scored down to a 'modest' 128.

This period of domination in the Southern League did not go unnoticed by the fans, particularly the older ones, and the crowds flocked to Penydarren in numbers that were rarely matched in their earlier Football League days. Typical attendances for the 'top' games were the 12,700 for Llanelli's F.A. Cup replay visit in October, 1950 (that was surprisingly lost by the Martyrs) and 11,000 for the visit of Ipswich in the first round proper of the Cup, the following year. But even these figures were eclipsed when fellow Welshmen contested with Merthyr for the Welsh Cup.

Between 1947 and 1952, Merthyr were twice winners and three times runners-up for the National trophy - yet another record not equalled by a non-League Club. The 1951 semi-final attracted 32,000 to Ninian Park and a further 15,000 in the replay; 21,048 for the match in the final against Cardiff at Swansea and 18,000 at their 3-2 replay victory. 12,938 at Penydarren when the team from the Capital again lost to Merthyr in February 1952, and 16,000 attendances in Cardiff for the later semi-final victory over Wrexham and the final defeat to Rhyl.

It is something of a surprise that during these triumphant days, the Club made little real impact on the F.A. Cup, their 1946 victory over Bristol Rovers being the only giant-killing, and with progress through to the second round being made on just two occasions. But Merthyr's bubble burst as quickly as it was inflated; the 1954-55 season saw a drop to midway (12th) in the final table, and second from bottom one year later. This sudden drop would seem inexplicable, but the all-conquering team was not a young one, and as they faded away the replacements could not emulate their mentors. And what of the support? When Championship seeking Headington United visited Penydarren in 1956, the attendance was a pitiful 1,200, yet a run of the mill match just two or three years earlier would have seen at least four times as many.

This sorry state of affairs was to continue for several years, and the depths were reached in May 1958 with their bottom placing in the League. From 9 victories, 3 draws and 30 defeats, the Club were not only 9 points below their nearest rivals, but the goal difference was 69 - 137, a complete reversal of the level of figures that were achieved a few years earlier.

A moderate recovery was made the next year, but not sufficient to raise the team into the top half of the table and membership of the newly formed Premier Division of the Southern League for the 1959/60 season.

Promotion was achieved - on goal average - with a fourth place in the First Division at the end of the 1960/61 season, but the team's involvement with those teams of the Premier Division lasted for only three seasons, before the drop down. The appointment of Harry Griffiths as Player/Manager in 1964, and his notable signings - including former Welsh International Reg Davis and Graham Vearncombe - brought a new football interest to the town and from gates seldom rising above 400 they leapt up to the 3,000 level. But further years of mediocrity resulted in the Club paying the price at the turnstiles, and as the Martyrs desperately tried to find a winning team several Managers came and went.

It was not until 1965 that a Football League team was once again encountered in the F.A. Cup, the Club having only reached the first round once in the previous eleven years. The fans rallied round, and 2,000 of them accompanied the team to the County Ground Swindon to swell the attendance to 15,962. But the team's gallant bid could not overcome the superior homesters, and the Martyrs bowed out to a 5-1 defeat.

The Club's former glories in the Welsh Cup were not to be repeated (until 1987), and elimination at the quarter-final stage in 1971 was their best effort in nearly twenty years. Meanwhile the Club struggled on, with poor gates and similar form, never seriously challenging for promotion nor in real danger of re-election - until 1969. The end of the 1968/69 season left the Martyrs fourth from bottom of the First Division, having conceded 101 goals - the most in the League, except for the hapless Tonbridge who let in 137. One year later the Club dropped even further, and it was only the abysmal form of Tonbridge again that prevented the Welsh team from finishing bottom. By now Merthyr had reached its lowest ebb, and the battle to stay alive was a constant fight, with the Directors digging deep into their pockets and with frequent meetings to try to ensure a future for the Club.

When Maldwyn Davies, a Director of the Club, took over as Manager in the early 1970's, there were few amongst the team's small following that could foresee a successful, albeit brief, time ahead. But the 1970/71 season produced a complete revival in the team's fortunes on the field.

The Runners-up spot, to Guildford City, in the League ensured the Club's promotion, and that quarter-final Welsh Cup-tie brought a brief moment of remembrances of the good old days to the long suffering supporters. Although the Martyrs lost by a single goal to their Football League opponents (Wrexham), the attendance of 10,000 represented the best attendance at Penydarren for twenty years.

The 1972/73 season saw a further influx of Clubs into the Southern League, and Merthyr were relegated into the new First Division North, a division with a sister companion in the South. The gates dropped alarmingly again, from a first home attendance of over 1,400 to under 800 later. An F.A. Cup run through to the second round the next season had attracted 1,500 to the final qualifying round match with Macclesfield, and even more in the second round home defeat by Hendon, but the next League match at Penydarren could muster only 500 faithfuls!

The early seventies saw many player and Managerial changes, the most notable being the acquisition of Mel Nurse, and the legendary John Charles in a dual capacity. Seven uneventful seasons followed, until the 1978/79 season, when a closely fought finish ended with the Martyrs once again becoming runners-up in their Division. But the months of toil meant nothing at the end, for a further change in the constitution of the Southern League dictated a return to two divisions, one South and one Midland, for the forthcoming campaign! The Club's furthest run in the F.A. Challenge Trophy took them through to the quarter-finals in 1978, but further progress was stopped by Runcorn, in a replay.

The 1979/80 season was the first for the new Alliance Premier League, and the loss in the past of the Southern League 'giants', such as the United's of Oxford, Cambridge and Hereford to the Football League, meant a further devaluation with the added 'defection' of the likes of Worcester, Telford, Weymouth and Kettering. Another encouraging F.A. Cup run took the Club into the second round, and a home game with Chesham United. But, as in the past, they fluffed this relatively easy chance and lost in a Penydarren replay by 3-1 before a large - and very rare - attendance of 4,000.

Until the 1985/86 season, Merthyr Tydfil were unable to make a serious challenge for a Southern League Midland Division promotion position into either the Alliance Premier League or the Premier Division of the Southern League; the latter was again reconstituted when the League allowed yet another influx of Clubs, and the consequent forming of three Divisions for the 1982/83 season. As in past years the crowds deserted the Club, for although always there for the big matches, numbers at the bread and butter League matches were measured in low hundreds.

At the end of the 1985/86 season, and one year later, the Club just failed to make the upward move, when finishing in third place on both occasions, with only two Clubs being promoted each year. At least the end of the latter season saw the Club win a very handsome consolation prize. After so many years in the backwaters, and around a quarter of a century without making a real impact in the Welsh Cup, the Club shot to glory when they won the Competition after beating Newport County at Cardiff City after a replay.

It was not the winning of this Trophy that brought the Club to prominence, but their qualification for the following year's entry into the European Cup Winners Cup - an honour that has never been achieved, nor will conceivably be in the future, by any other Ex-football League team. Merthyr's progress in the (English) F.A. Cup had not reached beyond the second round - and even then defeats on two occasions had been at the hands of fellow non-Leaguers. But on the 17th of September 1987, the whole Football World got to hear of the little Welsh part-timers.

On that Autumn evening they were hosts to Atlanta of the Italian Football League in the First Round of the second most prestigious competition in Europe. But rather than just appearing they went on to win the first leg 2-1, before a ('safety of grounds' capacity) crowd at Penydarren of 8,000. Against all the odds, the Martyrs pounded the Italians goal and got their just reward after 35 minutes with a goal from Kevin Rogers.

The crowd's jubilation was shortlived for Atlanta equalised six minutes later. Rather than capitulate to their theoretically superior opponents, Merthyr continued to storm the visitors goal, and when it looked as if a highly creditable draw was on the cards, Ceri Williams - a Newport County cast-off - slammed in the winner with seven minutes to go. The victory was no fluke, for the little Welsh team could so easily have won by three or four goals.

There was to be no fairy tale ending in the second leg, for before a partisan 14,000 strong crowd, the Martyrs succumbed to two early second half goals, despite coming close near the end with an effort that would have earned the Club at least a period of extra time. But at least the team gained the impetus to strive on in their domestic competition, and the end of the season saw the Club head the Southern League Midland Division, by eight points, and a long overdue promotion into the Premier Division once again.

EUROPE SPECIAL / **Glory night for Welsh minnows**

Merthyr magic

'So much for a welcome in the hillsides and a welcome in the vales!'

Road layer Ceri paves the way for a Cup shock

Merthyr Tydfil ...... 2 Atalanta 1

BY PETER JACKSON

MERTHYR TYDFIL'S magnificent £40-a-week part-timers sprang from the Southern League last night to snatch a taste of European glory.

The unsung Welsh club's collection of mechanics, teachers and electricians have earned a place in British soccer history — whatever the result of the second leg of this Cup Winners' Cup tie in a fortnight's time.

They did more than merely beat the expensive Italians. Atlanta scuttled back to Bergamo in the early hours of the morning counting their blessings at escaping an even bigger beating.

Merthyr won the home leg on their European debut before an ecstatic crowd of 8,000 in the best tradition of football fairytales — with a goal seven minutes from the end by a young Welshman who was dumped on soccer's scrapheap three years ago.

CERI WILLIAMS . . . scrapheap star

KEVIN ROGERS . . . home-town hero

Ceri Williams, sacked by Newport and forced to earn a living laying tarmacadam on the roads around Merthyr, taunted Atalanta all night long and the Italians were just beginning to think they had seen the last of Merthyr's dancing left-winger when he struck.

A free kick just outside the penalty area gave Williams the chance for one final strike. 'I just hit it and hoped for the best,' he said. 'I could hardly believe it when it went in. But we could have won by three or four goals.'

Kevin Rogers, the only home town player in Merthyr's ranks, launched the Welsh Cup holders on their way with the opening goal of a carnival night at Penydarren Park.

'Nobody gave us a hope and you couldn't really blame them,' said Rogers. 'But we knew if we worked like we'd never worked before we might have a chance.

The first breakthrough came ten minutes before half-time, when the Atlanta goalkeeper carried the ball several steps too far. Merthyr made the most of the free kick, David Tonge teeing the ball up for Rogers to smash it home.

When Progna stole a simple equaliser six minutes later, it seemed as if Merthyr's fling would simply fade away. Instead they reappeared from their dressing-room to pound the Italian goal.

Scramble

As the corners rained in from both sides, Piotti made a series of scrambling saves to postpone Merthyr's glory until the final minutes.

Jubilant manager Lyn Jones said: 'We've struck a great blow for British football. It's a night none of us will forget and in a fortnight's time we'll go out to hold what we have. Remember, we've only lost one of our last 24 league games.'

In one sense history had repeated itself. Twenty-five years ago another non-League club from another corner of Wales, Bangor City, scored a first-leg win over Naples in the same competition.

Merthyr in Europe - 1987

The initial successes of Merthyr Town and Merthyr Tydfil produced well supported teams for both, but success that did not show on the field of play for the former, and has been difficult to sustain in the case of the latter. The current Club, after a long battle, has made it to the top competition in the non-League tree, the (currently named) GM Vauxhall Conference, by virtue of their promotion from the Southern League Premier Division in 1989 (following promotion one year earlier from the lower division) and a Championship win. The early days of the season had looked like being anything but a successful year, for after 22 games they languished fourth from bottom, but an incredible run which saw them record 21 victories in their last 28 games, ensured their table-topping at the end. The final two home matches each produced crowds of almost 3,500.

The Martyrs have held their own with the football elite, whilst never looking like achieving the final accolade - promotion to the Football League. The 1991/92 season saw their best effort, with a final fourth place, but conversely relegation was narrowly avoided two years later. The Club also have the extra 'threat' hanging over them of a possible 'demotion' to the Welsh National League, which has been bestowed upon them by the generally agreed ludicrous ruling of the F.A. of Wales. This ruling allows just a few years for promotion to the Football League, with the alternative of joining the other Welsh teams in the lower standard National League. But with the successful fight exhibited by Newport A.F.C., which has resulted in their continued membership of the Southern League - whilst playing in Wales - hopefully common-sense will rule and ensure that this particular millstone is taken from the Martyrs necks.

PENYDARREN PARK

The Ground has an historical significance that goes back well before its current use. For during the Roman invasion of Wales in 43 A.D., several legions were based in the area with one at (the later named) Penydarren Park. The fort that was located within the Ground's boundaries dates from the first century A.D., although the remains were not discovered until 1786. When Penydarren was first proposed as being a suitable locations for the town's football pitch in 1902, excavations were undertaken in detail and continued for several years. Several identifiable Roman remains were found, including two hypocaust (for heating water) and a bath house. With the present-day recognition of preservation, it is unlikely that the site could be converted into a football ground, but rather that the area be retained for its historical significance. The town of Merthyr gained a good football arena at history's expense!

Just outside the North-east boundary of the Ground stood Penydarren House which for several decades was considered to be the largest and most opulent house and estate in Merthyr.

By 1904, part of the site had been converted into use for sporting occasions, which included a cycle track of an unusual triangular shape - with rounded corners (running roughly East to West), and a running track at the wide (East) end, from approximately North to South. The entrance to this ground was via Pen-y-Darren Road, the main route leading to the East out of Merthyr. With the formation of Merthyr Town in 1908, work was put in hand to create an oval shaped arena - a football pitch surrounded by a running track - and located in the same position as the current football area. The only entrance to this new Ground was, and still is, at the end of the formerly named Park Terrace, now known as Windsor Terrace. A small timber seated Grandstand was built, with dressing rooms below, that ran about a quarter pitch length at the centre of the South-West side. There was little else at Penydarren, apart from mostly natural embankments that surrounded the pitch, and particularly notable at the South-East end.

The Club's rapid progress led to a paddock area being formed in front of the Grandstand (overlying that area of the former cycle track), plus a standing covered enclosure opposite the main Stand that extended about two thirds pitch length. To the Grandstand were added several small office extensions, etc, plus proper turnstile enclosures at the end of Park Terrace. No concrete terracing was provided, but the very large overall area of the Ground, coupled with the natural earth banks that sloped down towards the pitch, provided ample viewing areas for the club's record attendance.

Penydarren was available for the new team in 1945, and over the further passage of forty plus years, the Ground had seen little real changes. The strip surrounding the pitch that formed the much earlier cycle track was retained and used for a period for Greyhound racing. Although the dogs have now disappeared, the barriers that formed the boundaries of the football area have barely moved, and so there are wide perimeters to both sides and behind the goals.

The covered enclosure, albeit rebuilt, remains in the same location as in pre-war days, and the large natural grass banks are still present to a degree, although additional concrete terracing - whilst reducing the standing areas - now provides spectators with safer and more comfortable viewing positions. The small seated Grandstand was re-built, now with a capacity for 1,500, and is situated as before on the South-West side of the pitch, with nearby purpose built changing rooms. For a while the old Grandstand had narrow covered standing areas to the side, but were removed along with the debris that resulted from this Stand that burnt down. A large social Club was an innovation which provides income that cannot be generated at the Gate. Overall, the very large site is still of a most odd shape, and little has been lost over the years to change the overall area, although a narrow bank of concrete terracing was built behind the North-West goal, and was later covered. By the late 1950's the Club had installed somewhat rudimentary floodlights on fairly low poles down each side of the football pitch - even so they were suitable for competitive matches - but were later replaced with similar, but higher, installations.

Penydarren is probably close to being suitable for Football League status, with a total 10,000 capacity, and the overall area of the Ground, coupled with some more expenditure (more was spent in order to allow the European Cup match to take place) could raise it to the necessary standard. The Ground is frustratingly located well above, and adjacent to, the main East road out of the town, but can only be entered by way of Park Terrace via an intricate series of backroads.

PROGRAMMES

The existence of a well supported Club - at least for a period - in pre-war days has meant that some copies have survived. But such samples appear very rarely and fetch very high prices.

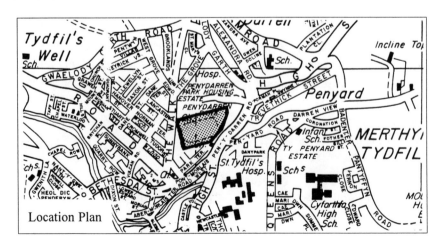

Location Plan

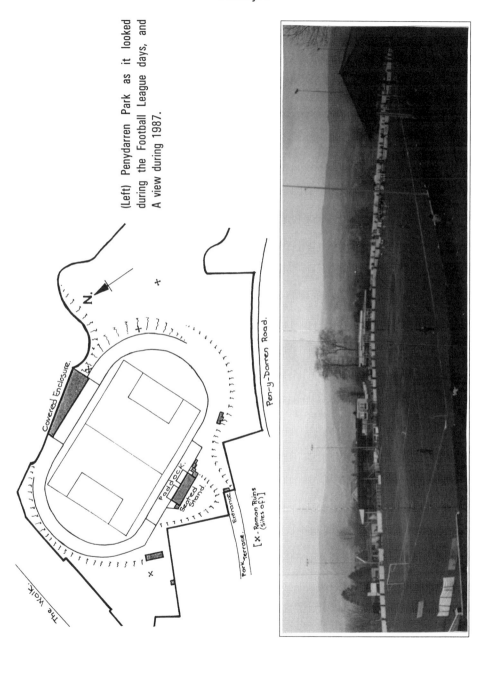

(Left) Penydarren Park as it looked during the Football League days, and A view during 1987.

THAMES F.C.

A rare team group, from the 1930/31 season.

THAMES F.C. OFFICIALS AND PLAYERS.

Back Row (left to right).—T. GIBBON (reserve trainer), RIDDOCH, McCULLOCH, CRAWFORD, LING, BAILEY, SPENCE, DURNION, COMBES, SMITH (G.), RUSSELL (W.).

Second Row (left to right).—ROBBIN, DONNELLY, THOMAS, BIRD, HAWKINS, PHILLIPS, TOWNSEND, PERRY, WARNER, JACKSON, W. HALES, HEAP.

Third Row (left to right).—F. SMITH, MR. H. R. MILHASK (secretary), MAJOR A. S. O'BRIEN (director), MR. C. H. McKNIGHT (director), RUSSELL (captain), MR. LOUIS DANE (chairman), MR. WRIGHT CUNDY (director), MR. W. REECE (director), MR. GRAHAM TILLEY, MR. DAVID BUCHANAN (manager), SMALLMAN.

Front Row (left to right).—W. DUFFY, L. McCARTHY, LINDSAY, MANN, JENKINS, BASSETT, IGOE, DAVIDSON.

230

THAMES ASSOCIATION

Founded: 1928, became defunct: 1932
Football League: 1930 - 1932

1928/29 -   1929/30 *Southern League Eastern Section*
1930/31 -   1931/32 *Football League Division 3 South*

****

SUMMARY OF FACTS

Ground
West Ham Stadium, Prince Regent's Lane
Custom House
London, E16
Colours (Football League):
Red & blue quartered shirts, white shorts.
Record Attendance
8,275 versus Exeter City, 29th August 1931, drew 0-0
Lowest League Attendance (Official)
469 versus Luton Town, 6th December 1930, (record low officially recorded for scheduled Football League Saturday game).
Achievements
None!

The entrance gates to West Ham Stadium
(note the 1930's art-deco) just prior to demolition.

FOOTBALL LEAGUE COMPLETE RECORD:
SEASON 1930/31

August	30th	Q.P.R.	(away)	0-3
September	3rd	Notts. County	(away)	0-4
	6th	Walsall	(home)	4-1
	11th	Clapton Orient	(home)	3-0
	13th	Coventry City	(away)	1-7
	18th	Clapton Orient	(away)	1-2
	20th	Fulham	(home)	0-0
	27th	Swindon Town	(away)	0-3
October	4th	Bournemouth & Bos.	(home)	1-4
	11th	Watford	(away)	0-1
	18th	Exeter City	(away)	3-4
	25th	Brighton & Hove Albion	(home)	0-0
November	4th	Torquay United	(away)	1-5
	8th	Northampton Town	(home)	2-1
	15th	Brentford	(away)	1-6
	22nd	Crystal Palace	(home)	0-2
December	6th	Luton Town	(home)	1-0
	17th	Bristol Rovers	(away)	0-4
	20th	Newport County	(home)	3-1
	25th	Gillingham	(away)	1-3
	26th	Gillingham	(home)	2-2
	27th	Q.P.R.	(home)	1-0
January	3rd	Walsall	(away)	0-6
	10th	Southend United	(away)	0-1
	17th	Coventry City	(home)	1-2
	24th	Fulham	(away)	2-4
	31st	Swindon Town	(home)	3-2
February	7th	Bournemouth & Bos.	(away)	3-3
	16th	Watford	(home)	3-2
	21st	Exeter City	(home)	1-0
	28th	Brighton & Hove Albion	(away)	4-2
March	7th	Torquay United	(home)	1-1
	14th	Northampton Town	(away)	1-4
	21st	Brentford	(home)	2-0
	28th	Crystal Palace	(away)	1-2
April	3rd	Norwich City	(home)	2-0
	4th	Southend United	(home)	3-0
	6th	Norwich City	(away)	0-0
	11th	Luton Town	(away)	0-8
	18th	Bristol Rovers	(home)	1-2
	25th	Newport County	(away)	1-1
May	2nd	Notts. County	(home)	0-0

	Played	W	D	L	F	A	Pts	Pos.
	42	13	8	21	54	93	34	20th

Average Attendance: 2,315 (Lowest average in Football League)
F.A. Cup - 1st Round

November	29th	Q.P.R.	(away)	0-5

Season 1931/32

August	29th	Exeter City	(home)	0-0
September	3rd	Brentford	(home)	1-1
	5th	Coventry City	(away)	0-2
	7th	Southend United	(away)	1-1
	12th	Gillingham	(home)	3-0
	17th	Southend United	(home)	1-3
	19th	Luton Town	(away)	0-2
	26th	Cardiff City	(home)	1-2
October	3rd	Northampton Town	(away)	0-4
	10th	Reading	(home)	0-0
	17th	Torquay United	(home)	1-1
	24th	Clapton Orient	(away)	1-1
	31st	Swindon Town	(home)	1-1
November	7th	Norwich City	(away)	0-7
	14th	Brighton & Hove A.	(home)	1-2
	21st	Mansfield Town	(away)	0-4
December	5th	Crystal Palace	(away)	1-2
	12th	Bournemouth & Bos.	(home)	2-4
	19th	Q.P.R.	(away)	0-6
	25th	Bristol Rovers	(home)	0-2
	26th	Bristol Rovers	(away)	1-4
January	2nd	Exeter City	(away)	1-4
	9th	Reading	(away)	1-5
	16th	Coventry City	(home)	2-5
	18th	Watford	(home)	1-2
	23rd	Gillingham	(away)	0-2
	30th	Luton Town	(home)	2-4
February	6th	Cardiff City	(away)	2-9
	13th	Northampton Town	(home)	0-2
	27th	Torquay United	(away)	1-3
March	5th	Clapton Orient	(home)	3-3
	12th	Swindon Town	(away)	0-2
	19th	Norwich City	(home)	1-0
	25th	Fulham	(home)	0-0
	26th	Brighton & Hove A.	(away)	1-4
	28th	Fulham	(away)	0-8
April	2nd	Mansfield Town	(home)	6-3
	9th	Watford	(away)	2-3
	16th	Crystal Palace	(home)	1-3
	23rd	Bournemouth & Bos.	(away)	2-4
	30th	Q.P.R.	(home)	2-3
May	7th	Brentford	(away)	0-1

Played	W	D	L	F	A	Pts.	Posn.	
42	7	9	26	53	109	23	22nd

Average Attendance: 2,623 (Lowest average in Football League)

F.A. Cup. Ist Round

November	28th	Watford	(home)	2-2

Replay:

December	1st	Watford	(away)	1-2 A.E.T.

When the facts are looked at in the cold light of day, and these are borne out by the Club's short existence, Thames Association never really stood a realistic chance of success! But over the decades, the heart has often overruled commonsense. And thus in 1928 a brand new Club was born.

For a football team founded in relatively modern times, it is surprisingly difficult to trace detailed facts relating to the origins of Thames Association F.C. The Club's formation was credited to being the brainchild of Major O'Brien, who not only became a Director, but also took on the role of Commercial Manager - the latter seldom heard of at this period in connection with football. The creation of the Club soon became a financial disaster, and when the facts are considered, it is quite amazing that a gamble against such poor odds was ever undertaken.

The East side of London and outlying districts were admittedly heavily populated, but so also was the area already well served with football clubs. Tottenham Hotspur, Arsenal and West Ham - all no more than a short train or bus ride away - captured the support of the majority of football fans, with the Hammers right on the new Club's doorstep. Meanwhile another local team Clapton Orient, just relegated from the Second Division, could vouch for the poor support perpetually given to a local team that had never been able to emulate the big London teams. In addition to the Football League representatives, there was a multitude of lesser - but top Amateur - teams, notably Walthamstow Avenue, Leyton, Leytonstone and Ilford. The facts appear to speak for themselves, but the opportunity to make use of a brand new Stadium, possibly added to the desire to form a completely new team.

The home venue had earlier been the site of the Custom House Sports Ground, an unpretentious arena that occupied part of the future stadium area. This earlier Ground was surrounded by allotments, with just one entry point in Bingley Road. Over many years, the West Ham Stadium was to play host to many sports, but the principal uses were to be for Speedway and Greyhound racing; the first Dog meeting attracted no less than 56,000 spectators - a record for the Sport - on the 4th of August, 1928, a far cry from the paltry crowds that were to come and watch the local Football team!

In a flurry of activity following the formation of the new football club, various experienced personnel were appointed, showing that the Club were aiming for a rapid climb to the top. D. Buchanon as Manager was enticed away from Charlton where he had for three years been the Assistant Manager and Coach, which had followed a playing career with Clapton Orient, Plymouth and Middlesbrough. To assist the Manager Bellamy (ex-Arsenal, Dundee and Burnley) was enroled as Trainer/Coach. Meanwhile a squad of fourteen professional ex-Football League players was signed on.

At the very outset, the Club was accepted as a viable proposition, for despite the untried capabilities of the team, they were immediately accepted into the Southern League - Eastern Section. With no reserve team, players that were not considered as League team members would have to show their worth in various friendly matches that were to be played during the season.

August the 23rd, 1928 became the day of the first League match for Thames Association F.C., when they drew 2-2 with Aldershot Town, in Hampshire. The first half was an even affair, and although a penalty was missed, the score after 45 minutes was one goal apiece - Robinson becoming the first ever marksman for the 'Dockers'. Right-winger, Martin, then put the visitors into the lead, but an initial victory was denied with a late equaliser from Aldershot.

The big day arrived, seven days later, when the team's first home match was played. Brighton Reserves were the visitors, and the auspicious occasion was marked with the presence - amongst other V.I.P.'s - of Football League Official, F.J. Wall. Although there was an attendance of some 3,000 - perfectly satisfactory from the financial viewpoint - the vast stadium looked empty and completely lacking in atmosphere. Thames were represented by: Kelly, Gilroy, Phizacklea, McIlvany, Hirst, Hilley, Martin, Robinson, Gilson, Tonner and Springwell.

The Brighton team started strongly, with the home defence looking decidedly uncertain, but gradually Thames came into the game and were only let down by their erratic shooting. But there was no dream home debut for the Club, for they eventually succumbed to two second half goals.

Individually the team members showed a fair degree of skill, but since they were little more than eleven individuals 'thrown' together, the collective play was more like that of strangers. *"On this showing, Thames F.C. are likely to develop into a good side. It seems likely that they will get good support, and they should be successful..."* These somewhat erroneous comments were made by the local press.

A variable start to the season was made and was completed when the third match - which produced the Club's first victory - ended 5-2, at home, to a poor Dartford team on the 15th of September. Two weeks later, when Bournemouth's Reserve XI were entertained - before a 2,000 crowd - the play as a team had improved considerably. The first Cup match, the London Challenge Cup, produced a close result when Millwall ran out 3-2 winners. But by the late Autumn there was already cause for concern, with attendances not reaching expectations - even the local derby game with West Ham Reserves (a 3-2 victory) attracted only a, *"meagre attendance"*.

A shot in the arm was provided with the capture, in December, of Ivor Jones - a Welsh International. He gave a good showing on his debut in the return fixture with Dartford, which resulted in an odd goal in five victory to the Dockers. As the season wore on the team gradually settled in, and to a certain extent the attendances improved. By the end of the campaign, however, the picture was not particularly encouraging, with a final placing of only 14th in the League of 19 teams; 13 wins, 5 draws and 18 defeats had been recorded, with a goal difference of 67 to 74 against. Not to be deterred, the Club made a somewhat audacious bid for Football League status, but secured only one vote in their bid for election.

Jack Hebden (ex-West Ham)
Another Aug. 1929 signing; he never played
for Thames in the Football League

The 1929/30 season started in fine style with a 3-1 win over Northfleet, a match which was recognised as being probably the best to date at the Custom House Stadium, and the double was completed with a 2-1 victory in the return. Following a two unopposed goals win over Brighton reserves, the team proudly lay in third place by early October, a position that the team was never to improve upon.

The F.A. Cup was competed for, but the match was postponed on November the 16th due to heavy snow! In the final event, the Dockers opponents, Winchester, were overcome, to provide the team with a money spinning visit to Fulham in the next round. Only one goal in arrears at half-time, the non-Leaguer's defence eventually cracked under continuous pressure, although overall it was an encouraging display, despite a final 4-0 defeat. But successes continued in the Southern League, and a fifth placing at the end of April was improved to 3rd by the season's end; 17 victories and 9 defeats in 32 matches, with a goal difference of 80 to 60.

A concerted effort was made for the Club's election to the elite, with the Directors pointing out in a circular letter to all Football League Clubs of their excellent stadium, financial stability and hugh catchment area for support. Regarding the latter item, it must have been obvious that the Club was already completely overshadowed by their successful and very near neighbours West Ham United, and consequently their gigantic home venue could never realistically expect more than a sprinkling of spectators for home matches! This was borne out with average attendances during the just completed season of less than one thousand; there were many other Football League aspirants who could call upon support several times this number. Financially viable they may have been, although even this was questionable since the Club were - in common with many clubs - in debt; the Dockers to the sum of nearly £3,000.

In spite of all the obvious reasons why the Club should not be accepted into the Football League, somewhat amazingly, on June the 2nd, Thames were elected into the Third Division South. They took the place of struggling Merthyr Town. Gillingham were easily re-elected with 33 votes, but for Thames it was a close thing. Their 20 votes were just one more than Southern League Champions, and surely far more eligible, Aldershot, and six more than Merthyr's. What made the whole question of Thames F.C.'s election even more perplexing was the obvious close relationship with the Greyhound Authority with whom they shared the Stadium; an allegiance between the two sports that the Football authorities were becoming increasingly unhappy about. This new canine sport was soon to prove that its activities were not compatible with football, and the Football League were to later positively discourage such dual uses.

There was great enthusiasm when the result of the voting was announced, with the optimistic followers of the Club confidently expressed their feelings that there was plenty of room for another League team in East London. The company's Share Capital was increased from £2,000 to £10,000 with initially many applicants for the £1 shares. The firm intention was to get a good team together, and it was predicted that within the course of few years, Thames would be among the leaders of the Football League Division 1! A rash statement, but one that is not uncommon within football, where the heart can so easily rule over commonsense.

Prior to the start of the 1930/31 season, the Stadium's grass surface was improved by re-turfing and installing a special drainage system. A Reserve team was formed, which was to play in the newly created London Combination Division 2; the Club's founder - Major O'Brien was on the Management Committee.

The season started with a somewhat new look team. Of the 26 players that were to represent the Club, all but six were new faces, and of these two were amateurs, Smith and Duffy. Amongst the newcomers were a number of men from other Football League Clubs, notably Moses Russell - from Plymouth and a Welsh International. Heap (ex-Burnley), Smith (Bristol City), Warner (Watford), Spence from neighbours Clapton Orient, Phillips (Millwall), Bird (Huddersfield) and Perry from Bournemouth. Whilst Manager Buchanon still held the reins.

Inside-forward Wilf Phillips, and full-back and captain Moses Russell, both played in the Club's first Football League match.

The Supporters Club were confident of their team's coming success of course, and were supremely optimistic at a pre-season meeting on the 30th of July, when they announced that they hoped for an eventual membership of 25,000!

Following the two Public Practise matches on August the 20th and 23rd, the Supporters organised a Charabanc (Coach) trip for the first game across London at Queens Park Rangers ground.

The Dockers first Football League match

The Thames team for the first Football League match on 30th August, consisted: Bailey, Russell (Captain), Heap, Warner, McCulloch, Igoe, Bird, Phillips, Townsend, Durnion and Mann. The first half was a reasonably even affair, but despite the generally good defence of the visitors, they went in at the interval one goal down. The second half produced less from Thames for their attacking moves were poorly finished, and playing with only ten men in this period - due to an injury - the final score was a disappointing 0-3 defeat. Four days later a visit was made to the ground of the oldest club in the League, Notts. County. This was a severe test for the newcomers, and a four goal reverse was suffered to the Champions-elect.

A match had also been played on the opening day of the season at the West Ham Stadium, a friendly, between the Dockers reserve eleven and a Chelsea second string, but the 'big' day was set for September the 6th, the date of the first home game of the Thames F.C. Football League team. Several dignitaries attended a pre-match luncheon, notably Sir Frederick Wall (again) - the Football Association Secretary - and the Mayor of West Ham. Not to be deterred by the two comprehensive defeats of the Club, a new record attendance of close on 7,000 was present for the game versus Walsall. Lindsay replaced Warner at right-half from the first match line-up, and the home fans soon had something to cheer. After three minutes, a 30 yard free kick from the Thames inside-right Phillips, hit the back of the net to record the first League goal for the Club. Five minutes before half-time Perry doubled the home team's score. Despite pulling one goal back in the second-half, Walsall finally ran out 4-1 losers, after the homesters scored two more goals in the last 14 minutes. The home fans had plenty to celebrate, but such an attendance of these proportions was only very rarely repeated, and in the vast stadium even 7,000 spectators appeared little more than a sprinkling of faces around the terraces.

Although the next game gave further cause for hope - a three goal home win over neighbours Clapton Orient (in which Perry scored a hat-trick) - as the weeks passed by results took a definite turn for the worse. Two away defeats followed, 7-1 at Coventry and by the odd goal in three return at Clapton, leaving the Club in a lowly League table position. Just two scoreless home draws were achieved in the next seven matches, and the last of this set produced a 5-1 thrashing at Torquay. As so often happens in Football, luck was not with the Club as their confidence waned. The 4-1 defeat at Bournemouth was played with virtually nine men for the last 20 minutes as Perry was no more than a passenger and Warner had already left with an injury.

The programme versus Bournemouth (4th October 1930) and match action.

The Thames goalkeeper saves at the feet of Bournemouth's Eyre (in stripes)

At Exeter, despite taking an early lead through Butler - who had made his debut along with Curwen one week earlier - the team found themselves 1-4 in arrears with 15 minutes to go, but pulled two goals back to produce a final, respectable, scoreline. A two goal defeat to Fulham put paid to any hopes in the London Challenge Cup competition. Measures had to be taken to stem the run of defeats, and for the home game versus high-flying Northampton Town (who had suffered only one defeat) the Manager's 18 year old son, from London Caledonians, made his debut. His inclusion was well merited as he scored both goals in a 2-1 surprise win.

The line-up for the match at Brentford on November the 15th, included only five players from the first match just over two months earlier. One of the newcomers was the right-winger Le May, the ex-Clapton Orient and later Watford player, who was reputed to be - at five foot tall - the shortest player ever in the Football League. The game attracted a 15,000 attendance - the joint best League gate for the Bees - no doubt the interest centred on the homesters high placing in the table, the local derby content and a natural curiosity to see the new Club. The game became another disaster as the visitors slumped to a 6-1 defeat. The record of the Club at this time had produced only eight points from fifteen games, and a second from bottom position in the League.

On the 29th of November more gloom was in store, when the team lost by five unopposed goals to Queens Park Rangers in the first round of the F.A. Cup.

In the run-up to Christmas a much improved spell was enjoyed, which produced three victories, one draw and only two defeats, but by the turn of the year the Club was still in a perilous position in the table. Four straight defeats followed, the last by six goals at Walsall (despite being only one goal behind at half-time), and it wasn't until the 7th of February that the first away point was achieved. The match at Bournemouth being otherwise notable due to the Dockers being three goals down into the second period, but then surprisingly scoring a trio of goals at the last. This game was the second in a string of results which produced the best run of the season, undefeated in six games with only two draws, and including the Club's only away win - 4-2 at Brighton. But there was to be no real revival, and the run-in to the end of the season produced only three more wins, and defeats included an eight goal demolition at Luton.

Despite the overall improvement in the second half of the season, these results were insufficient to prevent the Club finishing 20th in the final League table, six points and two places above tail-enders Norwich City. The leading League match goalscorer was Perry with 16 whilst W. Phillips achieved the most appearances, totalling 37.

It had been a very disappointing first Football League season for the Club, and apart from the playing front, warning bells were already ringing with regard to money! After the initial moderate interest in the Club, attendances had rapidly dropped, sometimes to an alarming level. On December the 6th, an all-time Football League (official) record low gate - for a scheduled Saturday match - was recorded when a pathetic attendance of only 469 spectators were present. (Undoubtedly lower attendances had been present at League matches in earlier years, but these were at times when official attendances were rarely, if ever, given).

In March, a public meeting was held when appeals went out for more financial backing for the Club; the meeting was supported by the presence of Herbert Chapman, Sir Frederick Wall and the local Member of Parliament. A number of dismal facts were presented to those present including the fact that in the previous June, 8,000 more £1 shares were made available - but only 653 had been taken up. The Supporters Club, who by now had dropped their expectations of future membership, to a 'mere' 10,000, reported a current paid-up following of only 1,080. A 'Penny on the Ball' scheme had been started, which allowed donations to the Football Club of £50 plus match balls to be made. But one of the biggest obstacles affecting attendances at matches was, as prevalent throughout the Country, widespread industrial disputes and hence lack of money for would-be support.

The meeting had the desired effect, for it ended with a new feeling of optimism; a scheme was devised to raise £5,000, and a concerted effort to attract more fans to home games had an immediate reward. When Brentford came to the West Ham Stadium on March the 21st, a very healthy attendance of over 6,000 was present to see an encouraging victory by the Dockers over one of the Division's leading clubs. The defeat at Crystal Palace seven days later could have quelled the enthusiasm of the new found support, but even so, on April the 4th, the home game managed to attract 5,000.

The Club did not have long to enjoy this brief moment of interest, for despite the fair results over the final dozen or so games, support once again waned. It was a sobering thought that the other main users of the ground, the local Speedway Club, was attracting on average around 25,000 fans to their meetings!

At a Supporters Club meeting one month later, a Director of the Football Club, Major A.S. O'Brien, gloomily stated: *"It would be a tragedy if we did not go on"*. A new Manager, and Player, in the shape of James Donnelly, was to hopefully lead the Club to success in the 1931/32 season, and optimism once again prevailed at the start of the campaign. But for economic reasons, a reserve team had been abandoned, and the non-first team players had to rely for matches on the six team, London Professional Midweek League, plus occasional Friendly fixtures.

The two signings - Jimmy Dimmock (left) and Len Davies (right)

Two well respected ex-international players were signed; 29 year old Jimmy Dimmock from nearby Tottenham and Len Davies from Cardiff. Brown from Newport County was also added to the squad, whilst Le May moved on to Watford. Only seven playing members had been retained, and late signings included ('unknown') Woosnam, and McDonough from Brentford, plus Lennox from Charlton. The Stadium had undergone improvements during the close season with concreted standing areas and a fresh lick of paint to the Stand. Season ticket prices at this time cost £1.11s.6d. and two guineas (£2.10p) for Gents, and two thirds these amounts for Ladies; Club badges were also available at one shilling (5p).

On the 15th of August an attendance of over 5,000 - well in excess of most of the previous League matches - was present for the Public Trial game. Two weeks later, and with the Supporters Club now numbering almost 2,000, the Club's expectations were briefly fulfilled. An all time record attendance for Thames F.C. of 8,275 spread themselves thinly around the arena - in summer weather - to see the first game of the season, versus Exeter City. This produced a scoreless draw that was dominated by two good defences. For the Dockers it could be seen as a success, since the team were so unfamiliar to each other.

All five forwards had only played together once before - in a practice match - and in addition, one half-back, one full-back and the goalkeeper were all newcomers. The following Thursday, however, there was surprisingly little more than half the record gate, when Brentford were entertained, and another draw (1-1) was played out.

Overall, the season started in reasonable fashion, for after five games, one victory, 3 draws and one defeat were recorded, but this run was followed by three straight defeats. On October the 3rd, it really looked as if the team may be getting things right, as they triumphed by four unopposed goals at Northampton - a match that was to become the Club's best Football League victory. A short unbeaten home record has already been broken a week earlier when Cardiff had triumphed by 2-1 after a goalless first half. In an eventful match Lennox had missed several good chances, the Docker's winger Brown received a broken nose, and the winning goal came just five minutes from time.

The last four (of five) games in October were unusual in that they all finished as draws, but the game at Norwich on the 7th of November really brought the Club down to earth and started to rekindle the Club's worries. In a match that was not so one-sided as the score suggests, the Dockers went in at the interval four goals in arrears, and the rout continued, to finish 7-0 after 90 minutes. The Canaries were enjoying something of a revival as they were the past season's wooden-spoonists. This match was the start of a run the likes of which have seldom been equalled in the Football League; no less than 15 defeats in the next 16 games were suffered - the one exception being a notable 5-2 home win over Coventry. Some of the matches were, on paper, relatively close affairs, but a few were very bad reverses: 4-0, 6-0 and 5-1 at Mansfield, Q.P.R. and Reading respectively, and the heaviest of all, a 9-2 thrashing at Cardiff, on February the 6th.

At the start of this terrible run, a new Director was appointed, Captain C.R. Dane (son of Chairman Louis Dane), a man who had taken an interest throughout the Club's brief life, but his influence however had little effect. On December the 11th a letter from the Thames F.C. Management was issued stating that they were concerned with regard to the lack of public support at home matches (although in all fairness the low numbers were hardly surprising), gate receipts were hopelessly inadequate, and that every attempt to raise financial support had failed. An immediate decision had to be taken on whether the Club could carry on to the end of the season, which they would prefer to do. £2,000 was required within days or the Club would have to go into voluntary liquidation! It is not clear if and where the cash came from, but two weeks later, a further announcement was made that there was every chance of the Club carrying on.

By Christmas the team was firmly anchored at the base of the Third Division, and the attendances had dropped to a pitiful level. With several alternative, and far more successful local clubs that could be watched, and a Club too young to have gained any form of traditional support, there could never have been any real chance of the Club pulling through this dire situation.

Due to the financial struggles of the Club, it was necessary to transfer goalkeeper McDonough to Blackpool, for despite some highly adverse scorelines this custodian was one of the few good players in the team. The next victory, five months after the previous, was a one goal win over Norwich, which was followed by a scoreless draw with Fulham. But the next two games proved that any hope of a sustained revival were false. A 4-1 defeat at Brighton, was followed by an eight goal thrashing in the return at Fulham; the latter game producing five goals in the last 13 minutes.

Seven days later, the Dockers shocked the few locals that were interested, with a notable and rare victory, when Mansfield were beaten 6-3. A goal up after one minute, a low scoring match was on the cards until the last 25 minutes when no fewer than seven further goals were scored. But such results were too rare to save the Club, and although no more 'cricket score' results were suffered, the last four games all ended in defeat.

The last ever game was played at Griffin Park, Brentford - and was lost by a single goal - before a 7,000 crowd, on the 7th of May. The final team to represent Thames F.C. consisted of: Bailie, Graham, Smith, Pritchard, Spence, Woosnam, Handley, McCarthy, Lennox, Kemp and Dimmock.

BRENTFORD FOOTBALL & SPORTS CLUB, LIMITED.

Registered Office :—GRIFFIN PARK, BRAEMAR ROAD, BRENTFORD.

Directorate.

Chairman:
MR. L. P. SIMON.

COUNCILLOR W. FLEWITT.   MR. H. J. SAUNDERS.
MR. H. N. BLUNDELL.   MR. H. W. DODGE.
MR. W. ADAMS.   MR. C. L. SIMON.

Vice-Chairman:
MR. J. R. HUGHES, C.C.

MR. F. W. BARTON.
COUNCILLOR H. F. DAVIS.
MR. F. A. DAVIS.

Hon. Treasurer:
COUNCILLOR W. FLEWITT.

Secretary-Manager:
MR. H. C. CURTIS,
258, WINDMILL ROAD, EALING, W.5.

Hon. Surgeons:
R. CRASKE LEANING, M.B., B.S.(Lond.), D.P.H.
R. C. NEIL, M.R.C.S. (Eng.), L.R.C.P. (Lond.)

Telephones:
GROUND : EALING 1744.
PRIVATE HOUSE : EALING 1183.

Telegraphic Address:
CURTIS, FOOTBALL, BRENTFORD.

Ground: GRIFFIN PARK, EALING ROAD, BRENTFORD.

Telephone: 1096 EALING.

LAMB & [

Monumen

and G

RENOV

EALIN'

—

G. R. BUTTERY, M.P.S.,
186, SOUTH EALING ROAD,

We Stock the "Unusual" T...

We give personal attention to all
Orders.

We offer to get anything not in
Stock.

We have 60 years' experience, and
understand our Trade.

298, 299 & 300, HIGH STREET,

'Phone EALING 0242.   BRENTFORD.

Saturday, 7th May, 1932.   No. 23

Notes from the Hive.

VICTORY AT LAST.

Considering that the last victory recorded by
...es' first team was prior to Easter, the two
...ected against Bournemouth last week
...me out of turn ; in fact our success

... MORE GOALS.

take on the role of
scores four goals
...uth on Satur-
...t, had our
...I know
...ur

might
not let
that in
winners.
c goals.

DUE.

...nopolised the
...ndon Combina-
...e only time the
...ghbury has been
the list of winners
...rally, the resources
great, but it was a
...e part of the Highbury
...nship five years in suc-
...stounding consistence in
d for its vagaries, and it
...e that the Arsenal would
...urs after Brentford Reserves
...r the best part of the season.
...and perhaps the game in the run of
general, ... has taken place in the run of
success enjoy ... by the Arsenal for this season,
gallant little Brentford, without any "stars" and
without any recourse to the cheque book, have
pipped the Highbury Club. This all happened
last week-end, when Brentford, by winning at
Upton Park against West Ham, while the

The Dockers last ever game

247

The situation was succinctly summed up in the programme notes: *"Our visitors have experienced a most disappointing season not only from a playing, but financial standpoint, and their future as a League Club is in the laps of the Gods"*. This sentiment was echoed with a press announcement to the effect that owing to the poor support received during the season, it was doubtful if the Club would be able to carry on.

The resilience of Football Clubs is, however, quite amazing, and three weeks later a glimmer of hope for the floundering outfit was given, the *"Thames F.C. Big Appeal"*. Contrary to rumours, it was announced, the Club was not dead; an application for re-election to the League had been made, and this appeal was backed by all the local political parties, despite the appalling financial problems created in part by the continuing industrial depression. But the over optimism was apparent when the expressed hope for no less than 20,000 season ticket purchasers at one guinea per head was asked for! On June the 3rd, a press release stated that the Club had decided to withdraw its re-election application, for there had been virtually no response to the appeal, and the Secretary, Mr. H.R. Milbank stated: *"Lack of funds prohibits us from continuing in the League. Indeed we are disbanding altogether and will not compete in any competition"*.

The season had been a disaster throughout, and had ended with bottom spot in the League, 5 points behind next placed Gillingham, with only 7 wins, 9 drawn games and 26 defeats. The goal tally showed 53 for and 109 against. F. Smith was an ever-present in the team, bar one game, and the leading League match goalscorers were C. Davies and J. Dimmock with 12 apiece. A modicum of success had been achieved in the F.A. Cup, when the first round had brought Watford to the West Ham Stadium. Despite a goal lead by half-time - scored direct from a corner by Dimmock - the final result of four goals shared necessitated a replay. The match at Watford went to extra time, where Thames finally lost 1-2, and Dimmock had a 'goal' disallowed.

The last business of the Club was to put nine players on the open to transfer list, and ten were given the chance to move for no fee.

The Club had very briefly made an appearance, and been readily accepted into the Football League at a time when there was plenty of competition from other worthy aspirants.

Undoubtedly the Club's acceptance had been related to their financial standing - two years was hardly time to create a playing record - and yet they rapidly failed in their endeavours. Footballing history has proved on many occasions since, that success at the game cannot be necessarily purchased with an open cheque book, and which - in the Dockers' case - had remained open for too short a period!

THE GROUND

It can be argued that in the sad, short saga of Thames Association F.C., a Football Club was created to occupy a newly constructed Stadium, rather than the creation of an organisation which then went about finding a suitable home venue!

Up to the birth of Thames F.C., a sports ground had previously existed over part of the succeeding West Ham Stadium site. The venue, known as the Custom House Sports Ground overlaid the central portion of the later Stadium, with the only entrance - in the South-west corner of the ground - approached via Bingley Road. This earlier ground was virtually surrounded with allotments. The rectangular playing area was surrounded by narrow, soil embankments and a small enclosure centrally located on the South side.

The West Ham Stadium, was completed in 1928, and was created to fulfil the sporting requirements of a densely populated area. The most popular use of the Stadium proved to be for Greyhound and Speedway Racing, in the case of the latter, a record attendance for the arena of some 64,000 was created in its early days for an International meeting between England and Australia. The claimed capacity (never fulfilled) was 120,000, which put the Stadium on a par with Wembley and White City - of similar size to the former and larger than the latter. In this respect, the venue was without doubt the largest Ground ever used regularly by a Football League team in England; it is ironic that the Football team in question was also one of the poorest supported!

Information regarding the formation of Thames Association F.C. is notoriously difficult to find, but it would appear that the availability of the Stadium was to influence greatly the formation of the Club. Due to its multi-purpose usage, the playing arena was an enormous oval shape (as with the former White City and Wembley Stadium), and was surrounded with two vast banks of concrete terracing.

With two enclosures - but with seating for only around 5,000 - down both sides and extending partly around each end, the Ground was not dissimilar to its more famous counterpart - Wembley Stadium.

Although Thames F.C. occupation was for only a short period, the Stadium remained intact until the early 1970's, when it was demolished and replaced with housing. No traces whatsoever remain of the earlier enormous structure, and it is somewhat ironic that the discordant estate of houses that have replaced the Stadium - tightly packed, with little 'breathing space' - should contrast so much with the aspect that was presented when Thames F.C. occupied the area, with their sprinkling of spectators dominated by the large expanse of concrete!

PROGRAMMES

In view of the Club's short life, examples are much sought after by collectors - even the 'away' games fetching very high prices. Even so it would seem that quite a number of copies still exist despite just the two seasons of League Football.

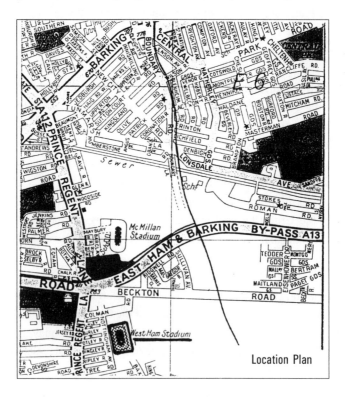

Location Plan

West Ham Stadium c.1930. Home of Thames Association F.C.
(The huge crowd is for a speedway meeting)

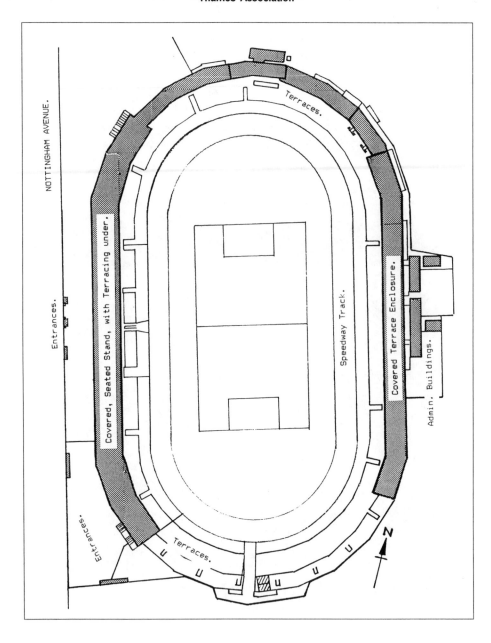

The layout of the Stadium (c.1930)

*Please turn the page for details of other
'Yore Publications' books, and videos*

From
'YORE PUBLICATIONS'
12 The Furrows, Harefield,
Middx. UB9 6AT

(Free lists issued 3 times per year. For your first list please send a S.A.E.)

Rejected F.C. Volume 1: (First published 1988, revised edition published 1992)
The first in this series, and which naturally follows the same path as this volume. Clubs included:- Aberdare Athletic, Ashington, Bootle, Bradford (Park Avenue), Burton (Swifts, Wanderers and United), Gateshead/South Shields, Glossop, Loughborough, Nelson, Stalybridge Celtic and Workington. 288 pages.
*** This reprint is now three years old ***
stocks are limited - and at this price is exceptionally good value
Rejected F.C. Volume 3: The close companion to this volume, contains the histories of:- Durham City, Gainsborough Trinity, Middlesbrough Ironopolis, New Brighton/New Brighton Tower, Northwich Victoria, Southport and Wigan Borough. 256 pages.
Rejected F.C. Scotland: Having dealt with England and Wales, the same treatment is given to the Scottish Clubs, many of whom were 'Rejected' during the ill-conceived Third Division of the 1920's.
Volume 1 'Edinburgh and The South' - Mid-Annandale, Solway Star, Nithsdale Wanderers, Armadale, Bathgate, Broxburn United, Peebles Rovers, Edinburgh City, Leith Athletic and St.Bernards. 288 pages.
Volume 2 'Glasgow and District' - Abercorn, Arthurlie, Beith, Cambuslang, Clydebank, Cowlairs, Johnstone, Linthouse, Northern, Third Lanark and Thistle. 240 pages.

All the above books are hardbacks, and priced £12-95 plus P/P £1-40 (U.K.)

Other books, by Dave Twydell, and published by YORE PUBLICATIONS:-
Football League Grounds For A Change: The well illustrated histories of every former Ground, of every Football League Club (published 1991 - limited stocks).
424 pages, Hardback. Price £13-95 (P/P £1-80 U.K.)
'Gone.. But Not Forgotten': A series of booklets published twice annually, each part providing well illustrated, abbreviated histories of a selection of defunct non-League Clubs, and Grounds that are no more.
(Parts 1 and 2 now sold out). 64 pages, softback. Each priced £4-95 (P/P 45p U.K.)

Since 1991, 'Yore Publications' have also published quality football books by other Authors, normally of an historical nature, including:- Large hardback Club histories (well illustrated and incl. detailed statistics) - Southend United, Bristol City, Kilmarnock, Shrewsbury Town, etc.

'Who's Who' books (Coventry City, Newport County, Lincoln City, etc.)
General interest - The Code War (The history of the different codes of 'football' upto 1918), Tommy Taylor (Manchester United 'Busby Babe') Biography, The Little Red Book of Chinese Football, etc.

For further details please send a S.A.E. in the first instance to:

YORE PUBLICATIONS